How to Write a Competitive Proposal
for Horizon 2020

A Research Manager's Handbook

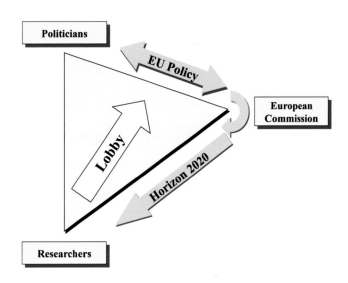

Seán McCarthy

Published by

Dr. Seán McCarthy,
Hyperion Ltd.,
Main Street,
Watergrasshill,
Co Cork,
Ireland.

sean.mccarthy@hyperion.ie
www.hyperion.ie

The information contained in this handbook is based on the author's experiences AND on official information published by the European Commission in December 2013. The official rules may change over time. The handbook describes how to monitor these changes.

ISBN 978-0-9546257-3-3

Table of Contents

About the Handbook

Horizon 2020 is the name of the European Union's research and innovation funding programme. The programme started on 1ˢᵗ January 2014 and will run until the end of 2020. Horizon 2020 has a budget of over €79 billion.

Horizon 2020 is divided into three 'Pillars' and each of these pillars is divided into programmes. Each programme publishes a 'call for proposals' annually. Researchers from all over Europe have to submit proposals in response to these calls.

This handbook is designed to assist researchers in writing competitive proposals for the Horizon 2020 calls for proposals.

The handbook is relevant to the following individuals:

- Coordinators of proposals
- Researchers who are partners in proposals
- Beginners who are trying to learn the basics of Horizon 2020
- Research Support Staff in Universities and Research Centres
- National Contact Points
- Consultants who support researchers in writing proposals

For proposal writers and coordinators, the handbook is designed to streamline the process of proposal writing and also to ensure that the person writing the proposal understands the background to each of the questions in the proposal.

For beginners, the handbook will show how to become involved and then how to progress to more advanced proposals.

For advisors and National Contact Points, the handbook can be used as a reference for answering the typical questions asked by researchers.

For financial and legal administrators, the handbook provides a quick overview of the key issues that must be understood in Horizon 2020 proposals and grants.

What the Handbook does NOT do!

- The handbook will not help researchers with poor science to access EU funds.
- The handbook will not help researchers with weak ideas to access EU funds.
- The handbook will not teach people how to bend the rules to access EU funds.
- The handbook does not replace European Commission documents. It should be used as a starting point before reading the European Commission documents.

The EU spends public money to undertake research for the benefit of the EU economy and to address social problems that are important to the EU. The handbook will show researchers how to put forward excellent proposals that will allow them to use their scientific knowledge to address important economic and social challenges.

Websites listed in the Handbook www.hyperion.ie/h2020-proposalwebsites.htm

This webpage is updated regurarly with new webpages and updates to the Handbook.

Handbook Layout

Chapter 1 provides a quick overview of Horizon 2020. It describes the key sources of information and the overall structure of the programme.

Chapter 2 describes how the research priorities of Horizon 2020 were selected. This Chapter could also be called 'How to Lobby for Horizon 2020'. It identifies the organisations and individuals involved in the preparation of Horizon 2020.

Chapter 3 provides a short overview of the different programmes. In particular, it identifies important background debates (lobbying) used in selecting research topics.

Chapter 4 describes the evaluation process and the evaluation criteria. It also describes how to become an 'expert evaluator.'

Chapter 5 discusses the 'Impact' of the proposal. It shows how to write the impact on Technology, the impact on the Economy, the impact on European Union Policy and Legislation, the impact on the Environment and the impact on Social Issues.

Chapter 6 describes the structure and content of a 'One Page Proposal'.

Chapter 7 describes a plan to simplify the proposal writing process.

Chapter 8 provides information on the selection of the best partners for the consortium. The chapter lists the different countries that can participate in Horizon 2020. It then provides a list of important websites where the best partners can be found.

Chapter 9 describes how to write the Implementation Plan of the project.

Chapter 10 provides a short overview of the rules and procedures for Horizon 2020. As the rules change throughout the programme, it is better to use the European Commission's handbooks as a reference for the detailed rules.

Chapter 11 provides organisations and individual researchers with a checklist that can be used to prepare a strategy for Horizon 2020.

ANNEXES

Annex I has a sample Part B of the proposal.

Annex II has samples of the evaluation criteria used during the evaluation process

Annex II is a list of the websites that are used in all of the above chapters. These can be accessed through the course Website www.hyperion.ie/h2020-proposalwebsites.htm

Structure of the Handbook

The chapters are written so that they can be used as independent reference documents. This entailed some repetition for the sake of clarification. The Handbook tries to avoid the use of Acronyms. When Acronyms are used, they are explained at the beginning of each Chapter. A Glossary is also provided at the beginning of the Handbook.

Updates to the Handbook
Discussions and updates on the Handbook can be accessed on Linkedin: Join Sean McCarthy Hyperion on Linkedin.

About the Author

Qualifications

Seán McCarthy has a PhD in Electrical Engineering. His research was done at the National Microelectronics Research Centre, (now Tyndall Institute), University College, Cork in Ireland. He is now Managing Director of Hyperion Ltd www.hyperion.ie

Research Activities

Seán McCarthy was manager of a research group in the National Microelectronics Research Centre in Cork, Ireland between 1980 and 1988. His research area was Photovoltaic (Solar Cells) Systems. His speciality was computer modelling of systems, electronic monitoring systems and battery problems in photovoltaic systems.

Hyperion Ltd.

In 1988, he established Hyperion Ltd., to sell the expertise that he had developed in his research activities. The company specialised in the development of electronic monitoring systems for industrial processes. Hyperion also continued research activities in photovoltaic and electronic monitoring systems. Today, Hyperion Ltd. specialises in the development and delivery of training courses for Research Managers.

Training Courses for Research Managers

Since 1980 Sean McCarthy has been involved in the writing of over 150 proposals for European Union Research and Development programmes. He has been a partner in over 60 research contracts and he has acted as the coordinator in 16 of these contracts. He has evaluated proposals in 10 different EU programmes.

This handbook is based on a training course titled How to Write a Competitive Proposal for Horizon 2020 (www.hyperion.ie/h2020-proposalcourse.htm).

Between 1999 and 2013, over 42,000 participants attended Hyperion's courses in 290 different locations throughout Europe. All courses were delivered by Seán McCarthy.

Linkedin: Sean McCarthy Hyperion
Twitter: @seanmccarthyhyp

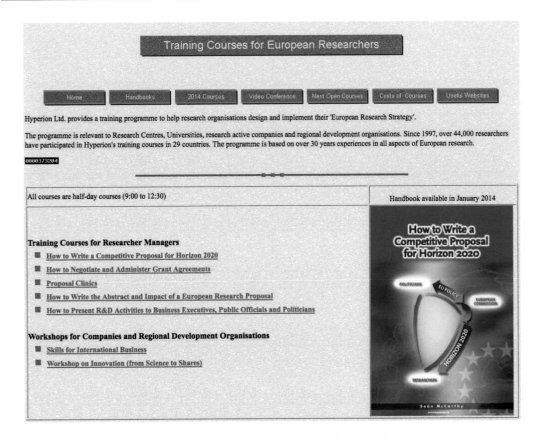

Hyperion Home Page www.hyperion.ie

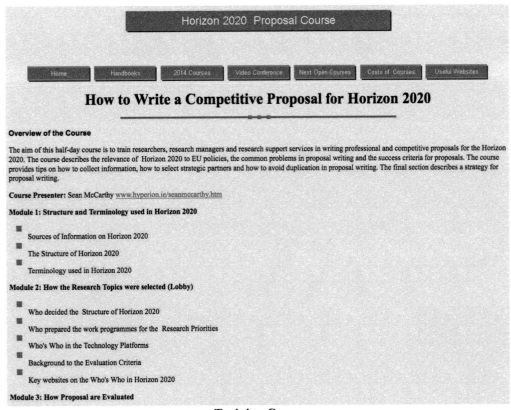

Training Course

How to Write a Competitive Proposal for Horizon 2020 www.hyperion.ie/h2020-proposalcourse.htm

Acknowledgements

This handbook is based on a training course that was presented to over 42,000 researchers since 1997. The courses were presented in 290 different research organisations throughout the European Union. These are listed in the following page. I would like to thank all of these researchers for attending the courses and the management of the research centres for inviting me to present the courses in their premises. During each course and after the course through emails, researchers had the opportunity to ask questions. These questions were most valuable in identifying the key issues that should be covered in this handbook. Also, the enthusiasm and commitment of research managers that I worked with gave me great encouragement.

I would like to dedicate this Handbook to my four children: Sylvia, Diarmuid, Grace and Jack

Seán McCarthy

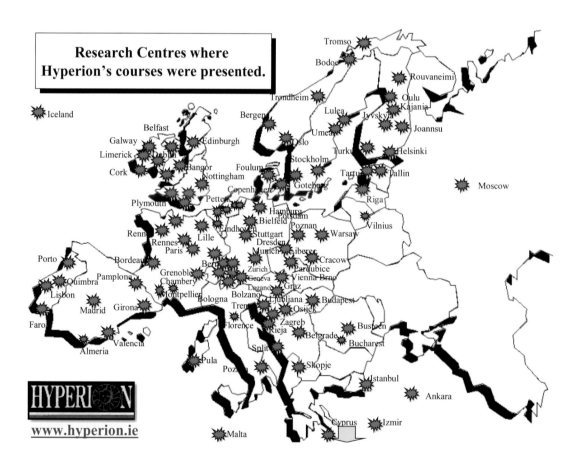

Training Locations in the European Union
The handbook is based on training courses presented in all of the following organisations:

European Organisations
EARMA
EUREKA
EARTO
International
WHO, Geneva
Joint Research Centre
Ispra, Italy
Geel, Belgium
Petten, The Netherlands
Austria
Joanneum Research, Graz
Medical University, Graz
CATT, Linz
fForte Women in Science
Belgium
SCK-CEN, Mol,
ITG, Antwerp
University of Leuven
ITG, Antwerp
Ernst and Young
Croatia
Ministry of Science and
Technology
University of Rijeka
Ruder Boskovich Institute
University of Split
University of Osijek
Czech Republic
University of Pardubice
RCP Liberec
MICEP, Prague
Cyprus
Research Promotion
Foundation
Denmark
AGRSCI
Eurocentre
University of Aahrus
DJOF, Albourg
Egypt
Finnish/Egypt Cooperation
Finland
TEKES
University of Jyvaskyla
University of Oulu
University of Helsinki
MTT
VTT
METLA
University of Vaasa
University of Lapland
University of Tampere
University Joensuu
ICT Turku
France
ILL, Grenoble
CEA, Paris
CNRS in Orleans, Paris,
Montpellier,Grenoble,Caen,
Rhone Alps ,Lille, Rennes

Germany
DLR, Bonn
UFZ, Leipzig,
Forschungszentrum Juelich
HGMU, Munich
Fraunhofer(FhG), Stuttgart
HLZ, Geestacht
Max Planck Institute, Bonn
GMD, Bonn
CEWS, Juelich
University of Stuttgart
KOWI (Brussels Office)
EADS, Munich
DKFZ, Heidelberg
University of Bielefeld
ZWM Speyer
LMU, Munich
Hungary
TET, Foundation
Iceland
RANNIS
University of Iceland
DeCode
Italy
EUI, Florence
University Bolzano
EUREC, Bolzan
University Padova
University de Roma
University of Bologna
Polaris, Sardinia
University of Potenza
Ireland
Teagasc
Dublin City University
DIT, Dublin
Enterprise Ireland
Marine Institute
Materials Ireland
WIT, Waterford
Cork Institute of Technology
Tyndall Institute, Cork
University College, Galway
University of Limerick
FORFAS, Dublin
DkIT, Dundalk
Sifco Ltd.
NUI, Maynooth
St. Patrick's College, Dublin
Hewlett Packard
DIAS, Dublin
Northern Ireland
IRTU, Belfast
Latvia
NCP Latvia
University of Agriculture
Lithuania
NCP Lithuania
Macedonia (FYROM)
Ministry of Science

Malta
Malta Council for
Science and Technology
Prime Minister's Office
Norway
Norwegian Research
Council
Agricultural University
of Norway
Oslo Agricultural
College
University of Bergen
University of Tromso
University of Trondheim
Veso, Oslo
University of Bodoe
Poland
NCP Poland
University of Krakow
Poznan Technology Park
Technology Partners
Portugal
FEUP Oporto
ICCTI
INESC Porto
PRELO
University of Coimbra
University of Algarve
GRICES, Lisbon
Romania
Uefiscsu
RARMA
RCTP, Timisoara
Russia
International Science and
Technology Centre
Scotland
Edinburgh University
Serbia
Ministry of Science
Slovenia
Innovation Relay Centre
Josef Stefan Institute
SBRU
Spain
Universidad Politecnica
de Valencia
Universidad de Alicante
AIDO, Valencia
University of Girona
ICT, Pamplona
ISDEFE, Madrid
Sweden
Research Council
Karolinska Institute
SLU
University of Lulea
University of UMEA
University of Uppsala
KTH
IRIS

Switzerland
EUresearch (NCPs)
SARMA
University of Basel
University of Lugano
Euroberatung
Network
Euro Info Centre
Uni. of Fribourg
Paul Scherrer Institut,
Würenlingen
EMPA, Dübendorf
University Nuchatel
ETH, Zurich
IBM, Zurich
University of Geneva
University Lausanne
Cern, Geneva
The Netherlands
International Training
School, Enschede
PNO Consultants
Universiteit von
Amsterdam
University of Utrecht
Vrije Universiteit,
Amsterdam
Philips Electronics
Netherlands BV
TNO, Delft
University of
Wageningen
Turkey
Tubitak (NCPs)
Izmir Business Park
MK Training Ltd.
United Kingdom
Medical Research
Council
CEFAS
Plymouth Marine
Research Centre
Universities of:
Surrey
Warwick
Sheffield
Nottingham
Central England
Manchester
Southampton
Wales
University of Wales,
Swansea
University of Wales,
Bangor

Glossary

Acronyms are rarely used in this handbook. When they are used, they are explained on the same page. The following is a summary of the key Acronyms used in Horizon 2020

AC	Associate Country
CFS	Certificate on Financial Statement
CSA	Coordination and Support Action
CSACA	CSA (Coordination Action)
CSASA	CSA (Support Action)
CIP	Competitiveness and Innovation Programme
CSO	Civil Society Organisation
DG	Directorate General (e.g. DG Research)
EAG	External Advisory Group
EEIG	European Economic Interest Group
EC	European Commission
EOI	Expression of Interest
EP	European Parliament
ERAC	European Research Area Committee
ERC	European Research Council
ESR	Evaluation Summary Report
ETP	European Technology Platform
EU	European Union
EURIAB	European Research and Innovation Advisory Board
FET	Future and Emerging Technologies
FP6	Framework 6
H2020	Horizon 2020
HLG	High Level Group
I3	Integrated Infrastructure Initiative
ICPC	International Cooperation Partner Country
IPR	Intellectual Property Rights
JTI	Joint Technology Initiative
MS	Member State (of the European Union)
NOE	Network of Excellence
OLAF	EU Anti-Fraud Office
OMC	Open Method of Coordination
PPP	Public Private Partnership
R&D	Research and Development
RTD	Research and Technology Development
RSFF	Risk Sharing Finance Facility
SICA	Specific International Cooperation Action
SME	Small and Medium Sized Enterprise
TP	Technology Platform
WP	Work Package

Chapter 1: An Overview of Horizon 2020

CONTENTS

1.1 The Success Criteria for Horizon 2020

1.2 Overview of Horizon 2020
Where to get information on Horizon 2020
The Structure of Horizon 2020
Example of a 'Call for Proposals'
The Research Priorities (Quick Overview)

1.3 What is your Strategy for Horizon 2020?

Success Criteria for Horizon 2020

Success in Horizon 2020 is about winning individual proposals. Successful proposals have the following characteristics.

Best ideas and Excellent Science

The essential part of any proposal is the idea and the excellence of the proposed science. In addition to having an excellent idea, researchers must 'sell' the idea to the evaluator. Unfortunately, most researchers are better at 'telling' than 'selling'. To 'sell' a concept to the evaluators, it is necessary to understand the mind of the evaluator. The best way to understand the mind of the evaluator is to become an evaluator. Researchers can apply to become an evaluator through the Participant Portal. The evaluation process is described in detail in Chapter 4.

Select the best partners and have an experienced Coordinator

The first step in any new proposal is to bring together the best researchers in the research topic. The best researchers have the best ideas. Researchers with ideas for proposals are always invited to participate. For newcomers to European research, this is a problem. Newcomers need to spend time networking and promoting their expertise to the best researchers. This can be achieved through participation in networks, associations, expert groups etc. This is the topic of Chapter 2 (Lobbying) and Chapter 8 (Finding Partners)

Who would you select if you were given the money and then told to select partners?

Impact

Impact is a political word. On 30th November 2011, the European Commission submitted a proposal to the Council and the European Parliament requesting €87 billion for Horizon 2020. The Council and the Parliament requested an *'Impact Assessment Report'* to justify why they should spend this money. The European Commission is now applying the same concept to researchers who are applying for individual research projects. How to write the 'Impact' of the proposal is described in Chapter 5 (Impact).

Science + Management + Financial Administration

In every proposal, there are four main parts:
>Scientific Excellence (B1) – written by the researchers
>Impact (B2) is written by the partner who wants the results
>Management and Implementation (B3) – normally written by an individual with experience in project management
>Financial Administration (A) – the budget – prepared by individuals familiar with financial calculations.

In other words, writing a proposal is a team effort. Chapter 7 presents a table that can be used as a template when planning and writing a proposal

Other issues that influence the success of a proposal are:
- **Start early**. The period of time from the publication of the draft work programmes to the call deadline is approximately 7 months. All this time must be used.
- **Use Research Support Services** at Institution level, National Level (National Contact Points) and Brussels level (National Offices). These support services are most effective if contacted at an early stage in the process.

Professional Coordinator and Research Manager

In Horizon 2020 proposals (and projects), one of the consortium partners is designated as 'Coordinator.' This job is normally done by two people. The 'Scientific Coordinator' ensures that the science is of high quality and the 'Research Manager' ensures that the contractual and financial aspects of the project are implemented properly. In many cases, the scientific coordination and management are done by one partner (organisation). Other times, the work can be divided between two partner organisations in the project. Finding a good scientific coordinator and research manager is essential. Chapter 9 (Implementation) describes the role of the scientific coordinator and project manager. The following are some of the criteria that must be considered when joining (or starting) a proposal:
- Does the coordinator have experience with previous Framework projects?
- Does the coordinator's organisation have the financial and legal experience to deal with all aspects of Horizon 2020 proposals/projects?
- Does the coordinator have personal contacts with the European Commission e.g. are they coordinator of an existing project?
- Has the coordinator received funding from their National Governments (or own organisation) to fund the writing of the proposal?
- Did the scientific coordinator evaluate Framework proposals in the past?
- Did the scientific coordinator participate in any European R&D networks, COST actions, Technology Platforms, Advisory groups? (Chapter 2).

Educate the Evaluator (with facts and figures)

This is, by far, the most important secret in writing any proposal. Researchers must understand the difference between a Horizon 2020 proposal and a scientific paper. When a scientific paper is submitted to a journal, the content of the document is purely scientific and scientific experts review the paper. In the case of Horizon 2020 proposals, the content is scientific, political, economic, and social. It also has a comprehensive management section. The different evaluators will have scientific, economic and political backgrounds. It is essential to educate all of the evaluators (with fact and figures) on ALL of these issues. The only exception are ERC Proposals – where excellence science is the only evaluation criteria.

Educating the Evaluator: Example: If a researcher is submitting a proposal entitled 'An eLearning System for Security Planning.' Who will evaluate the proposal? An expert on 'eLearning' or an expert on 'Security.' It is important to educate the eLearning expert on the security aspects of the proposal and to educate the security expert regarding the status of eLearning systems.

Facts and Figures: If an evaluator receives a proposal with 50 pages of words, the chances of success are limited. However, if the evaluator receives a 10 page proposal with facts, figures, graphs, tables, quotations and references, the proposal has a better chance of succeeding.

Networking, Networking, Networking

Networking is about establishing and staying in contact with people. It is about being out there building relationships. Then, when the time comes to form a consortium, researchers will work with the people they know and respect. It's a people, people, people business.

Researchers normally build their networks through scientific conferences, scientific networks or through previous projects. The European Commission funds European research networks in the Framework programmes for this reason. An example (described in Chapter 2) are the COST Actions.

Eliminate bad proposals early in the process (5 Key Questions)

The European Commission receives some terrible proposals. These proposals should never have passed an initial internal inspection. The 5 Key Questions should help in eliminating bad proposals. If the researcher cannot address these 5 key questions, it is an indication that the idea is not suitable for Horizon 2020 and that its chances of success are limited.

Chapter 2 will present the websites where the answers to the Five Key Questions can be found.

For applied research projects these 5 key questions are:

Why bother? (What problem are you trying to solve?)
Is it a European priority? (Could it be solved at National level?)
Is the solution already available? (Product, service, technology transfer)
Why now? (What would happen if this research was not completed now?)-(killer question)
Why you? (Do you have the best consortium to do this work?)

For ERC (Fundamental Research) projects the 5 Key Questions are:

What new knowledge will be generated in this project?
Will this project establish Europe as the leader in this scientific field?
Is this really beyond the state-of-the-art?
Why now? (Why was this not done before now?) – (killer question)
Why you?

Respect the European Commission's documents

The European Commission's personnel commit considerable effort and expertise to the design of the forms and guidelines for Horizon 2020. These documents are based on over 30 years of practical experience in administering research programmes. There are two important points to remember:

(1) Do not leave blanks in the forms – use '-', 0, 'Not Relevant' or something to show that the question has not been ignored. A blank in an insult to a bureaucrat.
(2) The proposal has three main sections in Part B (Scientific Excellence, Implementation and Impact). There are also three additional questions - Ethics, Gender and Security issues. This is not like an exam (answering some questions and attempting others). Each section has to be treated seriously. Really good proposals treat each section as if it is the most important section in the proposal.

Horizon 2020 forms tell the researcher exactly **WHAT** is required by the Commission.
The forms do not explain **WHY** this information is needed. This Handbook aims to provide this background knowledge because it is vital in producing a successful proposal.

Other Important Issues in Horizon 2020 Proposals

Avoid general statements.

For example, *'This proposal will improve the competitiveness of SMEs in the EU.'* The proposal must be more specific. A better example would be, *'This eLearning System will help Small and Medium Sized Enterprises in rural areas of the EU to adapt quickly to new EU legislation on Health and Safety. This will help them to meet the strict procurement criteria of multinational companies.'*

Professional layout of the proposal

Extra effort in the presentation of the proposal is very important. In some proposals, the quality is so excellent that it appears as if they are about to be published.

Repetition in proposals

Some sections of the proposal will be common to all researchers. These include the project management, the ethical strategy of the centre, the gender plan and the CVs of the partners. It is a good idea to develop templates for the research group on these topics. One research centre put these general topics on a central website. This simplified the proposal writing procedure.

Writing Style

The evaluators of Horizon 2020 proposals are from different European countries. In many cases, English is their second (or third) language. Also the evaluator has to read up to fifteen proposals in a short period. The text should be written in simple plain English. Sentences should be short. Use diagrams, tables and graphs to explain concepts. Use quotations to support arguments and print the quotations in *italics*. **If there is an important sentence in the middle of a paragraph highlight it so that the evaluator concentrates on it.**

Different parts of the proposal are written in different styles:

Abstract:	Written in journalistic style.
B1: Science	Written in scientific language – most important part of the proposal
B2: Impact	Written in journalistic style
B3: Implementation	Written in management style

Use diagrams to explain complex concepts.

One key diagram, at the beginning of the proposal, is a useful way of explaining, quickly and efficiently, the objectives of the proposal to the evaluator.

Label diagrams and tables.

Make the job of the evaluator easy by providing properly labelled tables and diagrams. Treat the proposal in the same manner as a scientific paper. It looks more professional.

Proof-reading and clarity

There is nothing worse than finding typing errors and spelling mistakes in excellent proposals. It is easy to make mistakes and it is worth asking somebody to proof-read the text for spelling mistakes and to check the flow of the language.

Where to get information on Horizon 2020

The official Website for Horizon 2020 is http://ec.europa.eu/programmes/horizon2020/

Participant Portal http://ec.europa.eu/research/participants/portal/page/home

This is where the 'Calls for Proposals' are published and where proposals are submitted electronically. Researchers, planning to participate in Horizon 2020, must have a thorough understanding of the Participant Portal. This handbook does not describe the Portal as the European Commission has a comprehensive set of guidelines and online training tools relating to the portal.

Cordis News: http://cordis.europa.eu/news/en/home.html
Cordis News publishes details of projects and their results.

IPR Helpdesk http://www.iprhelpdesk.eu/user/register
The IPR Helpdesk has an email newsletter dealing with all aspects of Intellectual Property issues in Horizon 2020

National Contact Points (NCPs)
National Contact Points are individuals in every member state who are responsible for the promotion of Horizon 2020. Each work programme in Horizon 2020 has an NCP devoted to it. The NCPs are in regular contact with the European Commission. In some countries, the governments provide funding to assist researchers in writing proposals for Horizon 2020. The National Contact Points can advise on the National funding for proposal writing.

National and Association Offices in Brussels www.iglortd.org
A number of countries/regions/organisations have established offices in Brussels and they act as a filter for information. Examples include Kowi (German Universities), UKRO (UK Research centres) and Swisscore (Swiss Research organisations).

European Research Associations www.hyperion.ie/euassociations.htm
Most research sectors are represented by European Research Associations or Networks. For example, EARTO (www.earto.eu) represents over 350 research organisations in Brussels. A list of over 200 EU associations are listed in the above website.

Linked Discussion Groups
Several Linkedin groups have been created for Horizon 2020. One very useful group is the Horizon 2020 group administered by EARTO (www.earto.eu)

Commercial Information Services
There are a number of commercial information services for EU information.

Research Europe www.researchresearch.com
Research Europe publishes a magazine on European research issues. Research Europe also has an online service: Research Professional

Euractiv www.euractiv.com
Euractiv is a private news service based in Brussels. Euractive publishes a daily news bulletin on general EU issues. Euractive also has a service 'Euractive Innovation' where a subscriber only receives news items relating to EU research and innovation issues

Companies providing training courses on Horizon 2020

A number of companies specialise in designing and delivering training courses on Horizon 2020. Hyperion is an example www.hyperion.ie.

Websites on Horizon 2020

The following webpage has been designed to support this Handbook.
www.hyperion.ie/h2020-proposalwebsites.htm

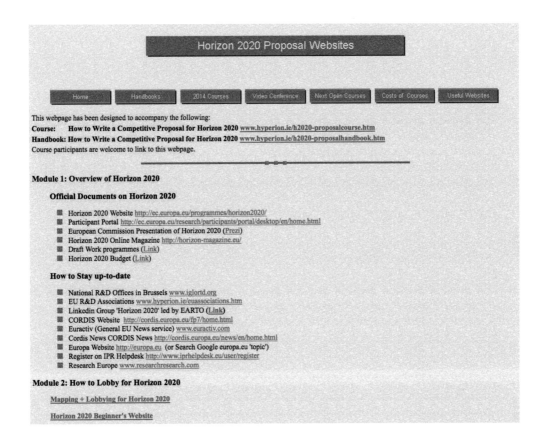

The webpage will be updated on a regularly. You are welcome to link to this page and use it when writing proposals or advising researchers.

Staying up-to-date with Horizon 2020

The best way of staying up to date with Horizon 2020 is to be involved directly in European Union activities.

Become a 'Scientific Expert' in Brussels.

The European Union needs scientific 'experts' to advise on the different policy areas. Chapter 2 will provide some examples of the different expert groups. *" 2 monitoring and one 5-year assessment exercise involved over 300 experts and produced 40 monitoring reports and 25 5-year assessment reports"* Source: European Commission.

European Associations and Networks.

Most research areas have European research networks or established research associations. For example, all of the top Renewable Energy centres in Europe have an association called EUREC (European Renewable Energy Research Centres www.eurec.be). Many European research associations and networks have offices in Brussels and have personal contacts with the scientific officers in charge of the different programmes. Examples can be seen on www.hyperion.ie/euassociations.htm. Other Networks, such as COST Actions and Coordination Actions will be described in Chapter 2.

European Science Conferences http://ec.europa.eu/research/conferences/index_en.cfm

European conferences are important sources of information on individual scientific topics. Many are funded as part of the Framework programmes and, in other cases, the European Commission provides speakers on topics related to Horizon 2020.

Become a Scientific Coordinator of EU R&D Projects.

A coordinator has a direct contact with the European Commission. Coordinators are invited to meetings in Brussels, invited to speak at conferences, asked to participate in advisory groups etc.

Evaluate FP7 Proposals
https://cordis.europa.eu/emmfp7/index.cfm?fuseaction=wel.welcome

The 'consensus meetings' of the evaluations are held in Brussels. The evaluators will have direct contact with the European Commission. It is estimated that over 5,000 evaluators are needed each year for the evaluations. In the Information and Communication Technologies programme, over 600 'expert evaluators' are needed to evaluate the proposals in each call. 25% of these must be changed annually and a person cannot evaluate more than three times in any programme.

The key word here is **NETWORKING** i.e. networking at EU level. This is an essential component of the whole process. This handbook will identify the best networks and the funding available through Horizon 2020 for networking.

The Structure of Horizon 2020

The structure of Horizon 2020 is shown in Figure 1.1.

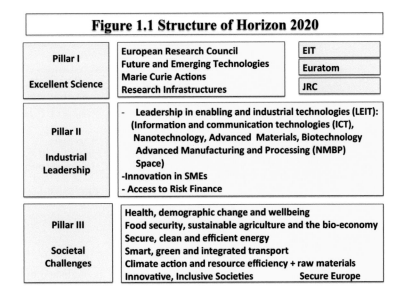

Figure 1.1 Structure of Horizon 2020

Pillar I Excellent Science	European Research Council Future and Emerging Technologies Marie Curie Actions Research Infrastructures	EIT Euratom JRC
Pillar II Industrial Leadership	- Leadership in enabling and industrial technologies (LEIT): (Information and communication technologies (ICT), Nanotechnology, Advanced Materials, Biotechnology Advanced Manufacturing and Processing (NMBP) Space) -Innovation in SMEs - Access to Risk Finance	
Pillar III Societal Challenges	Health, demographic change and wellbeing Food security, sustainable agriculture and the bio-economy Secure, clean and efficient energy Smart, green and integrated transport Climate action and resource efficiency + raw materials Innovative, Inclusive Societies Secure Europe	

In Chapter 3, each of these different programmes will be described. Each of the programmes (e.g. Health, Demographic Change and Wellbeing) has a 'Work programme' that contains 'Focus Areas' and 'Topics'. Proposals are submitted at topic level. This Handbook does not include the work programmes and topics as the topics change between calls. The work programmes can be found on the Participant Portal.

The following pages show three example of 'Topics' for Energy, Social Sciences and Humanites

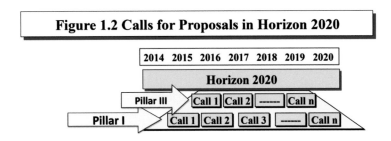

Figure 1.2 Calls for Proposals in Horizon 2020

Figure 1.2 shows that during the programme period (2014-2020), each programme has an annual Call for Proposals. The exact dates of the different Calls are announced on the Participant Portal.

Not all topics are covered in each call. The work programme and the individual calls define which topics are included.

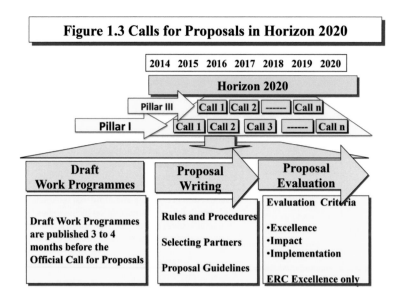

Figure 1.3 Calls for Proposals in Horizon 2020

Draft Work programmes

Before each call for proposals, a 'Draft Work programme' is published by the European Commission. This is not an official document. It is initially distributed to the Programme Committee – these are the National Delegates to the different Horizon 2020 programmes. During this period (before the official Call), researchers and research organisations have an opportunity to comment on the draft or to start planning future proposals.

Proposal Writing

The official proposal writing period is between the Official Call for Proposals and the proposal deadline. This period is normally between 3 to 4 months.

Rules and Procedures: It is important to remember that Horizon 2020 funding is public funding ('Tax Payers Money'). This is why there are so many rules and procedures on how the money can be spent. Chapter 10 provides and overview of the Legal and Financial Rules of Horizon 2020.

Selecting Partners: Horizon 2020 is a European programme. All programmes (except ERC and some Marie Curie fellowships) require consortia with partners from different countries. This is described in detail in Chapter 8.

Proposal Guidelines: Proposal writers have to follow strict guidelines and have to use an electronic proposal writing system on the Participant Portal. All proposal submissions will be completed electronically under Horizon 2020.

Evaluation of the Proposals

When the proposal arrives in Brussels, it goes through a very systematic evaluation process. In a typical year, the European Commission receives 16,000 proposals involving 84,000 partners and they may fund 2,000 projects. Chapter 4 describes the Evaluation Process. The evaluation criteria are described in Chapter 5 (Evaluation Criteria: Impact) and Chapter 9 (Evaluation Criteria: Implementation).

Example of a Call for Proposals

Call title: Marie Skłodowska-Curie Innovative Training Networks (ITN)

Call Identifier: H2020-MSCA-ITN-2014

Date of Publication: 11th December 2013

Closure Dates: 09 April 2014 at 17.00.00 Brussels time

Indicative Budget EUR 405.18 million from the 2014 budget.
   EUR 25.5 million is allocated to European Industrial Doctorates
   EUR 30 million is allocated to European Joint Doctorates.

Evaluation criteria: The selection and award criteria for Marie Skłodowska-Curie actions apply. Please read the dedicated section in this part of the work programme.

Evaluation procedure: The evaluation procedure for Marie Skłodowska-Curie actions apply. Please read the dedicated section in this part of the work programme.

Proposal page limits and layout: The maximum length of the proposal is 30 pages, excluding the annexes. Experts will be instructed to disregard any excess pages.
The minimum font size allowed is 11 points. The page size is A4, and all margins (top, bottom, left, right) should be at least 15 mm (not including any footers or headers). Ensure that the font type chosen is clearly readable (e.g. Arial or Times New Roman).

Indicative timetable for evaluation and grant agreement:
Information on the outcome of the evaluation (*one stage*): Maximum 5 months from the final date for submission.

Indicative date for the signing of grant agreements: Maximum 3 months from the date of informing applicants.

Consortium agreement:
Participants in ETN and EJD resulting from this call are NOT required to conclude a consortium agreement, as the main focus of activities is on research training and career development.

The Structure of a Proposal

The templates for the proposals can be found on the Participant Portal under 'Reference Documents'. This section provides a list of the headings of the proposal. The detailed forms are not included in this Handbook as the Participant Portal provides a comprehensive list of all the different templates.

The following is an indication of the layout of a proposal. It is important to stress that this is an example and that each 'Call for Proposals' may specify changes to this general format.

Research and Innovation Actions

PART A   Administrative information and costs
PART B
   1. Excellence
   2. Impact
   3. Quality and efficiency of the implementation
   4. Ethics Issues
   5. Consideration of gender aspects
   6. Security sensitive issues

ERC (European Research Council) Grants
(Starting, Consolidator and Advanced Grants)

Extended Synopsis: 5 pages
Curriculum Vitae: 2 pages
Track Record: 2 pages
Scientific Proposal: 15 pages
Host Institution Binding Statement of Support
Ethics Review Table
PhD record and supporting documentation for eligibility checking (for Starting and Consolidator Grants only).

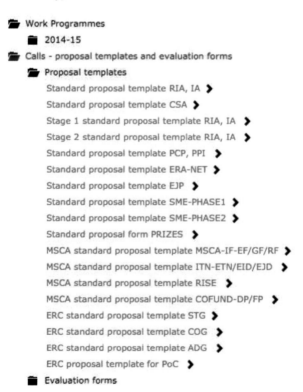

Types of Grants

Each topic, published in a work programme and call for proposals, clearly states which type of grant can be used in the topic.

Research and Innovation Actions

"Actions primarily consisting of activities aiming to establish new knowledge and/or to explore the feasibility of a new or improved technology, product, process, service or solution. For this purpose, they may include basic and applied research, technology development and integration, testing and validation of a small scale prototype in a laboratory or simulated environment. Projects may contain limited demonstration or pilot activities to show technical feasibility."
Research and Innovation Actions are funded 100% of eligible costs.

Innovation Actions

"Actions primarily consisting of activities directly aiming at producing plans and arrangements or designs for new, altered or improved products, processes or services. For this purpose, they may include prototyping, testing, demonstrating, piloting, large-scale product validation and market replication. Projects may include limited research and development activities"
Innovation Actions are funded 70% of Eligible Costs.

Coordination and Support Actions (CSA)

This type of grant does not fund research. It funds actions such as *"standardization, dissemination, awareness-raising and communication, networking, coordination or support services, policy dialogues and mutual learning exercises and studies. This includes design studies for new infrastructures and may also include complementary activities of strategic planning, networking and coordination between programmes in different countries".*
Coordination and Support Actions are funded 100% of eligible costs.

SME Instrument

The SME instrument is targeted at *"all types of innovative SMEs showing a strong ambition to develop, grow and internationalise".*
- SME Instrument (Phase 1) funds a feasibility study to verify the viability of the concept. Funding is provided at a fixed lump sum o f €50,000
- SME Instrument (Phase 2) funds demonstration, testing, prototyping, piloting, scaling-up, miniaturization, design and market replication. Funding rate is 70% (100% for exceptions).
- SME Instrument (Phase 3) facilitates access to public and private risk capital.

ERAnet Cofund

This is a merger of two previous actions (ERAnet and ERAnet plus). This is designed to bring national and regional funding agencies together to fund joint calls for proposals. The participants in this programme are organisations that are mandated to implement national or regional funding programmes.

Public Procurement Cofund Actions

These actions are designed to coordinate public procurement organization to promote:
- o (PCP) Pre-commercial public procurement which encourages public procurement bodies to fund research, development and valorization of new solutions;
- o (PPI) Public procurement of innovative solutions where the procurer acts as an early adopter of innovative solutions.

Prizes

Actions may be funded in the form of a prize. In the first Transport work programme the following topic was included:
An inducement prize for the cleanest engine (Indicative budget: €5 million)

The Rules of Participation

Official Title:
REGULATION OF THE EUROPEAN PARLIAMENT AND OF THE COUNCIL
laying down the rules for participation and dissemination in "Horizon 2020 - the Framework
Programme for Research and Innovation (2014-2020)

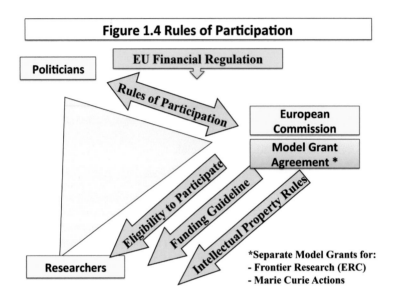

'Rules of Participation': this is the official document defining the rules of Horizon 2020.
All of the rules and procedures described in this Handbook are based on this document.
These rules define minimum criteria (e.g. number of partners in a consortium) or clear facts
(e.g. overhead rate of 25%).

The Rules are divided into three main parts:
    Eligibility Rules (Which organisations can participate)
    Funding Rules
    Rules on Intellectual Property

Below is a complete list of all the articles. Research Support Staff and Coordinators of
projects must be familiar with these rules. Throughout this Handbook, reference will be
made to the relevant article in the Rules of Participation

INTRODUCTORY PROVISIONS
    Article 1 Subject matter and scope
    Article 2 Definitions
    Article 3 Confidentiality
    Article 4 Information to be made available

GENERAL PROVISIONS
    Article 5 Forms of funding
    Article 6 Legal entities that may participate in actions
    Article 7 Independence

How Proposals are Submitted

Proposals can be submitted in one stage or in two stages. In the call for proposals, the European Commission clearly states which option is relevant to each topic. Figure 1.5 shows the flow of electronic documents between the research community and the European Commission.

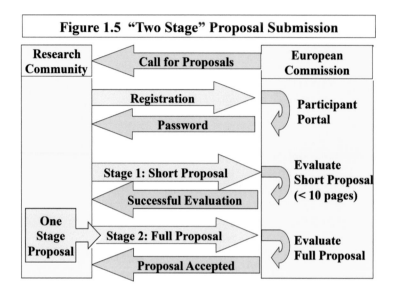

The process starts when the European Commission publishes a 'Call for Proposals.'

The Coordinator of the proposal must register the proposal in the Participant Portal. All proposal submissions in Horizon 2020 will be completed electronically.

Two Stage Submission

Some proposals involve a '*Two Stage Submission*.' In Stage 1, short proposals are submitted (usually less than 10 pages). These are evaluated and some of the proposals are rejected. The proposals that pass Stage 1 are then invited to submit a 'Full Proposal' and this is evaluated. In one Call for Proposals, one of the programmes received 554 proposals. 72 passed Stage 1 and 30 of these were approved in Stage 2. A good 'rule of thumb' is that 50% of the proposals that get to Stage 2 will be funded.

Most proposals are '*One Stage*' where full proposals are submitted. The *Call for Proposals* clearly states if it is '*One Stage*' or '*Two Stage*' proposals.

Two Stage Proposals are used in cases where:
- A large number of proposals are expected. The aim of the two stages is to remove bad proposals in Stage 1.
- The proposals will be very large. The aim of the two stages is to reduce the cost of proposal preparation for the researchers.

Evaluation Criteria of Stage 1 and Stage 2 Proposals.
In Stage 1 only the criteria 'Excellence' and 'Impact' will be requested and evaluated.

In Stage 2 the evaluation will be based on the three criteria – 'Excellence', 'Impact' and 'Implementation'.

Two Step Evaluation

Figure 1.6 shows a 'Two Step Evaluation' In this case, a full proposal is submitted by the researcher but the evaluation is done in two steps. Step 1 is a short evaluation and many proposals may be rejected in this step. A Step 2 evaluation is a full evaluation of the remaining proposals.

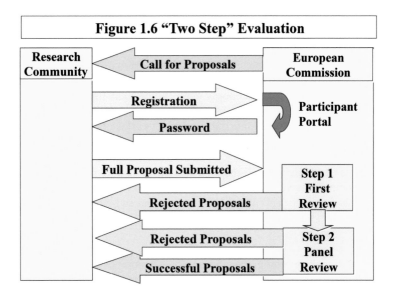

Evaluation of ERC Proposals (2-step)

A 'two step evaluation' is used for European Research Council (ERC) proposals.

"At step 1, the extended synopsis and the Principal Investigator's track record and CV will be assessed (and not the full scientific proposal). At step 2 the complete version of the retained proposals will be assessed (including the full scientific proposal)."
Source: ERC Evaluation Guidelines

Example of a 'Topic' (Social Science)

II) The Young Generation in an Innovative, Inclusive and Sustainable Europe

YOUNG-1-2014 Early job insecurity and labour market exclusion

Specific challenge:
Unemployment among young people in the EU has risen very sharply since the beginning of the financial crisis in 2008 reaching unprecedented levels. However, for over a decade the unemployment rate of young people in the EU remained approximately at double the rate of the overall unemployment in the economy while, at the same time, the use of flexible, fixed term contacts and alternative forms of employment has been increasing. This results in growing job insecurity and systematic labour market exclusion of young people at the very beginning of their professional careers with many of them moving directly from education to unemployment or taking up temporary jobs below their qualifications. The crisis has exacerbated this trend raising the threat of a 'lost generation' in particular in some European countries. A comprehensive understanding of the long-term consequences of these developments is crucial for successful economic, social and labour market policies that could address this problem now and in the future.

Scope:
The research will make a profound analysis of the situation of young people in the labour market across the EU in a comparative perspective. In particular, research should investigate the important differences in the performance of the labour markets that exist across Member States, especially from the young people's point of view, in order to identify the most effective ways of labour market organisation and education systems. Research will also investigate the economic, social, personal and psychological consequences of early job insecurity and labour market exclusion in the short, medium and long term, including for example such issues as income situation throughout the life course, establishing an independent household, family formation, physical and mental health and wellbeing. In this context, research could take into account the experiences of past generations which were exposed to high unemployment and job insecurity in their youth.

Expected impact:
Research is expected to explore in a comprehensive way the short- and long-term consequences of job insecurity and unemployment of young people in order to analyse their impact on the economy, society and politics. These activities will contribute to an effective anticipation of the potential challenges facing the EU in the future allowing for an early policy response. Through a better understanding of the mechanisms driving the labour market, this research should lead to a more robust labour market policy in the EU as well as to a better informed economic, social and education policy. Activities under this topic will also shed light on broader societal questions related, for example, to demographic developments, population ageing, health and wellbeing, as well as the potential of economic development in the EU, both from the historical and the forward-looking perspective.

Type of Actions: Research and Innovation Action (100% funded).

Example of a 'Topic' (Humanities)

II) Focus area: Reflective Societies, European values and identities

Topic 4. The role of creativity in a reflective society

Specific challenge:
The notion of creativity in its modern meaning has developed since the Renaissance and the Enlightenment as the individual and collective capacity to use imagination or original ideas to create new things, ideas, concepts, etc. Contemporarily, creativity, associated with the capability of continuous self-inquiry, is commonly considered as a self-evident value in modern Western societies and a major factor facilitating successful adaption to a globalised, fast changing world. As such, the past and present role of individual and collective creativity needs to be explored as one of the central European values and a living and inspiring part of European cultural heritage.

Scope:
The multidisciplinary research will aim at exploring the interpretations of "self-reflective societies" in a diachronic and synchronic European perspective by combining a wide range of approaches. Research should include the analysis of the different sources of creativity and the role of different factors fostering creativity in the contemporary society. The research should look, on the one hand, at the role of creativity in the artistic or scientific methods and processes, while on the other hand, it should provide an innovative analysis and new interpretations of creativity (including both its positive and negative aspects) in the context of social transformation and adaptability to change. Particular attention should be paid to provide new insights into the role of creativity in developing new products, ideas, concepts and theories.

Expected impact:
Research in this field is expected to contribute to a better understanding of the scope, mechanisms and perspectives of contemporary European reflective societies, also in comparison with other regions of the world as well as explore in depth the role of creativity and values associated with it.
The activities are also expected to provide insights into the contemporary dynamics of creativity and the factors that determine it in order to draw policy recommendations for developing a motivating educational, cultural and scientific environment.

Type of Actions: Research and Innovation Action (100% funded) – Single stage

Example of a 'Topic' (Energy)

EE 2 – 2015: Buildings design for new highly energy performing buildings

Specific Challenge: By the end of 2020 (2018 for buildings occupied and owned by public authorities), all new buildings should comply with the Energy Performance of Buildings Directive obligations and thus meet 'nearly zero-energy' performance levels using innovative, cost-optimal technologies with integration of renewable energy sources on site or nearby. Moreover, the construction of 'plus-energy' buildings - i.e. buildings producing more energy than they consume - should also be encouraged in order to reduce energy use whilst increasing the share of renewable energies. However the costs of these highly energy performing buildings still represent a barrier for investors. Therefore the construction industry needs to deliver more affordable solutions.

Scope: Projects should focus on development and demonstration of solutions which significantly reduce the cost of new buildings with at least 'nearly zero-energy' performance levels, whilst accelerating significantly the speed with which these buildings and their systems are taken up by the market. The focus should lie on solutions for appropriate indoor air quality and comfort, design adapted to local climate and site, passive solutions (reducing the need for technical building systems which consume energy) or active solutions (covering a high share of the energy demand with renewable energies), building energy management systems (where appropriate), highly efficient Heating, Ventilation and Air-Conditioning (HVAC, e.g. low temperature systems, solar cooling), electric and/or thermal energy storage of renewable energy onsite and nearby. Projects should also provide solutions for automated and costeffective maintenance of the installed equipment, and assess differences between predicted and actual energy performance. Such differences should be documented and minimized. The applied solutions should address the challenge to move towards a 'nearly-zero energy' buildings standard at large scale with demonstration projects that go beyond 'nearly-zero energy' buildings levels to the point where buildings are active contributors to energy production and environmental quality in particular when new districts are planned (e.g. netzero energy neighbourhoods). The energy balance should be calculated by means of a LCA approach, considering among other issues embodied energy.
Projects should also focus on design methods for on-site and nearby-generation of renewable energy for new buildings (electricity as well as heating and cooling generation, e.g. heat pumps, integrated photovoltaics, or other options) accompanying energy efficiency measures to achieve standards higher than those of 'nearly zero-energy' buildings.
The performance of innovative technologies may be verified through technology verification schemes such as the EU Environmental Technology Verification (ETV) pilot programme25. The Commission considers that proposals requesting a contribution from the EU of between EUR 3 and 5 million would allow this specific challenge to be addressed appropriately. Nonetheless, this does not preclude submission and selection of proposals requesting other amounts.

This topic will be implemented under the **PPP on Energy-efficient Buildings.**

The activities are expected to be implemented at **TRL 5-7** (please see part G of the General Annexes).

Expected Impact: Significant increase of the share of 'nearly zero-energy' buildings with the aim of 100% market uptake by the end of 2020. Costs reductions of at least 15% compared to current situation, with additional benefits in terms of energy reduction. Demonstration for netzero energy districts taking advantage of onsite or nearby-generation of renewable energy.

Type of action: Innovation Actions

Technology Readiness Level (TRL)

Technology Readiness Level (TRL) is a concept that was developed in the Space and Aeronautics industries. It is now used in most technology sectors to describe the state of development of a technology. Several definitions of TRL exist. The model that is used in Horizon 2020 is based on the OECD Definition. Annex G of the General Annexes of Horizon2020 defines the TRLs as shown in Table 1.1.

Table 1.1 Technology Readiness Level

TRL	Definition
TRL 1	Basic principles observed
TRL 2	Technology concept formulated
TRL 3	Experimental proof of concept
TRL 4	Technology validated in laboratory
TRL 5	Technology validated in relevant environment (industrially relevant environment in the case of the Key Enabling Technologies)
TRL 6	Technology demonstrated in relevant environment (industrially relevant environment in the case of the Key Enabling Technologies)
TRL 7	System prototype demonstration in operational environment
TRL 8	System complete and qualified
TRL 9	Actual system proven in an operational environment (competitive manufacturing in the case of Key Enabling Technologies or in space)

Examples in Call for Proposals

NMP 1 – 2014: Open access pilot lines for cost-effective nanocomposites
"The implementation of this proposal is intended to start at TRL 4-5, target TRL 6. Implemented as cross-KET activities."

"Expected impact: A European eco-system for high TRL testing and validation of nano-composites, affordable and accessible for SMEs, through technical collaboration between RTOs and composite producers and through identification of all critical value chain players for the market introduction of the final product."

Transport Programme:
1 Aviation
"The SESAR Joint Undertaking develops solutions for a seamless, efficient and cost effective management of air traffic, including services of European GNSS and covers the full range of TRL from 1 to 6."

TRLs and Social Sciences
The concept of Technology Readiness Levels (TRL) was designed for industries. It is not realistic to apply TRLs to Social, Economic and Political Sciences. However, phases such as basic principle observed, concept formulated, data collection and validated in a relevant environment. Closer to use terminology could be scenario planning, recommendations, strategy and implementation could be used to explain the relevant phases. There is a need to develop an SRL (Society Relevance Level).

Funding the Whole Innovation Chain

Horizon 2020 claims that it is designed to cover the 'whole innovation chain'. This section provides a map showing the relationship between the different funding programmes. Before describing these relationships, a number of concepts must be explained.

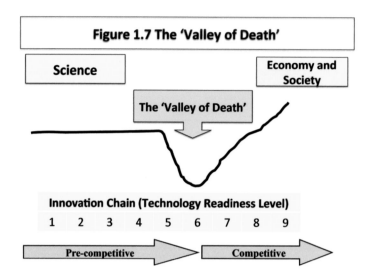

Innovation Chain
The Innovation Chain refers to the different Technology Readiness Levels described in the previous section.

'Valley of Death'
This is a term used to describe the gap between the research that is done by academics and researchers (TRL 1 to TRL 4) and the needs of industry (TRL 8 and TRL 9). The 'Valley of Death' is estimated to cover TRL 5, TRL 6 and TRL 7. These activities are not interesting to academic researchers as there is no scientific benefit from this work i.e. no publication. Industry is not interested in TRL 5,6 and 7 as it is considered expensive and risky. Large companies with research laboratories can fund these type of activities. For small and medium sized enterprises, this is often not practical. It is estimated that only 6% of European companies can undertake these activities.

Competition Law and State Aid Rules
Under European competition legislation, public funding cannot be used to help one company be more competitive than another European company. At the international level governments agree 'State Aid Rules' that limit how public money is spent on Research.
Public funding in Europe (Member States and European Union) only fund 'pre-competitive' research. For example, in the case of biotechnology, there are three different trials –Phase I, Phase II and Phase III. Phase I trials are considered 'pre-competitive' and can be funded as part of National or EU programmes. Phase II and Phase III trials are considered 'competitive' and consequently are not funded in public programmes. In the case of other research fields pre-competitive can mean pre-standard or pre-regulation. Most researchers are not aware of this debate as their research is in the range TRL1 to 4.

"If the risk benefit sharing does not take place under market conditions, and the price paid for the services provided is higher than market price, this will normally be regarded as State Aid that will have to be notified to and assessed by the Commission according to Articles 87-88 of the EC Treaty and the State aid Framework for Research, Development and Innovation."
Source: Pre-commercial Procurement: Driving innovation to ensure sustainable high quality public services in Europe {SEC(2007) 1668}

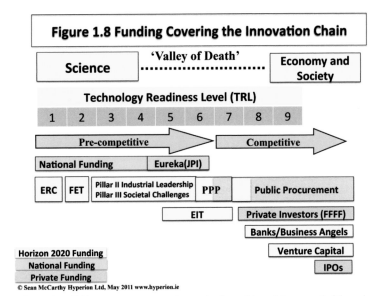

Figure 1.8 shows how the different programmes are designed to address activities along the Innovation Chain. These programmes are described in Chapter 3 (Research Priorities).

National Research Programmes: These programmes fund activities from TRL 1 to 5 (Fundamental research to pilot)

JPI (Joint Programming Initiative) **Eureka** is not a European Union programme. Eureka is an example of how different countries come together to fund research. If a consortium submits a proposal to Eureka, the Irish partner is funded in Ireland, the German partner in Germany etc. The concept of 'Joint Programming' uses Eureka as a model.

ERC (European Research Council) funds fundamental research (TRL 1) www.hyperion.ie/erc.htm

FET (Future and Emerging Technologies) funds radicals research, where known concepts are brought together in a novel way. www.hyperion.ie/fet.htm

Pillar II (Industrial Leadership) and **Pillar III** (Societal Challenges) fund TRL 3 to TRL 5

PPP (Public Private Partnerships) involve public funding and private funding being brought together to fund activities closer to the market (TRL 5,6,7). www.hyperion.ie/ppp.htm

Public Procurement is a term used when public bodies (local authorities, public hospitals, etc.) use their purchasing power to request innovation solutions to address their problems. Two concepts are used here. More information can be found on www.hyperion.ie/publicprocurement.htm

EIT (European Institute of Innovation and Technology) is designed to bridge the 'Valley of Death'. It brings together Universities, Research Centres and Companies to stimulate innovation at a regional level. www.hyperion.ie/eit.htm

FFFF (Founder, Friends, Fools and Family) – the traditional way of funding the first phase of a start-up company. This is not funded as part of Horizon 2020.

Banks and Business Angels: These are the main source of funding in the region €30,000 to €100,000 In Horizon 2020, there is funding for banks willing to invest in high potential growth companies.

Venture Capital: this is the primary source of funding for investments of €1 million +. In Horizon 2020, funding is provided to venture capital companies to invest in high potential growth companies.

IPO (Initial Public Offering). This is the term used to describe companies that float on the market. This is not funded in Horizon 2020.

Horizon 2020 Budget

Source: Horizon 2020 website (official figures)

Pillar	Programme	€ (2013 prices)
Pillar I Excellent Science 31.73% of budget €24.441 billion	ERC (European Research Council)	€13.095 billion
	Future and Emerging Technologies	€2.696 billion
	Marie Curie Actions	€6.162 billion
	Research Infrastructures	€2.488 billion
Pillar II Industrial Leadership 22.09 % of budget €17.016 billion	Leadership in Enabling and Industrial Technologies	€13.577 billion
	Access to Risk Finance	€2.842 billion
	Innovation in SMEs	€0.616 billion
Pillar III Societal Challenges 38.53 % of budget €29.679 billion	Health, Demographic Change, and Wellbeing	€7.472 billion
	Food Quality and Marine Research	€3.851 billion
	Secure, Clean and Efficient Energy	€5.93 billion
	Smart, Green and Integrated Transport	€6.339 billion
	Climate Action, Resources and Raw Material	€3.081 billion
	Inclusive and Innovative Societies	€1.309 billion
	Secure Societies	€1.695 billion
EIT	European Institute of Innovation and Technology	€2.711 billion
JRC	Direct Actions of Joint Research Centre	€1.903 billion
	Spreading Excellence and Widening Participation	€0.816 billion
	Science for and with Society	€0.462 billion
Total Horizon 2020 (excluding EURATOM)		**€76.7 billion**
EURATOM	(2014-2018)	€1.603 billion
Total Horizon 2020 Package		**€79.0 billion**

Chapter 2: How the Research Priorities are Selected (How to Lobby)

CONTENTS

The Players in Horizon 2020
Political Background to Horizon 2020
Background to the Research Priorities
Background to the Evaluation Criteria
Other Political Priorities influencing Horizon 2020
The Technology Platforms
Expert Advisory Groups

Chapter Webpage: www.hyperion.ie/h2020-mapping.htm

Political Background to Horizon 2020

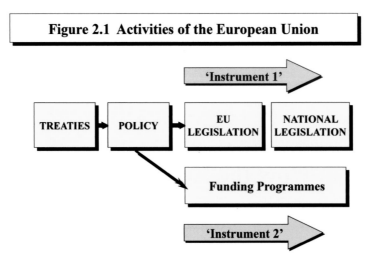

Figure 2.1 Activities of the European Union

The Treaty

The Member States of the European Union come together and they prepare a Treaty. The Treaty describes the policy areas where the Member States wish to cooperate. Examples include Energy, Agriculture, Transport, Environment etc. The Treaty on the Functioning of the European Union states *"The Union shall have the objective of strengthening its scientific and technological bases by achieving a European research area in which researchers, scientific knowledge and technology circulate freely, and encouraging it to become more competitive, including in its industry, while promoting all the research activities deemed necessary by virtue of other Chapters of the Treaties."*

Policy

The Institutions of the European Union prepare Policies based on the agreements in the Treaty. Policies describe exactly how the Member States will work together to meet the objectives defined in the Treaty. Examples include Agricultural Policy, Enterprise Policy, Regional Policy and Social Policy. Policy is only paper, and on its own, it has no impact. To implement these policies, the European Union says it has two 'instruments' - **Legislation** and **Funding Programmes.**

Legislation

EU Legislation is the most powerful instrument used in implementing EU Policies. For example, the European Union has a policy on the quality of drinking water. This policy is implemented through the Water Framework Directive.

Funding

European Union funding programmes are designed as 'instruments' to implement EU policies. There are many different funding programmes. Most researchers, preparing proposals for Horizon 2020, take time to study the funding rules. From the above diagram, it is clear that researchers should also study the policies behind the research topics in Horizon 2020.

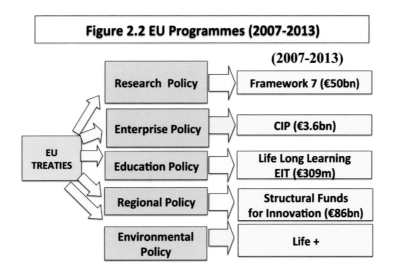

The financial cycle of the European Union is a seven year cycle. The current cycle is from 1st January 2014 to the end of 2020.

2007 to 2013 Financial Cycle
The previous financial cycle was from 2007 to 2013. Figure 2.2 shows some of the programmes that existed in the period 2007 to 2013.

Framework 7   http://cordis.europa.eu/fp7/home.html
Framework 7 was the name of the €50 billion programme that funded research and development.

CIP (Competitiveness and Innovation Programme)
http://ec.europa.eu/enterprise/enterprise_policy/cip/index_en.htm
CIP was a €3.6 billion programme that was designed to take research results closer to the market or closer to the end user application.

Structural Funds for Innovation:
http://ec.europa.eu/regional_policy/funds/2007/index_en.htm
Structural Funds were solely used in the past to develop infrastructure (roads, telecommunications etc) in the lesser developed regions of the European Union.
During the period 2007 to 2013, the programme was extended to the funding of Innovation. 15% of the Structural Funds (2007-2013) were allocated to Innovation.

EIT (European Institute of Innovation and Technology) http://ec.europa.eu/eit/
In 2010 the EIT was established as part of the Directorate General for Education. This was not part of Framework 7. It had a budget of €309 million for the period 2010 to 2013.

In 2010, there was a mid-term review of all the European programmes. The main conclusion of this review was that the different programmes operated independently ('silos'). One of the main recommendations of this review was that there should be more integration between the different programmes.

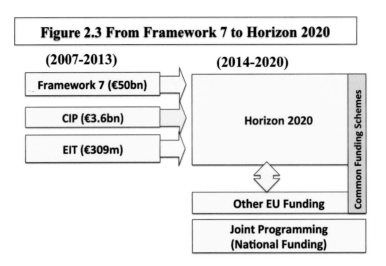

The official debate on Horizon 2020 started on 30th November 2011. The unoffical debate started in 2010. Following the mid-term review of the European programmes, the European Commission proposed the structure shown in Figure 2.3.

Framework 7, part of CIP and the EIT were brought together to become Horizon 2020. (This is why it was not called 'Framework 8').

Horizon 2020 will also be closely linked to the other European programmes such as the European Structural and Investment Funds (ESIF), Erasmus + and COSME (part of the old CIP programme). (These programmes are not described in this handbook)

Joint Programming
Horizon 2020 has more links with national funding programmes. This concept is called 'Joint Programming'. These links are described in Chapter 2. Background information in Joint Programming can be found on www.hyperion.ie/jointprogramming.htm

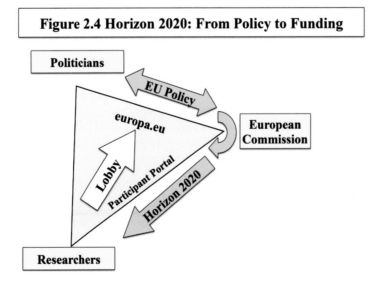

The main players in the design of Horizon 2020 are:

Politicians

The Council of Ministers represents the Member State Governments. The permanent representatives of the member states is known as COREPER.

European Parliament – members (MEPs) are directly elected at regional level. The Parliament is divided into 'Committees' and the committee responsible for Horizon 2020 is:
ITRE (Industry Trade Research and Energy).

The European Commission

The European Commission are the officials (similar to civil servants) responsible for the day to day running of the European Union activities. The European Commission has two main roles:
- It is the only institution that can 'propose' new legislation. For example, on 30th November 2011, the European Commission sent a proposal regarding Horizon 2020 to the European Parliament and Council of Ministers. This was the official start of the debate on Horizon 2020.
- it implement programmes – it is the only institution that spends money on programmes.

The European Commission is divided into Directorates General (DG). The full list of these (and their Acronyms) can be found on http://ec.europa.eu .

Table 2.1 Directorates General (DG) responsible for Horizon 2020 Programmes

Horizon 2020 Programme	Directorate General (DG)
Health, Demographic Change and Well-being	DG RTD
Food Security, Sustainable Agriculture, Marine..	DG RTD + DG AGRI
Secure, Clean and Efficient Energy Challenge	DG RTD + DG ENTR
Smart, Green and Integrated Transport Challenge	DG RTD +DG MOVE
Resource Efficiency and Climate Challenge	DG RTD
Inclusive, Innovative Societies	DG RTD
Security	DG RTD + DG CNECT
FET (Future and Emerging Technologies)	DG RTD + DG ENTR
Enabling and Industrial Technologies (inc. KETs)	DG RTD + DG ENTR
Support for SMEs	DG RTD +DG ENTR

The European Commission administers some of Horizon 2020 though 'Executive Agencies'.
"The task of executive agencies is to manage (literally to "execute") specific activities that would normally have been carried out by specific departments within the European Commission. As they concentrate on this management role, and have no policy remit, executive agencies can be more effective and more efficient in addressing the needs of their client base (in this case the research communities). " http://ec.europa.eu/research/rea/.

REA: Research Executive Agency
             REA administers the Marie Curie Programme

ERCEA: European Research Council Executive Agency
             ERCEA administers the ERC Programme

EACI: Executive Agency for Competitiveness and Innovation
EAHC: Executive Agency for Higher Consumers

Figure 2.5 shows the relationship between the different institutions in Horizon 2020. European Union Policy is first prepared between the Political Institutions (Council of Ministers and the European Parliament) and the European Commission (civil servants). When the policy is agreed, the European Commission implements its Policies through funding programmes such as the Horizon 2020 Programme. The important point here is that the topics in Horizon 2020 are political priorities. Another important point is that the European Commission is the only European Union Institution that has money for research (or indeed for any other activity).

One researcher summarised the above as: *"I always thought that the Call for Proposals was the beginning of the process. Now I realise it is actually the end of the process."*

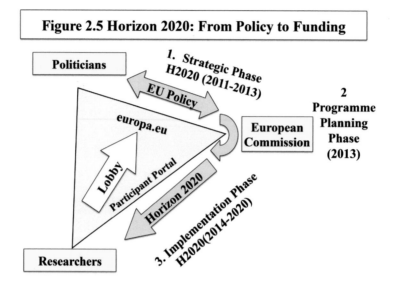

Figure 2.5 Horizon 2020: From Policy to Funding

Strategic Phase (2011 to 2013)
The debate on Horizon 2020 started on 30th November 2011 and was completed at the end of 2013. This was a debate between the European Commission and the European Parliament/Council of Minister.

Programme Planning Phase
During 2013, the European Commission began to draft the work programmes based on the discussion from the Strategic Phase. The draft programmes were published in July/August 2013 and the official work programmes were published in December 2013

Implementation Phase (2014 to 2020)
During this phase, the European Commission is responsible for the implementation of Horizon 2020. This is done through calls for proposals and is the main subject of this Handbook.

Lobbying
During the Strategic Phase and the Programme Planning phase, the European Commission 'consults the stakeholders'. They invite members of the research community to contribute to the debate on the structure of Horizon 2020. This process is described in Chapter 2.

Participant Portal
This is where the official forms and procedures for Horizon 2020 can be found

europa.eu
This is the official website of the European Union. This is where all the policy documents can be found. Examples will be presented in the Chapter 2.

When writing a proposal the forms can be found on the Participant Portal. The arguments for the proposal (especially impact) can be found on europa.eu.

Background to the Research Priorities

To fully understand EU policy, it is necessary to understand the political priorities of the European Union i.e. *'How do they think in Brussels?'* Policy making is about planning ahead 10 to 15 years. Policy makers try to identify the 'challenges' that will face Europe in this future period.

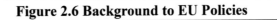

Figure 2.6 Background to EU Policies

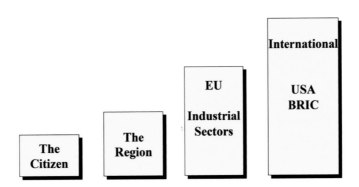

European policies focus on four main areas:

The Citizen

The first level is the level of the **citizen**. 2013 was designated as the *'European Year of the Citizen'*. Phrases such as *'research for the benefit of the citizen'* figure frequently in Commission documents. *"We want a Europe built for the citizens by the citizens"* The importance of this emphasis on the welfare of the 'citizen' will be explained in the following pages.

The Region

In European Union policy debates, the politicians do not think about Germany, France, Portugal etc. The European Union has been divided into more than 275 'Regions.' A 'Region' is defined as the level where policies can be implemented. The importance of the 'Region' is based on the following: **The EU politicians make Policy at EU level but they implement the policies at Regional level.** In Brussels, there is a 'Committee of the Regions,' 'Regional Policy,' 'Regional Funds' (Structural Funds), Inter-regional cooperation etc.

If the proposal has a geographical dimension, it is good to base the research at this regional level. The following is an example:

'In our proposal, we will select a region of France, a region of Germany, a region of Poland and a region of Sweden. We will test the model in these regions and then we will disseminate the results to the other regions of the EU,'

European Union Industrial Sectors

The next level for the politicians is the **European Industrial Sector** level. e.g. aeronautics sector, IT sector, biotechnology sector, agricultural sector etc… One of the main differences, between national and EU R&D funding for industry, is that national R&D is focused on individual companies whereas EU funding is based on the EU industrial sectors.

International

The final level for the politicians is the **International** level and the role of the EU on the international stage. In practice, international usually means the USA and BRIC countries (Brazil, Russia, India and China). In the future, Europe will be one player on the international stage. In Horizon 2020, researchers are encouraged to think at International level. The different opportunities for international cooperation will be presented in Chapter 3.

Figure 2.7 The Background to European Union Policies

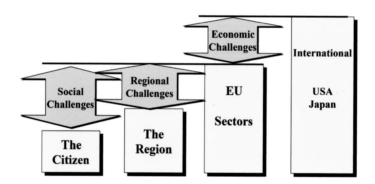

The European Commission funds many studies and collects considerable amounts of information through its statistical office, Eurostat (http://ec.europa.eu/eurostat). In addition to Eurostat, the OECD (www.oecd.org) provides European policy makers with reports on international issues. Eurostat and the OECD produce statistical data and reports relating to social, regional, sectoral and international issues. From this analysis, 'challenges' are identified. These are shown in Figure 2.7.

Social Challenges

If Eurostat or the OECD identify a group of European citizens, whose 'Quality of Life' is below the European average, then the European Institutions may decide to prepare policies to correct this disadvantage. Examples include: youth unemployment, the ageing society, the disabled, people with cancer, Alzheimer's disease, diabetes etc. Another interesting group are people who do not use the Internet – the 'digital divide.' In other words, researchers never go to Brussels looking for money – they only go there to help address a Policy challenge.

Humanities in Horizon 2020

Europe has over 400 different cultures – the motto of the European Union is *'Unity in Diversity'*. 2004 was designated as the 'European Year of Inter-cultural Communication'. Poor inter-cultural communication can result in conflict. Excellent intercultural communication can result in creativity (e.g. Silicon Valley). Projects funded in Horizon 2020, in the area of Humanities, focus on these two themes (intercultural communication and creativity).

The Regional Challenges (Smart Specialisation)

If the EU identifies a region where the economic development is below the European average then policies are designed to fill these regional gaps. Regional funds are used for the development of infrastructure such as roads, buildings, research centres etc. A new challenge has been identified for the regions of Europe. Some regions suffer from an 'Innovation Divide'. In the Structural Funds (2014-2020), there is an emphasis on 'Smart Specialisation' – where regions are encouraged to develop a strategy for innovation. These Smart Specialisation Strategies will be used to allocate Structural Funding to the regions. There will be links between Horizon 2020 and the Structural Funds. For example, topics such as 'Smart Cities' and 'Smart Communities' are included in Horizon 2020 programmes. The 'Knowledge Innovation Community' (KIC) in the EIT can be used as a model for stimulating innovation at regional level. The Marie Curie COFUND programme states: *"Programmes that prioritise specific research disciplines based on national or regional Research and Innovation Strategies for Smart Specialisation (RIS3 strategies) will also be supported"*.

Economic Challenges

In earlier Framework programmes, the focus was on 'catching up' with the USA. For example, if the USA was the leader in Information Technology then the justification for the programme was to help European organisations to fill the 'Economic Gap.' In 2006, an important report was published that changed this thinking. The report, entitled ***'Creating an Innovative Europe,'*** is better known as the 'Aho Report' after its author Mr. Esko Aho, former Prime Minister of Finland. In this report, Mr. Aho argued that scientific areas should be identified where Europe was or could be the leader. According to the report, these areas could then be referred to as 'Lead Markets.' The European Commission stated: "The *Technology Platforms can play a strong role in developing the concept of Lead Markets"*. The Technology Platforms are described in the following section of this Chapter.

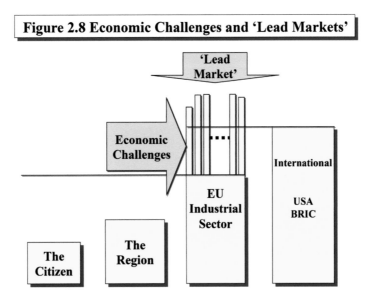

Figure 2.8 Economic Challenges and 'Lead Markets'

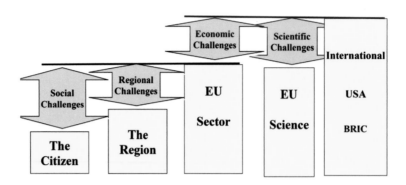

Figure 2.9 Policy Challenges and Horizon 2020

The Science Challenge

During the planning for Framework 7, a further gap was identified. Europe was seen to be falling behind in basic research in important scientific areas. The basic research community learned how to lobby.

"Although the EU remains the largest producer of scientific publications in the world, the US produces twice as many of the most influential papers (the top 1% by citation count). Similarly, international university ranking exercises show that US universities dominate the top places. And 70% of the world's Nobel Prize winners are located in the US. " (Impact Assessment Report 2011)

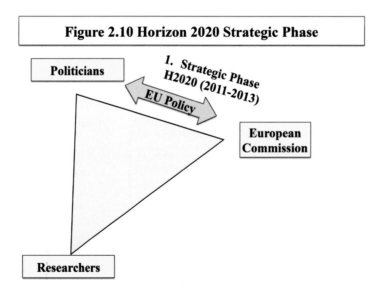

Figure 2.10 Horizon 2020 Strategic Phase

The above arguments were used during the Strategic Phase of Horizon 2020. It was a debate between the European Commission and the European Parliament/Council of Ministers.

How the Research Priorities were selected

Following this debate, the European Commission proposed the structure for Horizon 2020 shown in Figure 2.11.

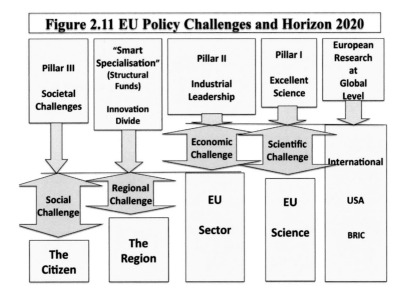

Pillar I: Social Challenges

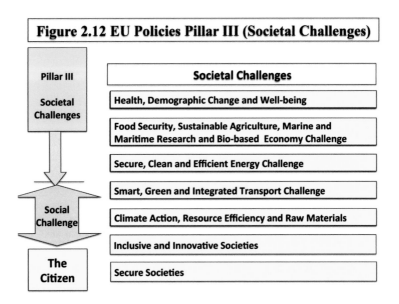

The key social challenges identified are:
* The health of the European Citizen (background to **Health Programme**)
* The quality and safety of food (**Food Programme**)
* The security of the European citizen (**Security Programme**)
* The social issues that are important at European level (**Social Science Programme**)

Pillar II: Industrial Leadership

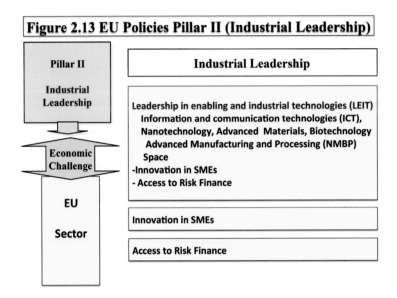

Figure 2.13 EU Policies Pillar II (Industrial Leadership)

The sectors where Europe would like to have Lead Markets are: **Biotechnology, Nanotechnology, Information and Communication Technologies, Materials, Aeronautics, and Aerospace.** This is why these topics have been included in Pillar II of Horizon 2020.

Pillar I: Excellent Science

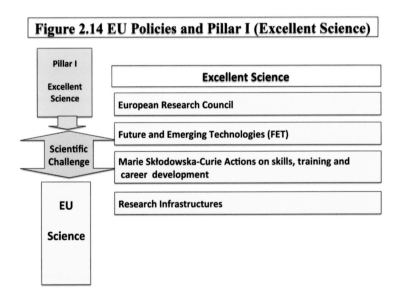

Figure 2.14 EU Policies and Pillar I (Excellent Science)

The aim of the ERC programme is to establish Europe as the international leader in different scientific fields. The aim of the Marie Curie programme is to develop the careers of European researchers. The Research Infrastructure is designed to identify future research infrastructures that will be needed in Europe to promote scientific excellence.

International Issues in Horizon 2020

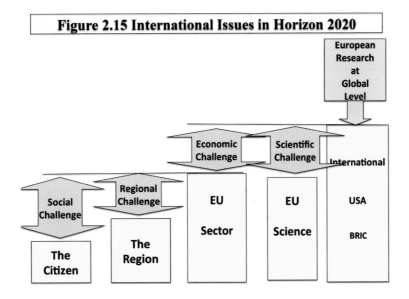

Figure 2.15 International Issues in Horizon 2020

International Agreements: The European Union has signed a number of international agreements. Examples of these International Agreements include:

*   Universal Declaration of the Human Genome and Human Rights (UNESCO)
*   Declaration of Helsinki on Human Rights and Biomedicine
*   Protocol on the Prohibition of Cloning of Human Beings (Paris 12/1/1998)
*   UN Convention on Biological Diversity (1992)
*   Millennium Development Goals (2000)
*   Kyoto Protocol (1997)
*   UN Convention on the Rights of the Child
*   Amsterdam Protocol on the Protection and Welfare of Animals

International Cooperation Agreements: The European Union has signed cooperation agreements with most countries. In these cooperation agreements, the European Union offers to help these countries on issues such as health, environment, energy, information technology etc. These agreements allow countries outside of the European Union to participate in Horizon 2020. The countries that can participate in Horizon 2020 are described in Chapter 9.

Where to find information on European Policies

The key sources of information on European Union policies can be found on:

*   Europa General Search Engine http://europa.eu/geninfo/query/advSearch_en.jsp
*   OECD (Organisation for Economic Cooperation and Development) www.oecd.org
*   EU White Papers (Policy) http://ec.europa.eu/white-papers/
*   EU Green Papers (Discussion documents for future policy) http://ec.europa.eu/green-papers/

'Top Down' and 'Bottom Up' Programmes

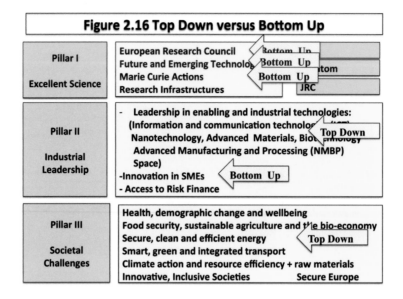

Figure 2.16 Top Down versus Bottom Up

'Bottom Up' Programmes

'Bottom Up' means that the researcher is free to decide on the content of the proposal.

In Figure 2.16 the main 'Bottom Up' programmes are:

> ERC (European Research Council)
> FET (Future and Emerging Technology)
> Marie Curie Programme
> Innovation in SMEs

Note that, in the FET programme, there is a part called 'FET Proactive' where broad areas are selected. This is a form of 'Top Down' but the researcher has considerable freedom to select ideas.

'Top Down' Programmes

'Top Down' means that the programme is designed to address a policy challenge. In Horizon 2020, the 'Top Down' programmes are written in a way that allows a lot of freedom to the researcher when selecting their project idea. The key message in Top Down programmes is that the researcher must be aware of the debate behind the topic i.e. *'Who wrote my topic?'*

Work programmes and Calls for Proposals

Horizon 2020 is a seven year programme. However, the planning for Horizon 2020 is done in the following ways. The process is shown in Figures 2.17 and 2.18. First, a 'Strategic Plan is prepared for the first three years (2014 to 2016). Based on this 'Strategic Plan', a 2-year 'Work programme' is designed. The first work programme defines the contents of the Calls for 2014 and 2015.

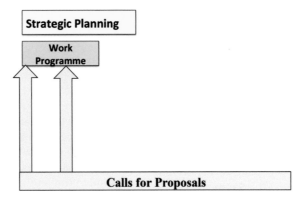

Figure 2.17 Work programme Design in Horizon 2020

This process will be repeated for the next 2-year work programmes (2016,2017) and for the final 3-year work programmes (2018, 2019, 2020)

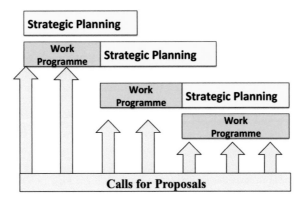

Figure 2.18 Work programme Design in Horizon 2020

It is important to stress here that this planning only applies to 'Top Down' programmes.

How the 'Top Down' Priorities are Identified

When the political priorities (Challenges) are identified, the European Commission then prepares detailed work programmes. Some of the work programmes are over 90 pages long. Figure 2.19 shows how the research community contributes to the preparation of the work programmes.

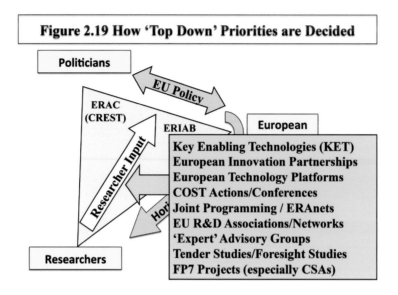

Figure 2.19 How 'Top Down' Priorities are Decided

Politicians

EU Policy

ERAC (CREST)

ERIAB

European

Researcher Input

Key Enabling Technologies (KET)
European Innovation Partnerships
European Technology Platforms
COST Actions/Conferences
Joint Programming / ERAnets
EU R&D Associations/Networks
'Expert' Advisory Groups
Tender Studies/Foresight Studies
FP7 Projects (especially CSAs)

Researchers

"Priority setting will equally be based on a wide range of inputs and advice. It will include, where appropriate, groups of independent experts set up specifically to advise on the implementation of Horizon 2020 or any of its specific objectives. These expert groups shall show the appropriate level of expertise and knowledge in the covered areas and a variety of professional backgrounds, including industry and civil society involvement."

"Priority setting may also take into account the strategic research agendas of European Technology Platforms or inputs from the European Innovation Partnerships. Where appropriate, public-public partnerships and public-private partnerships supported through Horizon 2020 will also contribute to the priority setting process and to the implementation, in line with the provisions laid down in Horizon 2020. Regular interactions with end-users, citizens and civil society organisations, through appropriate methodologies such as consensus conferences, participatory technology assessments or direct engagement in research and innovation processes, will also be a cornerstone of the priority setting process."

Source: Proposal for a COUNCIL DECISION establishing the Specific Programme Implementing Horizon 2020 - The Framework Programme for Research and Innovation (2014-2020)

"You are liable to have more influence if you can get together with a bigger grouping of people who can provide a unified view" Interview with Graham Stroud (Cordis Focus)

These sources can be found on www.hyperion.ie/h2020-mapping.htm

Key Enabling Technologies (KETs)

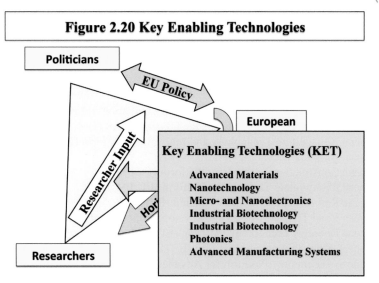

Figure 2.20 Key Enabling Technologies

Politicians

EU Policy

European

Researcher Input

Hor

Key Enabling Technologies (KET)

Advanced Materials
Nanotechnology
Micro- and Nanoelectronics
Industrial Biotechnology
Industrial Biotechnology
Photonics
Advanced Manufacturing Systems

Researchers

In 2009, the European Commission invited a group of European technology experts to establish an expert group on 'Key Enabling Technologies'. The six technologies identified were:

Advanced Materials
Nanotechnology
Micro- and Nanoelectronics
Industrial Biotechnology
Photonics
Advanced Manufacturing Systems

The expert group presented their first report in June 2011. (The proposal for Horizon 2020 was published by the European Commission on 30th November 2011). In 2013, an 'Implementation Group' was established to identify the research priorities in these six technologies. This plan was used in the writing of the Work programme for Pillar II (Industrial Leadership).

It is important to stress that the KETs are NOT projects or programmes. They are expert groups that are used to help the European Commission in identifying research priorities.

Beyond Horizon 2020, the KETs are being used by regions eligible for Structural Funds as a target for investments in research infrastructures.

KET Websites www.hyperion.ie/ket.htm

The Technology Platforms

Technology Platforms are not projects nor are they funding schemes. They are industry driven networks that are invited by the European Commission to submit 'Strategic Research Agendas (SRA). The European Commission uses these SRAs to prepare the workprogramm.

The following is a list Technology Platforms

(1) Advisory Council for Aviation Research and Innovation in Europe (ACARE)
(2) Association for R&D actors in Embedded Systems (ARTEMIS)
(3) European Aquaculture Technology and Innovation Platform (EATIP)
(4) European Biofuels Technology Platform (EBTP)
(5) European Construction Technology Platform (ECTP)
(6) European Photovoltaic Technology Platform (EU PV TP)
(7) European Rail Research Advisory Council (ERRAC)
(8) European Road Transport Research Advisory Council (ERTRAC)
(9) European Robotics Technology Platform (EUROP/euRobotics)
(10) European Steel Technology Platform (ESTEP)
(11) European Technology Platform for Advanced Engineering Materials (EuMaT)
(12) European Technology Platform for Global Animal Health (ETPGAH)
(13) European Technology Platform for High Performance Computing (ETP4HPC)
(14) European Technology Platform for Nanoelectronics (ENIAC)
(15) European Technology Platform for the Future of Textiles and Clothing
(16) European Technology Platform for Sustainable Chemistry (SusChem)
(17) European Technology Platform for Wind Energy (TPWind)
(18) European Technology Platform on Logistics
(19) European technology Platform on Nanomedicine
(20) European Technology Platform on Renewable Heating & Cooling (RHC-Platform)
(21) European Technology Platform on Smart Systems Integration (EPoSS)
(22) European Technology Platform on Sustainable Mineral Resources (ETP-SMR)
(23) Food for Life
(24) Forest Based Sector Technology Platform
(25) Integral Satcom Initiative (ISI)
(26) Manufuture
(27) Net!Works
(28) Networked and Electronic Media (NEM)
(29) Networked European Software and Services Initiative (NESSI)
(30) Photonics 21
(31) Plants for the Future
(32) Smart Grids European Technology Platform
(33) Sustainable Farm Animal Breeding and Reproduction Technology Platform (FABRE-TP)
(34) Sustainable Nuclear Energy Technology Platform (SNETP)
(35) Technology Research Platform for Organic Food and Farming (TP Organics)
(36) Water Supply and Sanitation Technology Platform (WssTP)
(37) Waterborne
(38) Zero Emissions Platform (ZEP)

During Horizon 2020, new Technology Platforms may be introduced, some of the existing ones may terminate and some may change their names or join with other platforms. This list is based on the Platforms listed on the website at the beginning of Horizon 2020.

The Technology Platforms and their Strategic Research Agendas can be found on
http://cordis.europa.eu/technology-platforms/individual_en.html

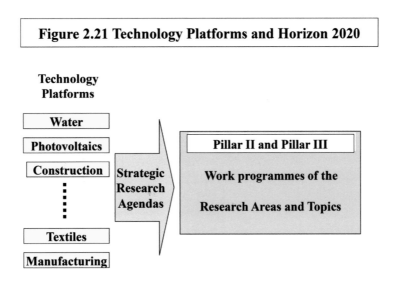

Figure 2.21 Technology Platforms and Horizon 2020

Each of the Technology Platforms prepares a **'Strategic Research Agenda.'** This document is used as an input to the preparation of the work programmes for the research priorities in Pillar II and Pillar III work programme. Details of each Technology Platform and their Strategic Research Agendas can be found on www.hyperion.ie/technology-platforms.htm.

Joint Technology Initiatives

Some of the Technology Platforms were considered to be too ambitious to be implemented through individual projects. One of the initiatives begun in Framework 7, set up an independent programme known as Joint Technology Initiatives (JTIs). In Horizon 2020, they are known as 'Institutional Public Private Partnerships (PPP)' These are described in Chapter 3.
The organisations that operate the JTIs are known as 'Joint Undertakings'.

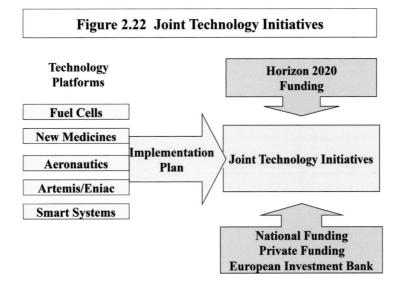

Figure 2.22 Joint Technology Initiatives

Relevant Hyperion websites
www.hyperion.ie/technologyplatforms.htm
www.hyperion.ie/jti.htm

European Innovation Partnerships (EIP)

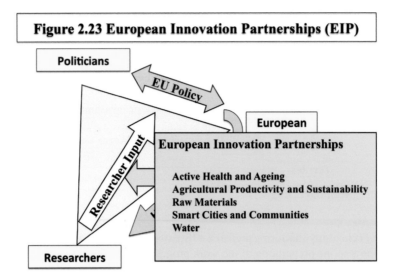

Figure 2.23 European Innovation Partnerships (EIP)

Politicians

EU Policy

European

Researcher Input

European Innovation Partnerships

Active Health and Ageing
Agricultural Productivity and Sustainability
Raw Materials
Smart Cities and Communities
Water

Researchers

In 2010, the European Commission established the European Innovation Partnerships as a means of identifying research priorities – mainly for the Societal Challenges programme. The five EIPs that existed when this book was written were:

> **Active Health and Ageing**
> **Agricultural Productivity and Sustainability**
> **Raw Materials**
> **Smart Cities and Communities**
> **Water**

The following information was provided on the launch of the EIPs

"When Commissioner for Research, Innovation and Science, Máire Geoghegan-Quinn, launched the Innovation Union package, a flagship Europe 2020 initiative, back in October 2010, she also unveiled new plans for EIPs. EIPs bring together public and private stakeholders across borders and sectors to address bottlenecks in the European research and innovation system that prevent good ideas from being developed and getting to market. This can be due to under-investment, outdated regulation, lack of standards, or market fragmentation."
Source: Cordis News March 2012

It is important to stress that the European Innovation Partnerships are not projects or programmes. They are expert groups that are used to advise the European Commission on research priorities for Horizon 2020.

Beyond Horizon 2020, the EIPs are also being used by Structural Funds (Smart Specialisation) to identify areas where funding can be directed.

Website on EIP www.hyperion.ie/eip.htm

COST Actions

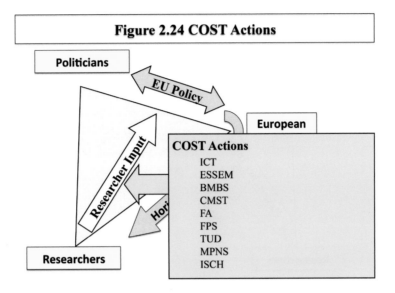

Figure 2.24 COST Actions

COST does not fund research. COST funds the networking of national researchers through seminars, fora, and conferences. According to the COST website, over 30,000 researchers attend these events annually.

COST is also used to identify new scientific directions and COST reports are used in identifying topics for work programmes. COST Actions are important for networking – especially in finding partners for projects.

COST is divided into nine themes:

<blockquote>
ICT (Information and communication technologies)
ESSEM (Earth Systems Science and Environmental Management)
BMBS (Biomedicine and Molecular Biosciences)
CMST (Chemistry and Molecular Sciences and Technologies
FA (Food and Agriculture)
FPS (Forests, their Products and Services)
TUD (Transport and Urban Development)
MPNS (Materials, Physics and NanoSciences
ISCH (Individuals, Societies, Cultures and Health)
</blockquote>

Table 2.1   Examples of Funded COST Actions

Theme	Example of Cost Action
ICT	Optical Wireless communications
ESSEM	Harmonizing global biodiversity modelling
BMBS	Next generation sequencing data analysis network
CMST	New drugs for neglected diseases
FA	Food for Health
FPS	Forest Management Decision Support System
TUD	Smart Low Carbon Regions
MPNS	Towards functional sub-wavelength photonics structures
ISCH	The role of the EU in UN Human Rights Reform

COST website www.cost.eu

Joint Programming Initiatives (JPI)

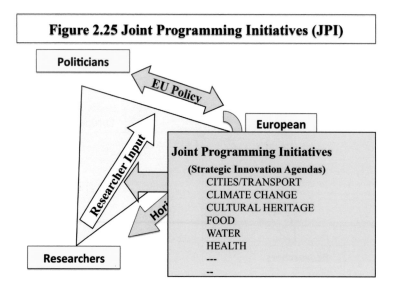

Figure 2.25 Joint Programming Initiatives (JPI)

Joint Programming is a Member State initiative (it is not driven by the European Commission). The aim of Joint Programming is to have more coordination between Member States in the planning and implementation of research programmes.

In 2008, a report was published entitled *'TOWARDS JOINT PROGRAMMING IN RESEARCH Working together to tackle common challenges more effectively'* This report showed that 85% of research funding in Europe was spent at National level and *"more than 95% of National R&D budgets are spent nationally without coordination across countries."*

The concept of Joint Programming is not new. The above report quotes examples from the past:

"Some of Europe's greatest scientific success stories have involved cross-border pooling of public R&D funds. Various inter-governmental research organisations have emerged over the last 50 years, (CERN), (EMBL) (ESA). In the 1970s and 1980s, inter-governmental schemes like COST and EUREKA were launched."

Table 2.2 List of Joint Programming Initiatives and Coordinating Country

Theme	Coordinator
Combat neurodegenerative Diseases and Alzheimers	
Agriculture, Food Security and Climate Change	UK
A healthy diet for a Healthy Life	The Netherlands
Cultural Heritage and Global Change	Italy
Urban Europe - Global Challenges, Local Solutions	Austria
Connecting Climate Knowledge for Europe	France
The microbial challenge – an emerging threat	
More Years, Better Lives – Potential and Challenges	
Water Challenges for a Changing World	Spain
Healthy and Productive Seas and Oceans	

Topic BG-16-2015: Coordination action in support of the implementation of the Joint Programming Initiative on 'Healthy and Productive Seas and Oceans.

Joint Programming websites www.hyperion.ie/jointprogramming.htm

ERAnets, ERAnet+, Article 185

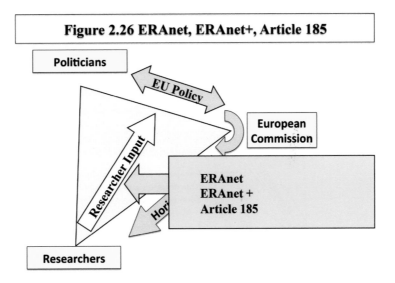

Figure 2.26 ERAnet, ERAnet+, Article 185

ERAnets

ERAnets are projects that are used to develop and strengthen the coordination of national and regional research programmes. An example is the HERAnet (Humanities ERAnet). In Heranet, national funding agencies come together and pool their funding for Humanities research. A Call for Proposals is published by the ERAnet. When a consortium submits a proposal, it is evaluated by the ERAnet. If the proposal is successful, the partners are funded by their own national funding agencies. This is modelled on the EUREKA programme.

Examples of ERAnets include:

ERA-IB Towards an ERA in Industrial Biotechnology
HERAnet: Humanities ERAnet

Example of ERAnet Call in Horizon 2020 (NMP Programme)

ERA-NET on Materials for Energy: *"The proposed ERA-NET aims at coordinating the research efforts of the participating Member States, Associated States and Regions in the field of materials for enabling low carbon energy technologies."*

ERAnet plus

ERAnet+ concept is similar to the ERAnet – except the European Commission makes a financial contribution to the project. This means that when a proposal is successful, partners are funded from their national funding programme and from the European commission. Examples include:

MATERA+ ERA-NET PLUS on Materials Research
PIANO+ ERA-NET-PLUS on photonics-based internet access networks of the future

ERAnet Cofund: ERAnet and ERAnet Plus are brought together as ERAnet Cofund

Article 185

Article 185 is an article in the European Treaty that allows European and National funding to be combined. In Framework 7, a number of projects were funded using this scheme;

EDCTP	European and Developing Countries Clinical Trials Partnership
AAL	Ambient Assisted Living
Bonus 185	Baltic Sea Research
EMRP	Metrology
Eurostars	Eureka programme for SMEs

ERAnet projects can be found on
http://netwatch.jrc.ec.europa.eu/web/ni/network-information/networks

European Policy Studies

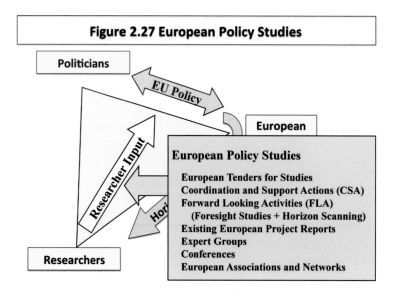

The European Union institutions (Council, European Parliament and European Commission) fund studies to support their policy debates. These studies are used by the European Commission to identify future trends and to define topics for research in future work programmes.

Tenders for European Policy Studies
The European institutions publish 'Calls for Tenders' for studies on the TED website. These published studies are available online (search on europa.eu). Research organisations can bid for these studies – and then contribute to the policy debates.

Coordination and Support Actions (CSA)
CSAs are a type of Grant in Horizon 2020 that fund networks, conferences and studies. They are included in the Call for Proposals. CSAs do not fund research but they fund studies that are the basis for future calls.

Forward Looking Activities (FLAs)
Forward Looking Activities is a term that is broader than foresight. It includes horizon scanning, forecasting, vision-building, participative technology assessment and scenario building. Examples of European FLAs are:
>**EFFLA** (European Forum for Forward Looking Activities) http://www.foresight-platform.eu/
>**EFP** (European Foresight Platform) http://foresight-network.eu
>**EFMN** (European Foresight Monitoring Network) www.efmn.info

Existing European Research Projects
Projects funded in Framework 7 and Horizon 2020 produce reports recommending future areas of research. (Projects funded in the last calls of Framework 7 (2013) will continue to operate up to 2018) These can be used by the European Commission when preparing work programmes. Projects funded in Framework 7 and Horizon 2020 can be found on the Participant Portal.

European Research Conferences
European funded conferences are used to identify trends in research and possible directions to address European Challenges. Examples of European funded conferences can be found on
http://ec.europa.eu/research/conferences/index_en.cfm

European Research Associations make formal contributions to the preparation of Horizon 2020. Examples of these R&D Associations can be seen on www.hyperion.ie/euassociations.htm .

Expert Groups contributing to Horizon 2020

Before leaving this chapter, it is worth listing the range of 'Experts' used by the European Commission in the preparation, running and assessment of Horizon 2020. These include:

ERIAB (European Research and Innovation Advisory Board)
http://ec.europa.eu/research/era/partnership/expert/eriab_en.htm
ERIAB acts as an advisor to the European Commissioner for Research and Innovation. According to the ERIAB website, its main functions are:

1. To advise the European Commission on European Research Area Issues, to provide recommendations on priorities and actions and in particular on how to increase the innovation impact and to evaluate the relevant part of Innovation Union Flagship initiatives on a continuous basis;
2. To deliver opinions on the development and realisation of the European Research Area and the Innovation Union at the request of the Commission, or on the Board's own initiative;
3. To provide the Commission with an annual report on the development of the European Research Area and of the Innovation Union;
4. To reflect on new trends in the European Research Area and the Innovation Union.

Programme Committees (National Delegates)
Each Member State nominates individuals who monitor Horizon 2020 on behalf of the national Government. Members of Programme Committees are called 'National Delegates'. When new work programmes are being prepared, these are the official National representatives that are consulted. There is no central database of National Delegates. Their names are usually found on national websites for Horizon 2020.

Advisory Groups:
http://ec.europa.eu/research/advisorygroups/
Each of the programmes has an 'Advisory Group' whose members are experts in the specific scientific field. They advise the European Commission on the content of the work programmes.

ERAC (European Research Area Committee)
http://ec.europa.eu/research/era/partnership/process/crest_en.htm
This is an advisory group whose representatives come from National Ministries i.e. public or civil servants. ERAC has been one of the main drivers for the Joint Programming Initiatives.

Reviews, Evaluations, Assessment, Monitoring

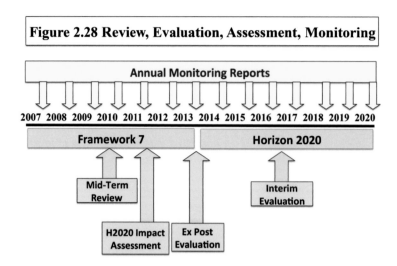

Figure 2.28 Review, Evaluation, Assessment, Monitoring

The Treaty on the Functioning of the European Union defines how the European Commission will report the progress of Horizon 2020 to the European Parliament and the Council.

Annual Monitoring Reports

http://ec.europa.eu/research/index.cfm?pg=reports
The Treaty on the Functioning of the European Union states
" At the end of each year the Commission shall send a report to the European Parliament and to the Council." (Article 190 Treaty on the Functioning of the European Union). This is a very important report as it provides information on the numbers of proposals submitted, success rates and typical size of projects.

Mid-term Reviews

This refers to a review that is undertaken mid-way through the financial cycle. This review has a considerable impact on the remaining half of the programme. It also has a considerable impact on the design of the following programme.

Impact Assessment Report

On 30th November 2011, the European Commission submitted a proposal to the Council and the Parliament. This was the first step in the preparation of Horizon 2020. In addition to the proposal, the Commission prepared a very comprehensive report justifying the investment in Horizon 2020. This report was called the 'Impact Assessment Report'.

Ex-post evaluation

At the end of each programme, the European Commission invites experts to prepare a report on the performance of the programme.

"Typically, monitoring is carried out during the lifetime of a programme or intervention, with the aim to provide information to the programme manager. Unlike evaluation, monitoring does not deal with impacts. The linkage between monitoring and evaluation is very important since monitoring can be a source of systematic evidence to support ex post evaluation.
In 2011, fifteen evaluation studies and six reports with evaluative information were completed by DG RTD3. In 2011, it took from three to eighteen months to produce a study or a report. The cost of evaluation studies ranges from € 14,400 to € 549,800 with an average cost of €162,594."
Source: 2011 Annual Monitoring Report

Chapter 3: The Research Priorities

CONTENTS

Pillar I Excellence Science
Pillar II Industrial Leadership
Pillar III Societal Challenges
EIT (European Institute of Innovation and Technology)
Euratom
JRC (Joint Research Centre)

Structure of Horizon 2020

This chapter provides an overview of the different programmes of Horizon 2020. As the work programmes change from 'Call' to 'Call', this chapter can only provide a general description and the background. The official description is contained on the Participant Portal. The description presented here is based on the information available at the beginning of Horizon 2020. The scope of each programme is liable to change during the period 2014 to 2020.

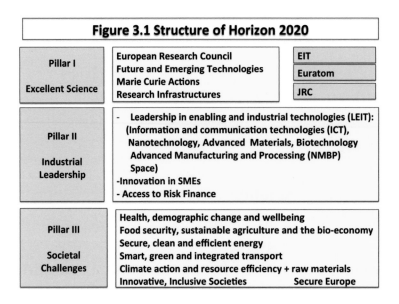

One of the biggest challenges facing researchers is in finding the best programme for their research. Each country, involved in Horizon 2020, has set up 'National Contact Points' who are responsible for advising researchers on the individual sub-programmes.

Terminology Used in Horizon 2020

Each programme has a 'Work programme' and this is divided into:
  -Areas
    -Topics
Examples of Topics were presented in Chapter 1.

It is important to stress that this Chapter is only an overview and the content will change during the lifetime of Horizon 2020.

Pillar I Excellence Science

European Research Council

ERC Website: http://erc.europa.eu/

The aim of ERC is to identify individuals who can establish Europe as the leaders in scientific research. *"Although the EU remains the largest producer of scientific publications in the world, the US produces twice as many of the most influential papers (the top 1% by citation count). Similarly, international university ranking exercises show that US universities dominate the top places. And 70% of the world's Nobel Prize winners are located in the US".*

No Consortium Required

The ERC grants will be carried out by *"individual teams which are headed by a single principal investigator of any nationality".* There is no need to have a 'Consortium' as in other programmes in Horizon 2020. However, the guidelines state that the team members can be of any nationality and *"these teams could be of national or trans-national character."*
A further definition of a 'team' is given: *'The term "team" is used in its broadest sense, including cases where a single individual works independently, or conversely, in cases when several investigators are working so closely together as to constitute a single team.'*

Host Organisation
ERC is open to any nationality. The Host must be located in a Member State of the European Union or in an Associated Country (e.g. Norway, Liechtenstein, Iceland, Israel, Switzerland and Turkey). The full list of Associated countries is listed in Chapter 9 (Partners).

Minimum Bureaucracy
The programme is designed to have a minimum of bureaucracy for the scientists. The evaluation criteria will be based on excellence – excellence in science and excellence in people. The programme is 'bottom up' – the researcher has total freedom in selecting the project idea.

Grants are Portable
The host institution will *"grant the Principal Investigator the independence to manage the research funding for the duration of the project".*

Table 3.1 Types of ERC Grants

Type of Grant	Role
ERC Starting Grants	Supports top researchers with 2 to 7 years of experience from their PhD
ERC Consolidator Grants	Support top researchers with 7 to 12 years of experience from their PhD
ERC Advanced Grants	Open to excellent, established researchers who have a recent research track record which identifies them as leaders in their research fields
Synergy Grants	Supports small groups of excellent researchers
Proof of Concept Grants	Open to ERC grant holders. Aim is to assess commercial potential of ERC research results

These are subject to change during the lifetime of Horizon 2020

FET (Future and Emerging Technologies)

FET Website www.hyperion.ie/fet.htm

The concept of FET originated in the Information and Communication Technologies programme of Framework 5. It continued in Framework 6 and 7 as a topic in the ICT programme. In Framework 7, the Energy programme published calls for FET projects. The original idea was to have a 'bottom up' topic in the ICT programme – to allow for rapidly changing technologies.

During Framework 6 and 7, it was found that FET provided researchers with an opportunity to propose ideas that were radical (rather than incremental). Some describe FET as allowing for 'crazy' ideas. **In Horizon 2020, FET is open to all research areas** (Health, Food, Social Science, Humanities..) Horizon 2020 describes FET as *'radically new technologies by exploring novel and high-risk ideas building on scientific foundation'.*

FET is implemented through three types of activities:

FET Open
This is an Open Call (no deadline) where researchers are free to submit any idea at any time. The proposals are evaluated on a regular basis and, if a proposal is considered interesting, the researcher will be invited to submit a full proposal. The European Commission states that FET Open will represent 40% of the total FET budget.

FET Proactive
In FET Proactive, a number of 'promising exploratory themes' will be investigated. Researchers will then be invited to submit 'bottom up' proposals to these themes. For example, at the beginning of Horizon 2020 nine themes were selected (based on a call published in 2012):
Time for time
Constructive symbiosis
Adaptive bottom-up construction
New possibilities at the nano-bio-chemistry interface
Knowing, doing, being
Ecological technologies
Nanoscale Opto-mechanical devices
Quantum Technologies
Global Systems Science (GSS)

FET Flagships
FET Flagships are designed to bring important scientific challenges together at national and European level. The European Commission describes FET Flagships as *"supporting ambitious large-scale science driven research aimed at grand interdisciplinary S&T challenges. Such activities will benefit from the alignment of European and national (research) agendas".*
At the beginning of Horizon 2020, two themes were selected for FET Flagships
Graphene http://www.graphene-flagship.eu/
The Human Brain Project http://www.humanbrainproject.eu/

Examples of FET Projects (ICT and Energy)
Novel design principles and technologies for a new generation of high dexterity soft-bodied robots inspired by the morphology and behaviour of the octopus (ICT)
The Body-on-a-Chip (BoC) (ICT)
The Listening Talker (ICT)
PLants Employed As SEnsor Devices (ICT)
Forecasting Financial Crises (ICT)
Synthetic pathways to bio-inspired information processing (ICT)
Reverse Electrodialysis Alternative Power Production (Energy)
PlantPower - living plants in microbial fuel cells for clean, renewable, sustainable, efficient, in-situ bioenergy production (Energy)

Marie Skłodowska-Curie Actions

The Marie Skłodowska-Curie programme is one of the success stories of the European programmes. All of the other programmes focus on funding for research. The Marie Skłodowska-Curie programme focuses on the funding of individuals to undertake research. The aim of the programme is to *stimulate researchers' career development*. The funding is done in the form of fellowships. Before describing each of the fellowships, it is important to distinguish between 'Individual Fellowships' and 'Marie Skłodowska-Curie Networks.'

Individual Fellowships
In the case of an Individual Fellowship, a proposal is submitted to Horizon 2020 - **naming the post-doctoral or experienced researcher in the proposal**. If the proposal is accepted, the named researcher can then join the research centre for the period specified in the grant.

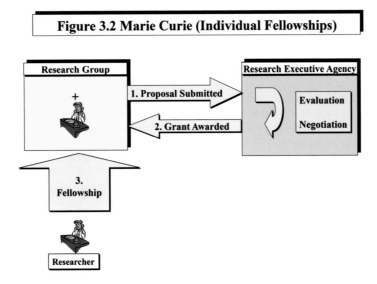

Marie Skłodowska-Curie Networks
In Marie Skłodowska-Curie Networks, a consortium of research centres submits a proposal requesting funding for a number of fellowships. **They do not have to name the researchers in the proposals**. If the proposal is successful, the consortium is given a grant for the fellowships. Researchers then apply directly to the individual research centres for the vacancies. Networks are used to fund PhDs and post-doctoral students

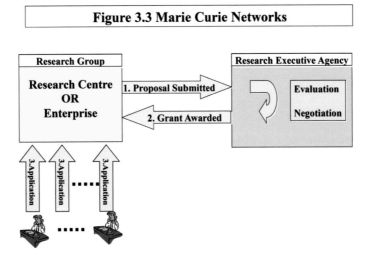

The Marie Skłodowska-Curie programme is a 'bottom up' programme where researchers have total freedom in selecting ideas for their proposals. Mobility is a key requirement in the Marie Skłodowska-Curie Actions. Researchers receive funding on the condition that they move from one country to another to broaden or deepen their competence.

Marie Skłodowska-Curie "Innovative Training Networks" (ITN)
This Action focuses on the initial and doctoral training of early-stage researchers. Partnerships may take the form of collaborative European Training Networks (ETN), European Industrial Doctorates (EID) or Joint Doctorates (EJD).

Marie Skłodowska-Curie "Individual Fellowships" (IF)
This Action supports experienced researchers. Three types of fellowships exist:

> *European Fellowships are held in EU Member States or Associated Countries and are open to researchers either coming to Europe or moving within Europe. Return and reintegration of researchers into a longer term research position in Europe, including in their country of origin, is supported via a separate multi-disciplinary reintegration panel of the European Fellowships.*

> *Global Fellowships The aim of this fellowship is to bring new knowledge or technologies to Europe and to establish contacts with international scientific organisations. For example, a European research centre can submit a proposal to send a Fellow to a research centre in the USA for two years and then return to the European research centre for one year.*

Marie Skłodowska-Curie Co-funding of Regional/National/International Programmes (COFUND)
Funding agencies in the Member States or Associated States can apply to the Marie Skłodowska-Curie programme for additional funding. This additional funding can be used to add an international dimension to their national mobility programmes. This is a way of combining European and national funding.

Marie Skłodowska-Curie Research and Innovation Staff Exchange (RISE)
The RISE action will promote international and inter-sector collaboration through research and innovation staff exchanges.
Inter-sector: exchanges between research groups and enterprises
International: exchanges between organisations at international level

Researchers Nights (Researchers exhibit their research to the public).

Transnational Cooperation among National Contact Points This action aims to reinforce the network of National Contact Points (NCP) for the Marie Skłodowska-Curie Actions (MSCA), by promoting trans-national co-operation.

NOTE: New activities may be added during the life of Horizon 2020.

Research Infrastructures

Research infrastructures are facilities, resources and services that are used by the research communities to conduct research and foster innovation in their fields. They include: major scientific equipment (or sets of instruments); knowledge-based resources such as collections, archives or scientific data; e-infrastructures, such as data and computing systems and communication networks; and any other infrastructure of a unique nature essential to achieve excellence in research and innovation. Such infrastructures may be 'single-sited', 'virtual' or 'distributed'. The programme can be divided into a number of activities.

Developing new world-class infrastructures

The aim is to facilitate and support the implementation, long-term sustainability and efficient operation of the research infrastructures identified by the European Strategy Forum on Research Infrastructures (ESFRI) as well as other world-class research infrastructures.

Design Studies for New Infrastructures.
The aim of this activity is to support the conceptual and technical design and preparatory actions for new research infrastructures.
Preparatory phase of ESFRI projects
The aim is to bring the project for the new and upgraded research infrastructure identified in the ESFRI roadmap, or in the European strategy for particle physics (CERN Council) to the level of legal, financial and technical maturity to implement it.
Individual implementation and operation of ESFRI projects
This is designed to help research infrastructures in the initial phase of implementation.

Integrating and opening research infrastructures of European interest

This call focuses on opening up key national and regional research infrastructures to all European researchers from both academia and industry and ensuring their optimal use and joint development.
Funding will be provided to support, in particular, the trans-national and virtual access activities provided to European researchers (and of researchers from Third Countries under certain conditions), the cooperation between research infrastructures, scientific communities, industries and other stakeholders, the improvement of the services the infrastructures provide, the harmonisation, optimisation and improvement of access procedures and interfaces.

Communities will be established in the following scientific fields:
(Starting Communities: research infrastructures with a low level of networking)
(Advanced Communities: research infrastructures with and advanced degree of coordination)

> *Biological and Medical Sciences* – Starting Communities
> *Biological and Medical Sciences - Advanced Communities*
> *Energy - Starting Communities*
> *Energy - Advanced Communities*
> *Environmental and Earth Sciences - Starting Communities*
> *Environmental and Earth Sciences - Advanced Communities*
> *Mathematics and ICT - Starting Communities*
> *Mathematics and ICT - Advanced Communities*
> *Engineering, Material Sciences, and Analytical facilities - Starting Communities*
> *Engineering, Material Sciences, and Analytical facilities - Advanced Communities*
> *Physical Sciences - Starting Communities*
> *Physical Sciences - Advanced Communities*
> *Social Sciences and Humanities - Starting Communities*
> *Social Sciences and Humanities - Advanced Communities*

e-Infrastructures

This call focuses integrating e-infrastructure resources and services across all layers (networking, computing, data, software and user interfaces).

Transnational Access to Research Infrastructures

All over Europe national governments have invested in research infrastructures. It is difficult for young researchers to access these facilities as the unit cost (e.g. daily rate to access a facility) is prohibitive. Travelling to these sites can be very expensive for young researchers. The aim of this action is to provide researchers with financial support to access specialised European research infrastructures.

Figure 3.4 shows how the 'Access' part of this programme operates. A research centre with a rare facility, where they can demonstrate a demand, can submit a proposal to this programme. If the proposal is accepted researchers can ACCESS the facility.

- **Benefit to the researcher:** Free access to a high quality research facility (travel and expenses are paid).
- **Benefit to research group:** Funding to allow researchers to access their facility and increased status as a 'European Research Infrastructure'

Examples of research centres funded under this programme can be found on
http://www.euroris-net.eu/transnational-access-opportunities

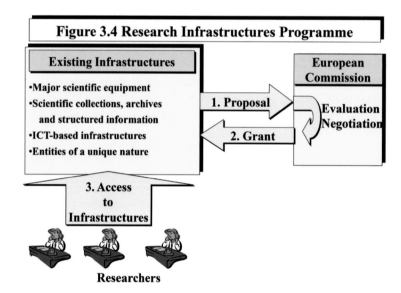

Examples of Research Infrastructures funded under the Transnational Access include:

- Centre for Application of Ion Beams to Materials Research
- ALOMAR (Arctic Lidar Observatory for Middle Atmospheric Research)
- The European Centre for Arctic Environmental Research
- Enhanced Transnational Access to Abisko Scientific Research Station
- Access to the Centre for the Theory and Application of Catalysis in Queens University Belfast
- Coal Mine Sites for Targeted Remediation Research
- The Jacob Blaustein Institutes for Desert Research, Ben-Gurion University of the Negev
- Centre for Analysis in the Social Sciences
- European Centre of Competence for Research and Education in Cutting Technologies
- Access to research in very high magnetic fields
- The Structure and Properties of Materials at High Pressure

Pillar II: Industrial Leadership

This aim of this Pillar is to address the challenges facing industry in Europe – namely competitiveness at a global level. Figure 3.6 shows the political background to the programme and the areas addressed. The topics in the programmes were identified using the Key Enable Technology expert groups and the Technology Platforms.

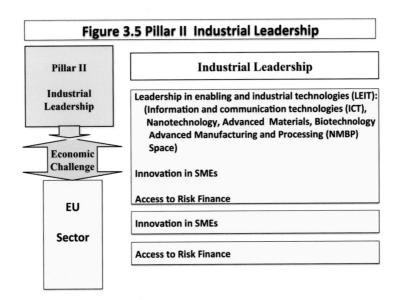

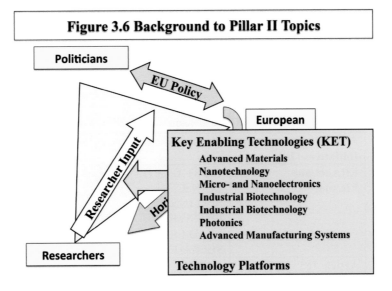

Information and Communication Technologies (ICT)

The aim of the ICT Work Programme under H2020 is to maintain a strong expertise in key technology value chains and secondly, to move more quickly from research excellence to the market.

The following are *examples* of research areas covered in the ICT programme.

A new generation of components and systems
Advanced Computing
Future Internet
Content technologies and information management
Robotics
ICT Cross-Cutting Activities
International Cooperation actions
Factory of the Future
EU-Brazil Cooperation in Advanced Cyber Infrastructure
EU-Japan Research and Development Cooperation in Net Futures

Table 3.2 Background to ICT Programme

Source	Examples
EU Policy	Digital Agenda for Europe
Key Enabling Technologies (KETs)	Nanoelectronics Photonics
Technology Platforms	ARTEMISIA AENEAS EPoSS EUROP ISI NEM NESSI Net!Works Photonics21
Joint Technology Initiatives (JTI)	ECSEL (ENIAC/ARTEMIS)
Public Private Partnerships (PPP)	CA-RoboCom FI - Future Internet
European Innovation Partnerships (EIP)	Smart Cities
Knowledge Innovation Communities (KIC)	EIT ICT Labs
Joint Programming Initiatives (JPI)	MYBL - More Years, Better Lives
ERAnet and ERAnet+	CHIST-ERA II DC-Net ECO-INNOVERA ERASynBio LEAD ERA SEERA-EI
Article 185 initiatives	AAL JP BONUS+

Nanotechnologies, Advanced Materials, Biotechnology, Advanced Manufacturing and Processing (NMBP)

This programme focusses on the nanotechnologies, advanced materials that are part of the Key Enabling Technologies implementation plan.

Challenge 1: Bridging the gap between nanotechnology research and markets
Challenge 2: Nanotechnology and Advanced Materials as enablers of applications in Health
Challenge 3: Nanotechnology and Advanced Materials for low carbon energy technologies and Energy Efficiency
Challenge 4: Tapping into the cross-sector potential of Nanotechnologies and Advanced materials to drive competitiveness and sustainability
Challenge 5: Safety of nanotechnology-based applications and support for the development of regulation
Challenge 6: Addressing generic needs in support of governance, standards, models and structuring in nanotechnology, advanced materials and production

Contractual Public Private Partnership (PPP)
This part of the Work Programme includes the EU support for the following contractual PPPs: Robotics, Photonics, Advanced 5G network infrastructures, Factories of the Future, Energy-efficient Buildings and Sustainable Process Industries (SPIRE).

Challenge FoF - Factories of the Future
The goal is to improve competitiveness through resource and energy efficiency; flexibility of production and customisation of products through new high-tech manufacturing processes; and addressing the human dimension.

Challenge SPIRE – Sustainable Process Industries
Resources are becoming increasingly scarce and resource efficiency has become an exceedingly important factor in industry. This is especially true for resource and energy intensive industries such as the process industries. The general goal is to optimise industrial processing, reducing the consumption of energy and resources, and minimising waste.
The Specific goals are:
- a reduction in fossil energy intensity of up to 30% from current levels by 2030.
- a reduction of up to 20% in non-renewable, primary raw material intensity compared to current levels by 2030.

Table 3.3 Background to NMP Programme (Materials and Manufacturing)

Source	Background to Materials Topics
Key Enabling Technologies (KETs)	Advanced Materials
Technology Platforms	EUmat (Advanced Materials and Technologies)
European Innovation Partnerships (EIP)	Raw Materials

Source	Background to Manufacturing Topics
Key Enabling Technologies (KETs)	Advanced Manufacturing
Technology Platforms	Manufuture
Public Private Partnership (PPP)	Factory of the Future
EIT (KIC)	Added value manufacturing (2016)
ERAnet	MANUNET II

Biotechnology (part of NMBP)

Biotechnology is seen as an enabling technology. The motivation for this programme is to secure European leadership in the Key Enabling Technology. *"This challenge is driven by the vision that cutting edge-biotechnologies are paramount to assure that the European industry is to stay at the front line of innovation."*

Examples of research areas covered in this programme are listed below.

Challenge 1: Cutting-edge biotechnologies as future innovation drivers
      1.1. Synthetic biology – design of organisms for new products and processes
      1.2. New bioinformatics approaches in service of biotechnology

Challenge 2: Biotechnology-based industrial processes driving competitiveness and sustainability
      "Industrial biotechnology enables industries to deliver novel products which cannot be produced by current industrial methods; in addition it makes possible replacing industrial processes by more resource efficient biotechnological methods with reduced environmental impact."

      2.1. Building the enzyme toolbox: widening industrial application of enzymatic bio-transformations
      2.2. Downstream processes unlocking biotechnological transformations
      2.3. Robust microbial platforms for next generation biomanufacturing

Challenge 3: Innovative and competitive platform technologies
      "Platform technologies are the main tools and techniques shared by nearly all biotechnology applications. The challenge aims at furthering technological development of metagenomics technologies in terms of increased accuracy and costs reduction in order to expand their potential."
      3.1. "Omics technologies" to drive innovation across economic sectors

Space

The main objective and challenge is to foster a cost-effective competitive and innovative space industry and research community to develop and exploit space infrastructure to meet future Union policy and societal needs.

The work programme has been structured to address these challenges by:
- Prioritising the existing two EU Space flagships of **European Global Navigation Satellite System (EGNSS)** and **Earth Observation** reaping the benefits they can generate in the coming years and ensuring their state-of-the-art also in the future;
- Ensuring support for the third programmatic priority of the EU space policy: the protection of space infrastructure and in particular the setting up of a **Space Surveillance and Tracking system (SST)** at European level;
- Ensuring support to EU industry to meet the objectives defined in the Commission communication on Space Industrial Policy, notably **to maintain and enhance industry's competitiveness in the global market**;
- Ensuring that Europe's investments made in space infrastructure are exploited to the benefit of citizens; as well as supporting European **space science;** and
- Enhancing Europe's standing as an attractive partner for international partnerships in space science and exploration.

Innovation in SMEs

SME Definition
Small and Medium Sized Enterprises (SMEs) have been identified as important contributors to growth and job creation in Europe. This programme has been designed to address SMEs that have the potential to grow at international level.

SME Instrument
"The SME instrument addresses the financing needs of internationally oriented SMEs, and particularly young entrepreneurs, in implementing high-risk and high-potential innovation ideas. It aims at supporting projects with a European dimension that lead to radical changes in how business (product, processes, services, marketing etc.) is done. It will launch the company into new markets, promote growth, and create high return on investment. The SME instrument addresses all types of innovative SMEs so as to be able to promote growth champions in all sectors."

The SME instrument consists of three separate, but inter-linked phases and a coaching and mentoring scheme for beneficiaries:

Phase 1: SMEs will receive funding to undertake innovation activities that explore and assess the technical and technological feasibility and the commercial potential/economic viability of a new breakthrough idea (proof of concept for new products, processes, services and technologies or new market applications of existing technologies). The output of this phase will be a business plan for submission to Phase 2. Funding will be provided in the form of a lump sum of € 50.000 and the duration will be six months.

Phase 2: Projects supported aim at bringing a breakthrough innovation idea (new products, processes, services and technologies or new market applications of existing technologies) close to deployment and market introduction. Projects underpinned by a strategic business plan, either developed under Phase 1 or through other means, will address a specific challenge and demonstrate high potential in terms of company competitiveness and growth. SMEs can subcontract or buy in work and knowledge that is essential for their innovation project in the spirit of the innovation voucher concept.

Phase 3: Support to commercialisation promotes the wider implementation of innovative solutions and customers and supports financing of growth by facilitating access to public and private risk capital. This stage will not provide for direct funding, but SMEs can benefit from indirect support measures and services as well as access to the financial facilities supported under Horizon 2020.

There is no obligation for applicants to sequentially cover all three phases.

The SME Instrument is only open to SME proposals. However, research organisations can act as sub-contractors on services such as technical feasibility, testing, prototyping, upscaling, demonstration and product development.

Other actions funded in this programme include:

EUREKA/Eurostars initiative that provides funding for transnational collaborative projects of research-intensive SMEs

Enhancing SME innovation capacity by providing better innovation
Cluster animated projects for new industrial value chains
European Intellectual Property Rights (IPR) Helpdesk
IPorta 2 - Increasing the quality of IP advisory services to SMEs
A European Label for innovation voucher programmes to support spin-in of technology

Access to Risk Finance

The aim of this programme is to attract private investments into research and innovation. This programme will help companies and other organisation engaged in research and innovation to gain easier access, via financial instruments, to loans, guarantees, counter-guarantees and hybrid, mezzanine and equity finance.

The programme is divided into three main areas:
> **Access to Risk Finance**
> **Capacity-Building in Technology Transfer**
> **Boosting the Investment-Readiness of SMEs and Small Midcaps**

Examples of instruments used to fund organisations include:

Loans Service for Research and Innovation:
This facility is designed to improve access to risk finance for projects coming from large firms and medium and large midcaps, universities and research institutes. This is modelled on the Risk Sharing Financing Facility of Framework 7 (www.eib.org/products/rsff/).

SMEs & Small Midcaps R&I Loans Service
This facility is part of a single debt financial instrument supporting the growth of enterprises and their research and innovation activities. It targets research and innovation driven SMEs and small midcaps requiring loans of between €25 000 and €7.5 million (subject to change during Horizon 2020). It is modelled on the Risk Sharing Instrument of Framework 7.

Equity Facility for Research and Innovation
This is part of a single equity financial instrument supporting the growth of enterprises and their research and innovation activities. It is designed to improve access to risk finance by early-stage research and innovation driven SMEs and small Midcaps through supporting early-stage risk capital funds. This facility succeeds and refines the GIF-1 scheme under CIP.

The European Investment Bank (EIB) and the European Investment Fund (EIF) are involved in implementing each financial instrument facility. Banks or funds that provide risk finance supported by the EU can be found on
http://access2eufinance.ec.europa.eu

In addition, organisations will be able to get advice on how to make themselves more attractive to banks and potential investors. Studies will be undertaken on how best to encourage more business angel and crowd-funding investments and the potential for pan-European venture capital (VC) funds-of-funds.

Horizon 2020's financial instrument facilities will operate in conjunction with those of COSME programme.

> SME definition: < 250 employees
> Midcap definition: 250 to 3000 employees
> Small midcap 250 to 499 employees
> Medium and large midcaps 500 to 3000 employees.

In addition to these financing instruments, this programme funds a number of studies and actions rrelating to financing of innovation. Examples include:
- Understanding the Nature and Impact of Angel and Crowd funding in Research and Innovation
- Assess the Potential for EU Investments in Venture Capital Funds-of-funds
- Capacity Building in Technology Transfer.

Pillar III Societal Challenges

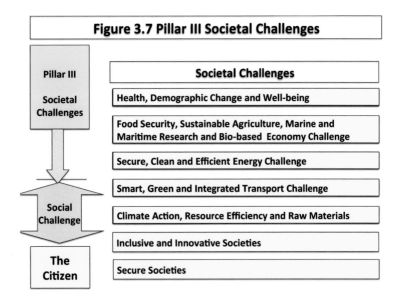

Figure 3.7 Pillar III Societal Challenges

Pillar III Societal Challenges

Social Challenge

The Citizen

Societal Challenges

Health, Demographic Change and Well-being

Food Security, Sustainable Agriculture, Marine and Maritime Research and Bio-based Economy Challenge

Secure, Clean and Efficient Energy Challenge

Smart, Green and Integrated Transport Challenge

Climate Action, Resource Efficiency and Raw Materials

Inclusive and Innovative Societies

Secure Societies

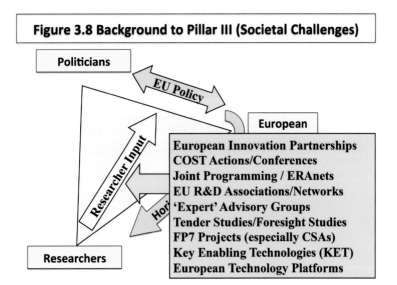

Figure 3.8 Background to Pillar III (Societal Challenges)

Politicians

EU Policy

European

Researcher Input

Researchers

European Innovation Partnerships
COST Actions/Conferences
Joint Programming / ERAnets
EU R&D Associations/Networks
'Expert' Advisory Groups
Tender Studies/Foresight Studies
FP7 Projects (especially CSAs)
Key Enabling Technologies (KET)
European Technology Platforms

Health, demographic change and wellbeing

The focus on personalising health and care is motivated by the ageing of the European population, an increase in the number of communicable and non-communicable diseases and the fall-out from the economic crisis. Another driver is the sustainability and equity of European health and care systems. Europe already spends nearly 10% Gross Domestic Product (GDP) on its health and care systems.

Areas covered in this programme include:

Understanding health, ageing and disease
Effective health promotion, disease prevention, preparedness and screening
Improving diagnosis
Innovative treatments and technologies
Advancing active and healthy ageing
Integrated, sustainable, citizen-centred care
Improving health information, data exploitation and providing an evidence base for health policies and regulation

Table 3.4 Background to Health Programme

Source	Examples
EU Policy	EU policies on Cancer, Diabetes, Alzheimers…
Key Enabling Technologies (KETs)	Industrial Biotechnology
Technology Platforms	Nanomedicine Innovative Medicines Initiative (IMI)
Joint Technology Initiatives (JTI)	Active and Healthy Aging
Knowledge Innovation Communities (KIC)	Innovation for healthy living and active ageing
European Innovation Partnerships (EIP)	Active Health and Ageing
Joint Programming Initiatives (JPI)	AMR - Antimicrobial resistance HDHL - A Healthy Diet for a Healthy Living JPND - Neurodegenerative Disease Research / Alzheimer
ERAnet and ERAnet+	EMIDA ERA-Age ERA-NET NEURON II E-Rare-2 EUROCOURSE EUROTRANSBIO (ETB-PRO) HIVERA LEAD ERA PathoGenoMics TRANSCAN
Article 185 initiatives	EDCTP (AIDs, Malaria and Tuberculosis)

Food Security, Sustainable Agriculture, Marine and Maritime Research and the Bioeconomy

Activities under Societal Challenge "Food Security, Sustainable Agriculture, Marine and Maritime Research and the Bioeconomy" aim at making the best of our biological resources in a sustainable way. The objective is to help secure sufficient supplies of safe and high quality food and other bio-based products, by developing productive and resource-efficient primary production systems and fostering related ecosystem services alongside competitive and low carbon supply chains. This will accelerate the transition to a sustainable European bioeconomy.

Examples of the areas funded in the programme.

   Sustainable Agriculture and Forestry
   Sustainable and competitive agri-food sector for a safe and healthy diet
   Unlocking the potential of aquatic living resources
   Sustainable and competitive bio-based industries

Table 3.5 Background to Food Security, Sustainable Agriculture, Marine and Maritime Research and the Bioeconomy programme

Source	Examples
EU Policy	Agricultural and Food Policies, Marine Policies
Key Enabling Technologies (KETs)	Advanced Manufacturing Industrial Biotechnology
Technology Platforms	FABRE TP Food GAH Plants
Public Private Partnerships (PPP)	BbG - Biobased for Growth
European Innovation Partnerships (EIP)	Agriculture
Knowledge Innovation Communities (KIC)	Food4future
Joint Programming Initiatives (JPI)	FACCE - Agriculture, food security and climate change Healthy & productive seas and oceans
ERAnet and ERAnet+	ANIHWA ARIMNet COFASP CORE Organic II ERA-ARD-II ERA-CAPS ERA-IB-2 ERASynBio EUPHRESCO II EUROTRANSBIO (ETB-PRO) FORESTERRA ICT-AGRI MariFish RURAGRI SNOWMAN SUSFOOD

Secure, clean and efficient energy

This programme is divided into three main focus areas.

Energy efficiency

The overall challenge for EU action in the field of energy efficiency is therefore to close this gap ensuring that the energy efficiency target for 2020 is achieved and that the necessary framework is put in place to enable the achievement of a sufficient and cost-effective level of energy efficiency for 2030.

A Increasing energy efficiency in buildings

B   Increasing energy efficiency in combination with renewable energy use in heating and cooling

   C   Increasing energy efficiency in industry and SMEs

   D   Increasing energy efficiency of energy-related products

   E   Innovative financing for energy efficiency

F   Citizen engagement, capacity building, governance and communication for energy efficiency

Competitive low-carbon energy

One of the major challenges Europe will face in the coming decades is to make its energy system clean, secure and efficient, while ensuring EU industrial leadership in low-carbon energy technologies.

To help achieve such ambitious objectives, this Focus Area aims to develop, and accelerate the time to market of, affordable, cost-effective and resource-efficient technology solutions to decarbonise the energy system in a sustainable way, secure energy supply and complete the energy internal market, in line with the objectives of the Strategic Energy Technologies Plan (SET-Plan).

A – Development and demonstration of competitive renewable electricity and heating/cooling

B – Electricity grids: enabling an increased flexibility of the European power system, efficiently providing increased transfer capacity and enabling an active participation of users and new market actors

C - Providing the energy system with flexibility through enhanced energy storage technologies

D – Sustainable biofuels and alternative fuels for the European transport fuel mix

E - Enabling decarbonisation of the fossil fuel-based power sector and energy intensive industry through CCS

Smart Cities and Communities

The European Innovation Partnership on Smart Cities and Communities (SCC) aims at accelerating the deployment of innovative technologies, organisational and economic solutions to significantly increase resource and energy efficiency, improve the sustainability of urban transport and drastically reduce greenhouse gas emissions in urban areas. The SCC is an industry-led initiative that is tailor-made to correspond to the intended intervention at the level of cities and communities, and to the complexity of action at the interface of the three sectors.

A-Initialising the process for deploying replicable solutions for Smart Cities and Communities at the intersection of energy , transport, ICT through lighthouse projects

B-Enhancing the roll out Smart Cities and Communities solutions through common levers

Background to Energy Research in Horizon 2020

Table 3.6 Background to Energy Programme

Source	Examples
EU Policy	SET Plan (Strategic Energy Technology Plan)
Key Enabling Technologies (KETs)	Advanced Materials Nanotechnology
Technology Platforms	Biofuels Photovoltaics RHC SmartGrids SNETP TPWind ZEP
Joint Technology Initiatives (JTI)	JTI FCH (Fuel Cells)
Public Private Partnerships (PPP)	BbG - Biobased for Growth EeB - Energy-efficient Buildings EFFRA - Factories of the Future
European Innovation Partnerships (EIP)	Smart Cities
Knowledge Innovation Communities (KIC)	KIC InnoEnergy
Joint Programming Initiatives (JPI)	Urban Europe –Global Challenges, Local Solutions
ERAnet and ERAnet+	CHIST-ERA II DC-Net ECO-INNOVERA ERASynBio LEAD ERA SEERA-EI
Article 185 initiatives	AAL JP BONUS+

Smart, green and integrated transport

The specific objective of the Transport Challenge 'Smart, green and integrated transport' is *"to achieve a European transport system that is resource-efficient, climate- and environmentally-friendly, safe and seamless for the benefit of all citizens, the economy and society"*. The Specific Programme is structured in four broad lines of activities aiming at:

a) Resource efficient transport that respects the environment and public health

b) Better mobility and accessibility, less congestion, more safety and security

c) Global leadership for the European transport industry

d) Socio-economic and behavioural research and forward looking activities for policy making

Areas addressing mode-specific challenges

1. Aviation

2. Rail

3. Road

4. Waterborne

Areas addressing transport integration specific challenges

5. Urban

6. Logistics

7. Intelligent Transport Systems

8. Infrastructures

Areas addressing cross-cutting issues

9. Socio-economic and behavioural research and forward looking activities for policy making

10. Small business innovation research

Table 3.7 Background to Transport Programme

Source	Examples
EU Policy	White Paper: Towards a Single European Transport Area
Technology Platforms	Aeronautics (ACARE) Rail (ERRAC) Road (ERTRAC) Waterborne

Climate action, environment, resource efficiency and raw materials

The era of seemingly plentiful and cheap resources is coming to an end: raw materials, water, air, biodiversity and terrestrial, aquatic and marine ecosystems are all under pressure. In order to meet the needs of a growing global population it is necessary to work within the sustainable limits of the planet's natural resources and eco-systems.

Examples of Focus Areas and Topics in this programme

WASTE: A RESOURCE TO RECYCLE, REUSE AND RECOVER RAW MATERIALS
Moving towards a circular economy through industrial symbiosis
A systems approach for the reduction, recycling and reuse of food waste
Recycling of raw materials from products and buildings
Towards near-zero waste at European and global level
Preparing and promoting innovation procurement for resource efficiency
Promoting eco-innovative waste management and prevention as part of sustainable urban development
Ensuring sustainable use of agricultural waste, co-products and by-products

WATER INNOVATION: BOOSTING ITS VALUE FOR EUROPE
Bridging the gap: from innovative water solutions to market replication
Integrated approaches to water and climate change
Stepping up EU research and innovation cooperation in the water area
Harnessing EU water research and innovation results for industry, policy makers and citizens
Strengthening international R&I cooperation in the field of water

GROWING A LOW CARBON, RESOURCE EFFICIENT ECONOMY WITH A SUSTAINABLE SUPPLY OF RAW MATERIALS
Fighting and adapting to climate change
Protecting the environment, sustainably managing natural resources, water, biodiversity and ecosystems
Ensuring the sustainable supply of non-energy and non-agricultural raw materials
Developing comprehensive and sustained global environmental observation and information systems

BLUE GROWTH: UNLOCKING THE POTENTIAL OF THE OCEANS
Improving the preservation and sustainable exploitation of Atlantic marine ecosystems
Developing in-situ Atlantic Ocean Observations for a better management and exploitation of the maritime resources
Strengthening international cooperation in the field of marine sciences
European polar research cooperation

Europe in a changing world: inclusive, innovative and reflective societies

This programme funds research on Social and Economic Science and the Humanities. The following are examples of the areas funded.

Overcoming the crisis; new ideas, strategies and governance structures for Europe
Examples of topics:
1. The institutional foundation of economic development – The European growth perspective
2. Innovation based growth strategy in Europe for better jobs, higher employment and less inequality
3. Innovative social investment approaches for the modernisation of social policies and services

Reflective Societies: Cultural Heritage
Examples of topics
1. ERA Net on Uses of the past
2. Emergence and transmission of European cultural heritage and Europeanization
3. Cultural heritage and the development of European tourism

Inclusive and sustainable Europe for the young generation
Examples of topics:
1. Traditional and new ways of societal and political engagement of young people in Europe
2. The young as a driver of socio-ecological transition
3. Early job insecurity and labour market exclusion

Europe as a Global actor
Examples of topics:
1. Europe's contribution to a value-based, just global order and its contestants
2. Alternative models of governance and the European Union's foreign policy

Reflective Societies: European values and identities
Examples of topics:
1. Unity in diversity: prospects of a European identity and public sphere
2. European intellectual and artistic space as a basis for European construction
3. The role and contribution of European mobility programmes in the shaping of the European

Innovation Policy Studies
Achieving the Innovation Union (IU) and the European Research Area (ERA)
New forms of Innovation
Digital Empowerment of Citizens
Cooperation with Third Countries
Ensuring societal engagement with research and innovation
Strengthening the evidence-base for Research and Innovation policy making
Support the development of Research and Innovation Policies

Teaming and Twinning

Teaming focuses on the creation of new (or significant upgrades of existing) Centres of Excellence in regions and Member States that are currently identified as low performers in terms of research and innovation.

Twinning aims at significantly strengthening a defined field of research in an emerging institution by linking this institution with at least two internationally-leading counterparts in Europe.

Secure Societies

This programme focuses on research aimed at protecting citizens, society and economy as well as assets, infrastructures and services. The overall impact is to protect economic prosperity, political stability and well-being.

Fight against crime and terrorism
The aim is to prevent criminal or terrorist incidents and to mitigate the consequences of criminal or terrorists activities. This requires new technologies and capabilities for fighting and preventing crime (including cyber-crime), illegal trafficking and terrorism (including cyber-terrorism). Research is not only focussing on technology development but social research, including understanding and tackling terrorist ideas and beliefs. Examples include:
- Forensics;
- Law enforcement capabilities;
- Urban security;
- Ethical/societal dimension.

Disaster Resilient Societies
The objective of this area of research is to reduce the loss of human life, environmental, economic and material damage from natural and man-made disasters, including from extreme weather and geological events, crime and terrorism threats. Examples include:
- Crisis Management and Civil protection;
- Disaster Resilience and Climate Change;
- Critical Infrastructure Protection;
- Communication Interoperability;
- Ethical/Societal Dimension.

Border Security
In relation to movement of persons the European Union treats migration management and the fight against crime as twin objectives of its integrated border management strategy. Technologies and capabilities are required to enhance systems, equipment, tools, processes, and methods for rapid identification to improve border security, including both control and surveillance issues.

Cyber-security and Privacy
The proposed activities in this domain address the economic and societal dimension of security in the digital ecosystem, for the purposes of ensuring the well-functioning of the internal market. It entails preventing cyber-attacks on any component of the digital society (networks, access devices, IT services, ...) no matter what their nature or origin; as well as protecting physical (e.g. critical infrastructures) or intangible assets (e.g. finances, intellectual property, privacy). Examples include:

- Privacy;
- Access Control;
- Secure Information Sharing;
- Trust eServices5. Risk management and assurance models;
- The role of ICT in Critical Infrastructure Protection.

Background to Security Programme
The key policy documents are the Security Industrial Policy, the Internal Security Strategy and the Cyber Security Strategy.

EIT (European Institute of Innovation and Technology)

EIT Website http://ec.europa.eu/education/policies/eit/index_en.html

Background to EIT

Innovation has become the 'holy grail' of economies all over the world. In 2003, Henry Chesborough published a book entitled 'Open Innovation'. This book has become the bible of many industries and companies. 'Open Innovation' promotes the concept that companies must be willing to source ideas from outside their organisations – especially from public research organisations. While this appears logical in principle,the reality is that there is a 'valley of death' between the world of academic research and the needs of companies. Many attempts have been made to overcome this 'valley'. The aim of the EIT is to address this dilemma.

Terminology used in by the EIT

Knowledge Triangle: This describes the interaction between Academic Institutions, Research Centres and Industry

Knowledge and Innovation Communities (KICs) *"bring together the three elements of the knowledge triangle and are excellence-driven partnerships between universities, research organisations, companies and other innovation stakeholders"*

In 2010 the European Commission funded three KICs to test the concept. The three KICs were:
> ICTLabs KIC (www.eit.ictlabs.eu)
> Climate KIC (http://eit.europa.eu/kics1/climate-kic.html)
> INNOenergy KIC (http://eit.europa.eu/kics1/kic-innoenergy.html)

"To date, the 3 KICs bring together a total of 195 partners including 61 universities, 51 research institutes, 73 businesses and 10 local/regional agencies in 12 countries and at 16 co-location centres." (EIT Strategic Innovation Agenda , 2013)

Table 3.8 The structure of the ICTlabs KIC

Colocation Centres	Partners
Berlin	Fraunhofer SAP Siemens TU Berlin DFKI Deutsche TeleKom
Helsinki	VTT Nokia Aalto (TKK)
Stockholm	SICS KTH Acreo TeliaSonera Ericsson
Eindhoven	Philips 3TU.NIRICT Novay TNO-ICT
Paris	Université Pierre et Marie Curie Université Paris-Sud INRIA Institut Telecom Alcatel-Lucent Orange-France Telecom Thomson
Trento	Trento RISE + Italian Universities + Telecom Italia + Engineering Ingegneria Informatica S.p.A

(Membership of this KIC may change)

Co-location Centres: These are geographical locations where existing world-class partners interact and work together face-to-face. For example, in Table 3.7 Helsinki co-location centre brings together VTT (research centre), Nokia (Company) and Aalto (University)

Strategic Innovation Agenda (SIA) means a policy document outlining *"the priority fields and the long-term strategy of the EIT for future initiatives, including an overview of planned higher education, research and innovation activities, over a period of seven years."*

EIT in Horizon 2020

The EIT aims at boosting innovation in Europe by pooling together excellent resources, allowing innovative businesses, research organisations and higher education institutions to interact with each other in new ways and to exploit fully their creative potential for finding new solutions to major societal challenges.

The EIT gives the vision, the KICs provide the forum for strategy making in the selected areas of societal challenges and the Co-location Centres are the primary delivery mechanisms for the KICs.

The Impact of EIT in Horizon 2020
- The transfer and valorisation of higher education, research and innovation activities in a business context
- New business creation through innovation
- Cutting edge and innovation-driven research in areas of key economic and societal interest
- Development of talented, skilled and entrepreneurial people through education and training activities
- Dissemination of best practice and systemic knowledge sharing

Table 3.9 Proposed KICs for Horizon 2020

Year	KIC
2014	Innovation for healthy living and active ageing
2014	Raw materials- sustainable exploration, extraction, processing, recycling and substitution
2014	Food 4 Future -sustainable supply chain from resources to consumers
2018	Added-value manufacturing
2018	Urban mobility
2018	Smart Secure Societies

(These areas and dates are subject to change)

Key Documents on EIT
CATALYSING INNOVATION IN THE KNOWLEDGE TRIANGLE
Practices from the EIT Knowledge and Innovation Communities
http://eit.europa.eu/fileadmin/Content/Downloads/PDF/Key_documents/EIT_publication_Final.pdf

EIT: Criteria for the Selection of Knowledge and Innovation Communities (KICs)
http://ec.europa.eu/eit/doc/kicselectioncriteria_20090302.pdf

EIT's Strategic Innovation Agenda (SIA) – Investing in Innovation beyond 2014
http://eit.europa.eu/fileadmin/Content/Downloads/SIA/EIT_Strategic_Innovation_Agenda_FINAL_-_Copy.pdf

EIT Websites www.hyperion.ie/eit.htm

Euratom

The Euratom programme focuses on two main research themes: (a) Research on Nuclear Fission and Radiation Protection and (b) Fusion Research

Nuclear Fission and Radiation Protection

This programme existed in Framework 7. In Horizon 2020 the programme has been thoroughly reviewed, in the context of the post-Fukushima disaster. Euratom in Horizon 2020 focuses on nuclear safety and improved interaction with civil society. Nuclear technology also includes other applications of ionising radiations (e.g. radioisotope production for medical radio-diagnosis, -imaging and -therapy). A key background document to this programme is the Strategic Research Agenda of Sustainable Nuclear Energy Technology Platform.
Areas covered include:

1. Support Safe Operation of Nuclear Systems
   1.1. Improved safety design and operation of fission reactors

   1.2. Faster and more reliable tool for reactor accident management.

   1.3. High density uranium targets for the production of medical radioisotopes

   1.4. Supporting the development of reactor infrastructures for irradiation

   1.5. Transmutation (conversion of one element into another)

2. Contribute to the Development of Solutions for the Management of Ultimate Radioactive Waste
   2.1. Joint development and management of Member State research programmes of pan European interest

   2.2. Development of harmonised regulatory requirements in the review of license applications of geological repositories

   2.3. Improved science, technology and accompanying measures and innovative solutions for safe and publically acceptable geological repositories

3. Radiation Protection

4. Education & training, and socio-economic aspects

Future areas of research in Horizon 2020

- materials for nuclear fission
- advanced partitioning of spent nuclear fuel
- new research infrastructures and numerical prediction tools of common interest
- pre-normative research in view of harmonisation of safety standards and practices
- improvement and dissemination of nuclear safety culture within the EU and abroad.

Fusion Research

The areas covered in this section of the programme are based on the document 'Fusion Electricity – A roadmap to the realisation of fusion energy'. The principal aim of the Euratom work programme 2014-15 is to provide Community support to the joint programme of activities implemented by the current EFDA members (national fusion laboratories) in line with the EFDA roadmap. One of the key elements of the Fusion Research programme is ITER (International Thermonuclear Experimental Reactor http://www.itercad.org/index_en.html .)

JRC (Joint Research Centres)

The European Commission has seven research institutes of its own, known as the Joint Research Centre (JRC). The JRC Website (http://ec.europa.eu/dgs/jrc/) states that *'The JRC supports policy makers in the conception, development, implementation and monitoring of policies.'*

These research centres are located in five different sites throughout the EU (Belgium, Germany, Italy, The Netherlands and Spain). Even though they are part of the European Commission, they can participate as partners in Horizon 2020 projects. If the grant is awarded, the Commission makes payments to the Joint Research Centre directly (not through the coordinator as for other partners).

The Joint Research Centres are:

- Institute for Reference Materials and Measurement (IRMM)
- Institute for Transuranium Elements (ITU)
- Institute for Energy (IE)
- Institute for the Protection and Security of the Citizen (IPSC)
- Institute for Environment and Sustainability (IES)
- Institute for Health and Consumer Protection (IHCP)
- Institute for Prospective Technological Studies (IPTS)

Fast Track to Innovation

This is an initiative to promote innovation in any technological field. It is a 'bottom up' initiative open to any new ideas. The focus will be on 'impact' – where the proposers can demonstrate a clear innovation that is relevant to a market demand. The programme is Open – proposals can be submitted at any time.

Widening Participation

There is a divide between the regions in Europe in terms of research infrastructures and attractiveness as a centre of excellence. The aim of this initiative is to develop links between research organisations with established international reputations and research organisations 'lower performing Member States and regions'. Four actions are funded to support the lower performing regions:

- Teaming aimed at creating or improving existing Centres of Excellence;
- Twinning promoting networking with excellent centres;
- ERA Chairs bringing outstanding researchers to universities and research centres;
- A Policy Support Facility to help in the formulation of research and innovation policies.

Science with and for Society

The aim of his part of the work programme is to build effective cooperation between science and society, to recruit new talent for science and to pair scientific excellence with social awareness and responsibility. *"It will make science more attractive (notably to young people), raise the appetite of society for innovation, and open up further research and innovation activities. It allows all societal actors (researchers, citizens, policy makers, business, third sector organisations etc.) to work together during the whole research and innovation process in order to better align both the process and its outcomes with the values, needs and expectations of European society. This approach to research and innovation is termed Responsible Research and Innovation (RRI)."*

Public Private Partnerships (PPP)

Public Private Partnership is the term use to describe funding arrangements that involve public (National or European) and Private funding. Public-private partnerships (PPPs) in research are defined by the OECD as: *"Any formal relationship or arrangement over a fixed-term/indefinite period of time, between public and private actors, where both sides interact in the decision-making process, and co-invest scarce resources such as money, personnel, facilities, and information in order to achieve specific objectives in the area of science, technology, and innovation".*

In Horizon 2020 PPPs are used to address industrial challenges. Two approaches are used: Institutional PPP and Contractual PPP

Institutional PPP (also known as Joint Technology Initiatives (JTI))

www.hyperion.ie/jti.htm

An Institutional PPP is a legal body. It is created using the same process that was used to create the Horizon 2020 programme. The European Commission submitted a proposal to the Council and European Parliament. The Council and the Parliament 'adopted' the proposal and a new legal body was created. This legal body is implemented using Article 187 of the Treaty on the Functioning of the European Union. The organisation that is responsible for the implementation of the Institutional PPP is called a 'Joint Undertaking'. In Horizon 2020 the following are the Institutional PPPs

- *Innovative Medicines*: to improve European citizens' health and wellbeing by providing new and more effective diagnostics and treatments such as new antimicrobial treatments;
- *Fuel Cells and Hydrogen*: to develop commercially viable, clean, solutions that use hydrogen as an energy carrier and of fuel cells as energy converters;
- *Clean Sky*: to radically reduce the environmental impact of the next generation of aircraft;
- *Bio-based Industries*: to develop new and competitive bio-based value chains that replace the need for fossil fuels and have a strong impact on rural development;
- *Electronic Components and Systems*: to keep Europe at the forefront of electronic components and systems and bridge faster the gap to exploitation.

Contractual Public Private Partnerships

www.hyperion.ie/ppp.htm

Contractual PPPs are NOT legal bodies. They are established on an ad-hoc basis. In Horizon 2020 the following Contractual PPPs exist. (This list may expand during Horizon 2020)

- Factories of the Future;
- Energy-efficient Buildings;
- Green Vehicles;
- Future Internet14;
- Sustainable Process Industry;
- Robotics;
- Photonics;
- High Performance Computing (HPC).

These challenges will be implemented through several of the programmes in Pillar II and Pillar III. For example, the Energy-efficient Buildings PPP (EeB PPP) will be implement as follows:

Energy Programme

EeB 1: Materials for building envelope
EeB 2: Adaptable envelopes integrated in building refurbishment projects
Etc.

NMPB Programme

EE1: Manufacturing of prefabricated modules for renovation of buildings
EE2: Building design for new high energy performing buildings
EE3: Energy strategies and solutions for deep renovation in historic buildings

Chapter 4: How Proposals are Evaluated

CONTENTS

Terminology used in the Evaluation Process
The Evaluation Process
Facts and Figures about the Evaluation Process
The Life of an 'Expert Evaluator'
Why bother being an 'Expert Evaluator'?
How to become an 'Expert Evaluator'

Chapter Webpage: www.hyperion.ie/h2020-evaluation.htm

The Evaluation Process

This Chapter first describes the evaluation process of Pillar II and Pillar III. ('Top Down' Programmes). It then describes the evaluation process for the Marie Curie Programme and the ERC (European Research Council) Programme ('Bottom Up' Programmes).

The standard evaluation criteria for Horizon 2020 are described in Annex H of the General Annexes of the Work programmes.

The evaluation process for Horizon 2020 is based on the European Commission's 30 yer experience of the Framework programmes. The administration of the process is very professional and the software systems to support the evaluation are very efficient. The evaluators are selected based on expertise in their fields.

The selection of the evaluators for each proposal can pose problems. The person that selects the evaluators is the Project Officer in charge of the topic. The Project Officer uses the Abstract of the proposal and the database of the evaluators to match the evaluators to the project. When writing the abstract, it is critical to provide the Project Officer with a clear description of the different disciplines in the project so that the most appropriate evaluators can be selected.

"Because of the range of topics and time constraints, it may not be always possible to find evaluators with specific detailed expertise for all detailed areas or niches of a proposal. Thus, in some cases multi-disciplinary evaluations have to be done. Therefore, experts should not only be competent in one specific area, but should also have a broad overview of their field"

"The Commission services selected a new set of evaluators for stage 2 of this two-stage process, which involved an extensive search for experts from all over the world. As a result, 76 evaluators were selected, of which 56% were non-European."

Source: Health Programme: Independent Observer's Report.

The evaluation process is like a production line. The European Commission has been improving the evaluation process since the early 1980's. The process, the documentation and the database have all been streamlined. It is impressive to see the whole administration system in operation.

Proposal page limits and layout
The maximum number of pages is specified, for each section of the proposal. Experts will be instructed to disregard any excess pages in each section in which the maximum number of pages has been indicated.

Request for Review
A request for review shall relate to a specific proposal, and shall be submitted by the coordinator of the proposal within 30 days of the date when the Commission or the relevant funding body informs the coordinator of the evaluation results.
The Commission or the relevant funding body shall be responsible for the examination of this request. This examination shall only cover the procedural aspects of the evaluation, and not the merit of the proposal.
An evaluation review committee composed of Commission staff or of the relevant funding body staff shall provide an opinion on the procedural aspects of the evaluation process. It shall be chaired by an official of the Commission or of the relevant funding body, from a department other than the one responsible for the call for proposals. The committee may recommend one of the following:
      (a) re-evaluation of the proposal *primarily by evaluators not involved in the previous evaluation;*
      (b) confirmation of the initial opinion.

Competition at Topic Level

The Top Down' Programmes in Pillar II and Pillar III are divided into 'Areas' and each Area is divided into 'Topics'. Examples of these 'Topics' were shown in Chapter 1.
Each 'Topic' has a Project Officer and this is the person responsible for the selection of the evaluators for the topic. The maximum score for a proposal is 15 and the scores are in steps of 14.5, 14.0, 13.5…

Table 4.1 Proposals Submitted by Topic (Example)

Topic	Topic Name	Proposals	Accepted
1.1	**Network of the Future**	145	23
1.5	**Networked Media & 3D Internet**	139	23
2.1	**Cognitive Systems and Robotics**	109	19
2.2	**Language-Based Interaction**	29	9
8.2	**Quantum Information Foundations and Technologies**	5	3
8.3	**Biochemistry based IT**	7	3

Table 4.1 is an example of proposals submitted by Topic in the ICT programme.

> Topic 1.1 received 145 proposals and 23 were funded.
> Topic 8.2 received 5 proposals and 3 were funded.
>
> In Topic 1.1, it would be necessary to obtain a score of 15.0 or 14.5 to succeed.
> In Topic 8.2, a proposal could be successful with a score of 13.5.

Where can the statistics of the evaluation be found?
It is impossible to predict how many proposals will be submitted per topic. One indicator is the budget for the topic. A bigger budget will attract more proposals – and more proposals will mean more competition. Smaller budgets may (but not always) have less competition.
After each Call for Proposals, the statistics are stored in a database called eCorda. These statistics include: the number of proposal per topic, the number of successful projects per topic and the Evaluation Summary Reports for each proposal. The National Contact Points have access to these statistics. When the statistics are finalised, it is important that the NCPs analyse this data to identify topics where competition is high and where competition is not so high.
As topics in one call may not be repeated in the following calls, these statistics can only be used as rough indicators. If a proposal can fit into one or more topics then this type of information can be important.

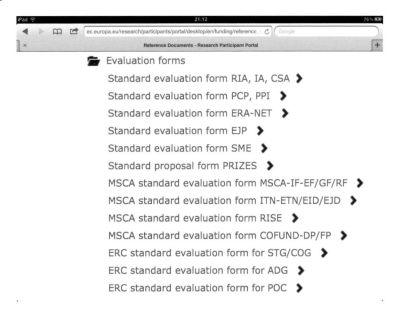

The Evaluation Criteria

In Horizon 2020, a standard set of evaluation criteria are defined in Annex H of the General Annexes. In the case of ERC, Marie Curie and FET, the evaluation criteria are defined in the individual work programmes. The following is a summary of the evaluation criteria as defined in Annex H. It is important to read the work programme to assess if additional criteria are used or if specific evaluation criteria are given more attention (weight). For example, in the case of 'Innovation Actions' and 'SME Instrument' , the impact score is given a weight of 1.5.

During Horizon 2020, these evaluation criteria may change due to lessons learned or due to changes in the programme.

This Chapter first describes the evaluation process and criteria for Pillar II and Pillar III. It then describes the evaluation criteria for ERC and the Marie Skłodowska-Curie Fellowships/

Table 4.2 Evaluation Criteria for 'Research and Innovation Actions', 'Innovation Actions'

Excellence	Impact	Implementatioon
The following aspects will be taken into account, to the extent that the proposed work corresponds to the topic description in the work programme:	The extent to which the outputs of the project should contribute at the European and/or International level to:	The following aspects will be taken into account:
Clarity and pertinence of the objectives; Credibility of the proposed approach; Soundness of the concept, including trans-disciplinary considerations, where relevant; Extent that the proposed work is ambitious, has innovation potential, and is beyond the state of the art (e.g. ground-breaking objectives, novel concepts and approaches).	The expected impacts listed in the work programme under the relevant topic; Enhancing innovation capacity and integration of new knowledge; Strengthening the competitiveness and growth of companies by developing innovations meeting the needs of European and global markets; and, where relevant, by delivering such innovations to the markets; Any other environmental and socially important impacts (not already covered above); Effectiveness of the proposed measures to exploit and disseminate the project results (including management of the IPR), to communicate the project, and to manage research data where relevant.	Experts will indicate whether the participants meet the selection criterion related to the operational capacity, to carry out the proposed work, based on competence and experience of the individual participant(s); Coherence and effectiveness of the work plan, including appropriateness of the allocation of tasks and resources; Complementarity of the participants within the consortium (when relevant); Appropriateness of the management structures and procedures, including risk and innovation management.

Table 4.2 Evaluation Criteria for the 'SME Instrument'

Excellence	Impact	Implementatioon
The following aspects will be taken into account, to the extent that the proposed work corresponds to the topic description in the work programme:	The extent to which the outputs of the project should contribute at the European and/or International level to:	The following aspects will be taken into account:
Clarity and pertinence of the objectives;

Credibility of the proposed approach;

Soundness of the concept, including trans-disciplinary considerations, where relevant;

Extent that the proposed work is ambitious, has innovation potential, and is beyond the state of the art (e.g. ground-breaking objectives, novel concepts and approaches). | The expected impacts listed in the work programme under the relevant topic;

Enhancing innovation capacity and integration of new knowledge;

Strengthening the competitiveness and growth of companies by developing innovations meeting the needs of European and global markets; and, where relevant, by delivering such innovations to the markets; Any other environmental and socially important impacts (not already covered above);

Effectiveness of the proposed measures to exploit and disseminate the project results (including management of the IPR), to communicate the project, and to manage research data where relevant. | Experts will indicate whether the participants meet the selection criterion related to the operational capacity, to carry out the proposed work, based on competence and experience of the individual participant(s);

Coherence and effectiveness of the work plan, including appropriateness of the allocation of tasks and resources;

Complementarity of the participants within the consortium (when relevant);

Appropriateness of the management structures and procedures, including risk and innovation management. |

The European Commission provides the following description of the evaluation process for the SME instrument.

"The criterion Impact will be evaluated first, then Excellence and Implementation. If the proposal fails to achieve the threshold for a criterion, the evaluation of the proposal will be stopped.

For Phase 1 the threshold for individual criteria will be 4. The overall threshold, applying to the sum of the three individual scores, will be 13.

For Phase 2 the threshold for the criterion Impact will be 4. The overall threshold, applying the sum of the three individual scores, will be 12.

The final consensus score of a proposal will be the median of the individual scores of the individual evaluators. The consensus report will comprise a collation of the individual reports, or extracts from them. Where appropriate, a Panel Review will be organised remotely.

Applicants can provide, during the electronic proposal submission, up to three names of persons that should NOT act as an evaluator in the evaluation of their proposal. This is allowed for competitive reasons. If any of the persons identifies is an independent expert participating in the evaluation of the proposals for the call in question, they may be excluded from the evaluation of the proposal concerned, as long as it remains possible to have the proposal evaluated."

Table 4.3 Evaluation Criteria for 'Coordination and Support Actions'

Excellence	Impact	Implementatioon
The following aspects will be taken into account, to the extent that the proposed work corresponds to the topic description in the work programme:	The extent to which the outputs of the project should contribute at the European and/or International level to:	The following aspects will be taken into account:
Clarity and pertinence of the objectives; Credibility of the proposed approach; Soundness of the concept; Quality of the proposed coordination and/or support measures	The expected impacts listed in the work programme under the relevant topic; Effectiveness of the proposed measures to exploit and disseminate the project results (including management of the IPR), to communicate the project, and to manage research data where relevant.	Experts will indicate whether the participants meet the selection criterion related to the operational capacity, to carry out the proposed work, based on competence and experience of the individual participant(s); Coherence and effectiveness of the work plan, including appropriateness of the allocation of tasks and resources; Complementarity of the participants within the consortium (when relevant); Appropriateness of the management structures and procedures, including risk and innovation management

Coordination and Support Actions (CSA)

This type of grant does not fund research. It funds actions such as *"standardization, dissemination, awareness-raising and communication, networking, coordination or support services, policy dialogues and mutual learning exercises and studies. This includes design studies for new infrastructures and may also include complementary activities of strategic planning, networking and coordination between programmes in different countries"*. Coordination and Support Actions are funded 100% of eligible costs.

Example of a Coordination and Support Action

Innovation in SMEs Programme

INNOSUP-9-2014: Community-building and competence development for SME instrument coaching
"The objective of the action is to create the conditions for a comprehensive and consistent delivery of the coaching and mentoring service....."

"Type of action: Coordinating and support action"

Table 4.4 Evaluation Criteria for 'ERA-NET Cofund'

Excellence	Impact	Implementatioon
The following aspects will be taken into account, to the extent that the proposed work corresponds to the topic description in the work programme:	The extent to which the outputs of the project should contribute at the European and/or International level to:	The following aspects will be taken into account:
Clarity and pertinence of the objectives; Credibility of the proposed approach; Level of ambition in the collaboration and commitment of the participants in the proposed ERA-NET action to pool national resources and coordinate their national/regional research programmes.	The expected impacts listed in the work programme under the relevant topic; Achievement of the critical mass for the funding of trans-national projects by pooling of national/regional resources and contribution to establishing and strengthening a durable cooperation between the partners and their national/regional research programmes; Effectiveness of the proposed measures to exploit and disseminate the project results to communicate the project.	Experts will indicate whether the participants meet the selection criterion related to the operational capacity, to carry out the proposed work, based on competence and experience of the individual participant(s). Coherence and effectiveness of the work plan, including appropriateness of the allocation of tasks and resources; Complementarity of the participants within the consortium (when relevant); Appropriateness of the management structures and procedures, including risk and innovation management.

ERAnet Cofund

This is a merger of two previous actions (ERAnet and ERAnet plus). This is designed to bring national and regional funding agencies together to fund joint calls for proposals. The participants in this programme are organisations that are mandated to implement national or regional funding programmes.

Example of an ERAnet Cofund Call

Supporting the development of a European research area in the field of Energy

LCE 18 – 2014/2015 84: Supporting Joint Actions on demonstration and validation of innovative energy solutions
"The proposals should aim at coordinating the research efforts of the participating Member States, Associated States and Regions in the areas and challenges targeted in this 'Competitive low-carbon energy' call or in the 'Smart Cities and Communities' call and to implement a joint transnational call for proposals resulting in grants to third parties with EU co-funding to fund multinational innovative research initiatives in this domain...."

"Type of Action: ERAnet Cofund Action"

Table 4.5 Evaluation Criteria for 'Pre-commercial procurement Cofund' and 'Procurement of innovative solutions Cofund'

Excellence	Impact	Implementatioon
The following aspects will be taken into account, to the extent that the proposed work corresponds to the topic description in the work programme:	The extent to which the outputs of the project should contribute at the European and/or International level to:	The following aspects will be taken into account:
Clarity and pertinence of the objectives; Credibility of the proposed approach; Progress beyond the state of the art in terms of the degree of innovation needed to satisfy the procurement needed.	The expected impacts listed in the work programme under the relevant topic Enhancing innovation capacity and integration of new knowledge; Strengthening the competitiveness and growth of companies by developing innovations meeting the needs of European and global markets; and, where relevant, by delivering such innovations to the markets; Any other environmental and socially important impacts (not already covered above); Effectiveness of the proposed measures to exploit and disseminate the project results (including management of the IPR), to communicate the project, and to manage research data where relevant.	Experts will indicate whether the participants meet the selection criterion related to the operational capacity, to carry out the proposed work, based on competence and experience of the individual participant(s); Coherence and effectiveness of the work plan, including appropriateness of the allocation of tasks and resources; Complementarity of the participants within the consortium (when relevant); Appropriateness of the management structures and procedures, including risk and innovation management.

Public Procurement Cofund Actions
These actions are designed to coordinate public procurement organization to promote:
- o (PCP) Pre-commercial public procurement which encourages public procurement bodies to fund research, development and valorization of new solutions;
- o (PPI) Public procurement of innovative solutions where the procurer acts as an early adopter of innovative solutions.

Example of a Public Procurement Cofund Action

Smart, Green and Integrated Transport Programme
MG 8.3-2015 Facilitating market take up of innovative transport infrastructure solutions
"Actions should lead to the improvement and capacity building in the field of public purchasing of innovative solutions in transport infrastructure leading to implementation of best available solutions on cross-border TEN-T network business cases representative of dtypical European situations……."

Type of action: *Public Procurement of Innovative Solutions (PPI) Cofund.*

The Evaluation Scores

Each of the three evaluation criteria has a maximum score of 5. The total maximum score is therefore 15. Each of the criteria has a threshold of 3 – a score below 3 in any of the criteria means that the proposal is rejected. The overall threshold is 10. Table 7.6 is a guideline for the evaluators on the relevance of each score.

Table 4.6 Evaluation Scores

Score	Comment
0	The **proposal fails to address the criterion** or cannot be assessed due to missing or incomplete information.
1	**Poor**. The criterion is inadequately addressed, or there are serious inherent weaknesses.
2	**Fair**. The proposal broadly addresses the criterion, but there are significant weaknesses.
3	**Good.** The proposal addresses the criterion well, but a number of shortcomings are present.
4	**Very Good.** The proposal addresses the criterion very well, but a small number of shortcomings are present.
5	**Excellent.** The proposal successfully addresses all relevant aspects of the criterion. Any shortcomings are minor..

The Evaluation Process

The proposal is submitted electronically through the Participant Portal. Figure 4.1 shows how the proposal is processed when it arrives in Brussels. The different steps are described in the following pages.

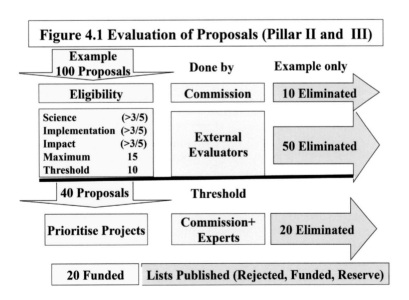

Figure 4.1 Evaluation of Proposals (Pillar II and III)

Check Eligibility	**Done by Commission**	**10 Eliminated**

The proposals are submitted electronically. The proposals are first checked for basic eligibility criteria. The 'eligibility criteria' are:

- Deadline: The computer stops accepting proposals at the deadline.
- Relevant Funding Scheme: The Commission checks the funding scheme of the proposal. If this scheme is not relevant to the call the proposal will be deleted.
- If Part A or Part B is not complete the proposal will not be read.
- Partners: If the legal minimum number of partners is not in the consortium, the proposal will not be evaluated.
- Proposals are clearly not 'relevant' to the call or the expected impacts are not 'relevant.'
- Funding thresholds exceeded. These thresholds are listed in the work programmes.

The proposal must meet the basic administrative criteria. **Up to 10% of proposals could fail these basic criteria.**

Science (>3/5) **Impact** (>3/5) **Implementation** (>3/5) **Maximum** 15 **Threshold** 10	**Decided by External Evaluators**	**50 Eliminated (Example only)**

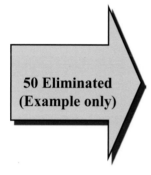

Normally, the proposal is sent to three evaluators. In most cases, the evaluation is done remotely (in the evaluator's office or home). The evaluators do not know each other. Each evaluator is aware that at least two other evaluators are reading the same proposal. The three evaluators eventually meet in Brussels to discuss the proposals and they agree a score for each criterion. (The process is described in the following section).

It is possible for a proposal to get 5/5 in Science, 5/5 in Implementation and to fail because of 2.5/5 in Impact. Each of the thresholds has to be passed.

At this point, the evaluators have completed their role in the evaluation.

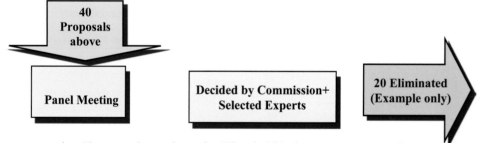

40 Proposals above → **Panel Meeting**	**Decided by Commission+ Selected Experts**	**20 Eliminated (Example only)**

Let us assume that 40 proposals are above the 'Threshold.' The European Commission then checks the budgets and may find that there is only funding for 20 projects. This means that 20 of the proposals that are above the Threshold will be rejected. (Generally only 50% of the proposals that get above the Threshold are funded).

The Commission then publishes three lists:
Proposals Rejected, Proposals recommended for funding and a Reserve List

The Life of an 'Expert Evaluator'

This section presents a short summary of what exactly is involved in becoming an evaluator.

A researcher must first enter her/his details in the expert database on the Participant Portal. The project officers in the European Commission have to select a team of evaluators to evaluate the proposals for each programme. The database is consulted and, using the key words on the database, a list is selected. Researchers who want to increase their chances of being selected should be very precise on the topics where they could evaluate.

The project officers study the list to find suitable evaluators. The criteria, judged by the project officers in the selection process, include the experts' academic backgrounds (minimum PhD), their research activities and their involvement in previous Framework Programmes. For industrial experts, the main criteria would be their practical expertise in industrial research.

It is estimated that the European Commission hires over 5000 evaluators every year and 25% of the evaluators have to be new each year. In one Call in the Health programme, over 50% of the evaluators were evaluating for the first time. The Commission tries to restrict the number of evaluations done by any individual researcher. Project Officers are always searching for suitable evaluators. Suitable 'experts' are identified through conferences, workshops, magazine articles, existing project coordinators and partners. Months before the evaluation, the selected researchers will be contacted to find out if they are interested in becoming evaluators.

Assume that the researcher has been invited and has agreed to become an 'expert evaluator.' The researcher will then receive an email with the details of the evaluation. This email will also state that 'this is not a formal offer'. This gives the Commission some flexibility in case there are some last minute changes. All the registration and payment of the experts is done through the Participant Portal. The evaluators must sign confidentiality agreements stating that any information seen in the proposals will be kept confidential. There is also a question asking if the researcher is part of any proposal that has been submitted to the 'Call for Proposals.'
Figure 4.2 is a summary of the process. Each step is described in the following pages.

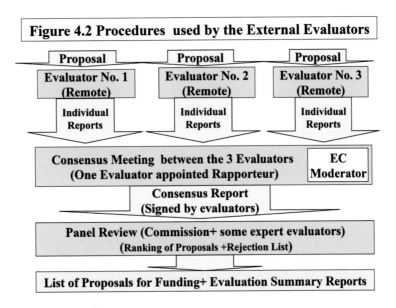

Each of the evaluators reads the proposal and fills in an 'Individual Report.' These reports are based on the evaluation criteria shown in Table 4.1 to Table 4.3. Each proposal could take between 2 to 4 hours to evaluate. The reports are submitted electronically and are stored in a database in the European Commission. The three evaluators then travel to Brussels to have a 'Consensus Meeting.'

An evaluator, arriving at the Commission in Brussels, will see a queue of other experts signing in at the reception. (In one call in the Information Society programme there were over 600 expert evaluators).

Each evaluator receives a badge and is given the details of a meeting room where all the evaluators for the topic will meet. Each evaluator receives a table listing the names of the other evaluators and the times of the Consensus meetings.

The Consensus meeting brings together the three evaluators and a European Commission official designated as the 'EC Moderator.' The Moderator is not involved in the discussion and is only there to answer questions on legal issues. If an evaluator changes a score during the discussion, the Moderator will ask him/her to sign a document confirming that the score was changed and explaining why the change was made.

One of the evaluators is appointed 'Rapporteur.' In some cases, a fourth person reads the proposal and acts as 'Rapporteur'. That person is responsible for writing a summary of the Consensus meeting. This document will be signed by the three evaluators. This is called the 'Consensus Report Form.' The duration of the Consensus meeting will depend on the variation between the scores of the experts. If everyone has a score of 14 out of 15, the meeting could be over in 20 minutes. However, if one expert gives a score of 11, another 13 and another 15 then the proposal will be discussed in detail. The meeting will continue until the experts agree on a score. This is why it is known as a 'Consensus' meeting rather than an 'Averaging' meeting. In exceptional cases, where the evaluators cannot agree, the Commission may select three new evaluators for the proposal.

The first discussion, between the evaluators, concerns their overall understanding and impression of the project. Some proposals are so badly written that the evaluators may have difficulty understanding the main theme of the proposal.

The first paragraph of the abstract should be a clear statement on the aims of the proposal and, in particular, the research question being addressed.

Each of the evaluation criteria is discussed individually. Each evaluator is asked to explain why they gave the score (e.g. 4.5) for the criteria (e.g. Excellence). This discussion is continued until the three evaluators come to a 'consensus'. The same procedure is then done for B2 (Impact) and B3 (Implementation).

Having signed the 'Consensus Reports', the evaluators will return home. Some evaluators are invited to stay for a 'Panel Review' where the Commission selects the projects for funding. In the example on the previous page, 40 proposals were above the Threshold but funding was only available for 20 projects.

FET Consensus Meeting

In the description of the FET evaluation process, the Commission states the following:
"Eligible proposals will be evaluated by four evaluators, selected to cover the appropriate range of expertise, who will deliver their assessment in an 'Individual Evaluation Report'. A consensus comment criteria will be based on the collection of the 'Individual Evaluation Reports' comments received, or extracted from them. An interdisciplinary panel of evaluators will be convened to examine and, where necessary, review the consensus comments and scores."

Observers

During the evaluation process, the Commission hires individuals called 'Observers'. They monitor and report on the evaluation process. Below is a sample of comments from one of these Observer reports.

"It was observed that many experts agreed on scores for the consensus report that were different from the scores they had given in their Individual Evaluation Reports."

"Because of the range of topics and time constraints, it may not be always possible to find evaluators with specific detailed expertise for all detailed areas or niches of a proposal. Thus, in some cases multi-disciplinary evaluations have to be done. Therefore, experts should not only be competent in one specific area, but should also have a broad overview on their field. Also, for that reason, the consensus meetings are playing a crucial role."

"All the discussions in consensus meetings seen by the Observers were of high scientific quality and were characterized by mutual respect and serious consideration of different and diverse opinions and by a common commitment to reach consensus. The experts appreciated the high level of scientific expertise of the other evaluators."

"Every proposal was discussed in detail even when it was clear that it was going to fail. This was done in order to give the best possible comments and feedback to the proposers."

Source: FP7 Health Observer's Report
ftp://ftp.cordis.europa.eu/pub/fp7/health/docs/observers-report-health-two-stage-2009_en.pdf

Panel Meeting (Selection of Proposals)

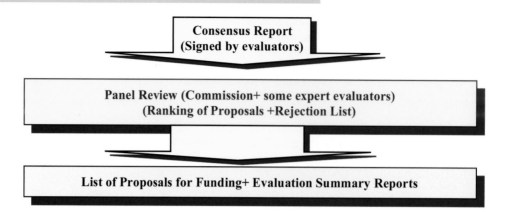

The Consensus Reports produced by the Evaluators are now used in the 'Panel Meeting'. During this panel meeting, senior European Commission officials (Heads of Unit) attend. It is also important to note that the original proposal documentation prepared by the researchers does not appear at this meeting. The only document that is discussed is the Consensus Report. This has the following format:

> **Title** (taken from the original proposal)
> **Acronym** (taken from the original proposal)
> **Abstract** (taken from the original proposal)
> **B1 Score** + Justification (Consensus agreement between the evaluators)
> **B2 Score** + Justification (Consensus agreement between the evaluators)
> **B3 Score** + Justification (Consensus agreement between the evaluators)

Annex H of the General Annexes (P31) describes the process.

"As part of the evaluation by independent experts, a panel review will recommend one or more ranked lists for the proposals under evaluation, following the scoring systems indicated above. A ranked list will be drawn up for every indicative budget shown in the call conditions.

If necessary, the panel will determine a priority order for proposals which have been awarded the same score within a ranked list. Whether or not such a prioritisation is carried out will depend on the available budget or other conditions set out in the call fiche. The following approach will be applied successively for every group of ex aequo proposals requiring prioritisation, starting with the highest scored group, and continuing in descending order:
(i) Proposals that address topics not otherwise covered by more highly-ranked proposals, will be considered to have the highest priority.
(ii) These proposals will themselves be prioritised according to the scores they have been awarded for the criterion excellence. When these scores are equal, priority will be based on scores for the criterion impact. In the case of Innovation actions, and the SME instrument (phases 1 and 2), this prioritisation will be done first on the basis of the score for impact, and then on that for excellence.

If necessary, any further prioritisation will be based on the following factors, in order: size of budget allocated to SMEs; gender balance among the personnel named in the proposal who will be primarily responsible for carrying out the research and/or innovation activities.
If a distinction still cannot be made, the panel may decide to further prioritise by considering how to enhance the quality of the project portfolio through synergies between projects, or other factors related to the objectives of the call or to Horizon 2020 in general. These factors will be documented in the report of the Panel."

The following sections will describe this process.

Figure 4.3 shows a possible scenario in a Panel Meeting. 24 proposals have been presented to the Panel and these are divided evenly between 8 topics. The proposals are sorted in order of priority by topic. (Reality is different as the number would be greater). This is a simplistic description to explain the decision making process.

"A ranked list will be drawn up for every indicative budget shown in the call conditions."

Figure 4.3 Panel Meeting (Possible Scenario)

Topic 1	15.0	14.5	14.0
Topic 2	14.5	14.0	14.0
Topic 3	15.0	14.5	14.0
Topic 4	14.0	14.0	14.0
Topic 5	13.5	12.5	10.5
Topic 6	13.5	12.0	11.0
Topic 7	9.5	9.0	9.0
Topic 8	13.5	12.0	11.0

Suppose there is only funding for 12 proposals. How are these selected?
Figure 4.4 identifies a number of key messages.

Figure 4.4 Panel Meeting (Possible Scenario)

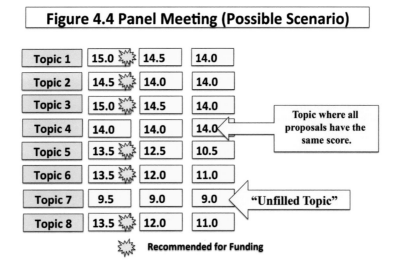

Topic 7 is called an 'Unfilled Topic'. The only proposals received in this topic were below the threshold (10). This is actually an important point. If this Topic appears in future calls it may be less competitive than other topics. In one Health call, a proposal with a score of 11 was funded – obviously it was the highest score in the topic.

The '*' shows the highest scoring proposal per topic. These are the most likely first 6 proposals to be selected. Note that it is possible to have a project with a score of 13.5 funded and a proposal of 14.5 not recommended for funding at this stage.

"(i) Proposals that address topics not otherwise covered by more highly-ranked proposals, will be considered to have the highest priority."

Topic 4 has three proposals – all with the same score.

When a topic has many proposals with the same score other criteria are needed to select the proposals. A possible scenario is presented in Figure 4.5

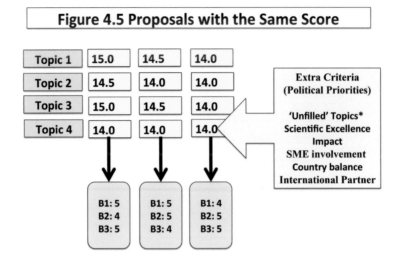

The scientific judgement of the experts is not to be questioned.

"(ii) These proposals will themselves be prioritised according to the scores they have been awarded for the criterion excellence."
At this point, proposals with the highest score in B1 (excellence) are selected. The competition is now between the first two proposals in topic 4. This is an important point. It reinforces the importance of gaining a high score in B1.

"When these scores are equal, priority will be based on scores for the criterion impact."
At this stage, proposal number 2 wins. (B1 = 5 B2 = 5 B3 = 4)
This is a critical point. As most researchers can gain a high score in B1 (Excellence), the next most important criteria is Impact (B2).

"In the case of Innovation actions, and the SME instrument (phases 1 and 2), this prioritisation will be done first on the basis of the score for impact, and then on that for excellence."

At this point in the selection there are several proposals with scores of 14.5 and 14.0. The guideline states:

"If necessary, any further prioritisation will be based on the following factors, in order:"

"size of budget allocated to SMEs" – at this point proposals with a number of relevant SMEs would be selected. The Commission has a target for SME participation and this is reported after each evaluation.

"gender balance among the personnel named in the proposal who will be primarily responsible for carrying out the research and/or innovation activities."
This stresses the importance of having a gender balance in the consortium.

"If a distinction still cannot be made, the panel may decide to further prioritise by considering how to enhance the quality of the project portfolio through synergies between projects, or other factors related to the objectives of the call or to Horizon 2020 in general. These factors will be documented in the report of the Panel."

Other issues that could be considered at this point include:

'strategic importance': this means proposals that are addressing important issues at political level. Many projects were funded on 'preventing future financial crises' after the financial crisis of 2008.

'industrial relevance': projects that address important industrial challenges (for example following the horse meat crisis, any proposal dealing with methodologies to improve the traceability on the food chain would have high priority).

'Third Country participation': the involvement of USA, China, Russia etc. could be a deciding point at this stage.

Some proposal writers think that selecting SMEs, partners from Eastern Europe and ensuring there is a gender balance are the most important part of a proposal. This is not true. These criteria are only important when the score is 14.0 and 14.5 i.e. when the science and impact are excellent.

After the panel review, the list of proposals recommended for funding is prepared. An *'Evaluation Summary Report'* is written for each proposal and this is the document that is sent to the Coordinator. All the statistics from the Panel Meeting are stored on the eCorda database. This can be accessed by the National Contact Points for analysis.

The evaluation process for Pilar II and III can be summarised in Figure 4.6

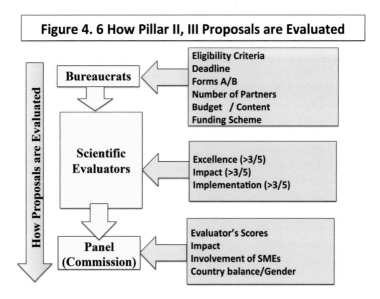

Figure 4. 6 How Pillar II, III Proposals are Evaluated

Evaluation Summary Reports (ESRs)

The following are examples of comments for ESRs.

General Comments

- *Absence of one of the compulsory components*
- *Too much focus on the description of only some components of the project*
- *Scattered sub-projects. Very interesting and innovative sub-projects are proposed – without any apparent coherence, integration or connection to each other*
- *Conditional project parts – where part of the project depends on a future decision or on the uncertain realization of another part of the project*
- *The proposed performance does not exceed that of normal commercial practices*
- *Unclear/ imprecise/ unstructured/ incomplete information*
- *A description which attempts to impress the evaluators – rather than convince them of the merits of the project*
- *Proposal text too long, with a structure that is difficult to read and extract meaningful information.*
- *Feasibility studies (or prior experience/analysis) are not completed or included in the information.*

Comments on Scientific Excellence
- *The S&T approach is not coherent with the identified objectives. The state of the art is not sufficiently described and contribution to advancement of knowledge and of technological progress is not clear.*
- *The methodology is weak and not sufficiently described, while technical limitations and risks have not been properly addressed.*
- *The technical solution...is not convincing.*

Comments on Impact
- *The project's specific contribution at the EU/ International level is weak. The potential impact is not correctly addressed.*
- *Dissemination, exploitation and IP management measures are all considered but should be more specific.*
- *The plans for knowledge and IPR management are confused in the proposal and impossible to evaluate.*

Comments on Implementation
- *The work plan is too general. Work packages, tasks, milestones, list of deliverables and time schedules are insufficiently described and documented*
- *The overall project management is inadequate and no management work package is planned in the work plan*
- *The experience in the leadership of European projects of the co-ordinator is not sufficiently presented.*

Comments on the Consortium
- *The individual participant description is very short and some participants are missing*
- *The contribution of the coordinating SME to the leadership of most workpackages and to most key activities may be a risk for the project; this may limit the other partners' involvement in the project. Two partners do not appear in the work plan.*
- *The experience in the leadership of European projects of the co-ordinator is not sufficiently presented.*

How Marie Curie Proposals are Evaluated

"More than 6,200 proposal evaluations were conducted, divided as usual into 25 different panels per call, involving more than 650 panel reviewers and around 1,800 external reviewers."

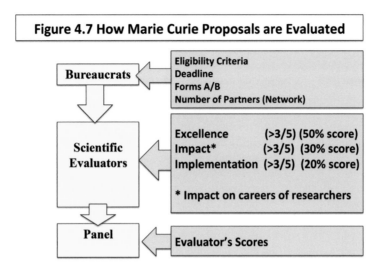

Figure 4.7 How Marie Curie Proposals are Evaluated

The procedures used in evaluating Marie Curie proposals are similar to the procedures described in the previous section. The following are the main differences

The focus of the Marie Curie programme is the development of the **career of the researchers** participating in the projects. This must be the primary aim of the project.

In Marie Skłodowska-Curie ITN, IF and RISE, proposals are allocated to one of the eight main evaluation panels: Chemistry (CHE), Social Sciences and Humanities (SOC), Economic Sciences (ECO), Information Science and Engineering (ENG), Environment and Geosciences (ENV), Life Sciences (LIF), Mathematics (MAT), Physics (PHY).

In ITN, separate multidisciplinary panels will be created for the European Industrial Doctorates (EID) and the European Joint Doctorates (EJD). In IF, separate multidisciplinary panels will be created for the Career Restart Panel (CAR) and the Reintegration Panel. COFUND evaluation will be organised in two different panels: Doctoral programmes and Fellowship programmes.

The 'impact' will be judged by considering the impact on the career of the Fellows.

The 'training plan' will be judged on its relevance to the training needs of the fellows. Guidelines on the contents of these training plans are included on the Marie Curie website.

"Training should aim at making them more independent and providing them with the skills to become team leaders in the near future." Source: Marie Curie Guide for Applicants

In the Marie Curie evaluations, the evaluators are not limited to scores of 5, 4.5, 4.0 etc. They can have scores of 4.1, 4.2 etc. The final score is converted in a % score.

During the panel meeting, the sorting of the proposals is done based on the evaluators scores.

Table 4.7 Evaluation Criteria: Marie Skłodowska-Curie Actions

ITN - Marie Skłodowska-Curie Innovative Training Networks		
Excellence	**Impact**	**Implementation**
Quality, innovative aspects and credibility of the research programme (including inter/multidisciplinary and intersectoral aspects)	Enhancing research- and innovation-related human resources, skills, and working conditions to realise the potential of individuals and to provide new career perspectives	Overall coherence and effectiveness of the work plan, including appropriateness of the allocation of tasks and resources (including awarding of the doctoral degrees for *EID* and *EJD* projects)
Quality and innovative aspects of the training programme (including transferable skills, inter/multidisciplinary and intersectoral aspects)	Contribution to structuring doctoral / early-stage research training at the European level and to strengthening European innovation capacity, including the potential for: a) meaningful contribution of the non-academic sector to the doctoral/research training, as appropriate to the implementation mode and research field b) developing sustainable joint doctoral degree structures (for *EJD* projects only)	Appropriateness of the management structures and procedures, including quality management and risk management (with a mandatory joint governing structure for *EID* and *EJD* projects*)*
Quality of the supervision (including mandatory joint supervision for *EID* and *EJD* projects)	Effectiveness of the proposed measures for communication and dissemination of results	Appropriateness of the infrastructure of the participating organisations
Quality of the proposed interaction between the participating organisations		Competences, experience and complementarity of the participating organisations and their commitment to the programme
50%	**30%**	**20%**
Weighting		
1	**2**	**3**

NOTE: These criteria are subject to change during Horizon 2020.

Table 4.8 Evaluation Criteria of Marie Curie Individual Fellowships

IF - Marie Skłodowska-Curie Action: Individual Fellowships		
Excellence	**Impact**	**Implementation**
Quality, innovative aspects and credibility of the research programme (including inter/multidisciplinary and intersectoral aspects)	Enhancing research- and innovation-related human resources, skills and working conditions to realise the potential of individuals and to provide new career perspectives	Overall coherence and effectiveness of the work plan, including appropriateness of the allocation of tasks and resources
Clarity and quality of transfer of knowledge / training for the development of researcher in light of the research objectives	Effectiveness of the proposed measures for communication and results dissemination	Appropriateness of the management structures and procedures, including quality management and risk management
Quality of the supervision and the hosting arrangements		Appropriateness of the institutional environment (infrastructure)
Capacity of the researcher to reach or re-enforce a position of professional maturity in research		Competences, experience and complementarity of the participating organisations and institutional commitment
50%	**30%**	**20%**
Weighting		
1	**2**	**3**

Table 4.9 Evaluation Criteria of Marie Curie RISE proposals

RISE - Marie Skłodowska-Curie Action: Research and Innovation Staff Exchange		
Excellence	**Impact**	**Implementation**
Quality, innovative aspects and credibility of the research (including inter/multidisciplinary aspects)	Enhancing research- and innovation-related human resources, skills and working conditions to realise the potential of individuals and to provide new career perspectives	Overall coherence and effectiveness of the work plan, including appropriateness of the allocation of tasks and resources
Clarity and quality of knowledge sharing among the participants in light of the research and innovation objectives.	To develop new and lasting research collaborations, to achieve transfer of knowledge between research institutions and to improve research and innovation potential at the European and global levels	Appropriateness of the management structures and procedures, including quality management and risk management
Quality of the interaction between the participating organisations	Effectiveness of the proposed measures for communication and results dissemination	Appropriateness of the institutional environment (infrastructure)
Capacity of the researcher to reach or re-enforce a position of professional maturity in research		Competences, experience and complementarity of the participating organisations and institutional commitment
50%	**30%**	**20%**
Weighting		
1	**2**	**3**

NOTE: These criteria are subject to change during Horizon 2020.

How ERC Proposals are Reviewed

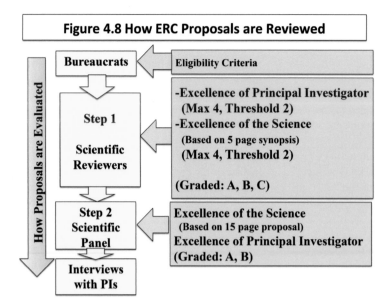

Figure 4.8 How ERC Proposals are Reviewed

The ERC Proposal consists of the following parts: Extended Synopsis (5 pages); Curriculum Vitae (2 pages); Track Record (2 pages); Scientific Proposal (15 pages) ; Host Institution Binding Statement of Support; Ethics Review Table; and PhD record.

The procedure used to review the ERC proposals appears similar to Pillar II and III. In fact, there are some very important differences.

ERC proposals are mainly submitted by individual researchers and the proposed idea is typically in one scientific discipline. The reviewers are selected based on their expertise in that specific field. ERC can attract high calibre reviewers for two reasons – it is an honour to be asked to review ERC proposals and researchers use the reviewing to gain experience on how to submit ERC proposals in the future.

The criteria used to assess the proposals are also different. There are only two criteria:
- Excellence of the principal investigator
- Excellence of the science

Criteria such as impact, partners, gender and country balance do not matter here.

At step 1, the extended synopsis and the Principal Investigator's track record and CV will be assessed (and not the full scientific proposal). At step 2 the complete version of the retained proposals will be assessed (including the full scientific proposal). It is important to stress that the European Commission is not part of the Scientific Panel.

At the end of step 1 of the evaluation, applicants will be informed that their proposal:
   A. is of sufficient quality to pass to step 2 of the evaluation;
   B. is of high quality but not sufficient to pass to step 2 of the evaluation;
   C. is not of sufficient quality to pass to step 2 of the evaluation.

At the end of step 2 of the evaluation, applicants will be informed that their proposal:
   A. fully meets the ERC's excellence criterion and is recommended for funding if sufficient funds are available;
   B. meets some but not all elements of the ERC's excellence criterion and will not be funded.

Principal Investigators, whose proposals are retained for step 2 of the evaluation for the Starting and Consolidator Grants, may be invited for an interview to present their project to the evaluation panel meeting in Brussels. This is a very serious interview. Professional training is required for this interview.

Table 4.10 ERC Evaluation Criteria (Starting and Consolidator Grants)

1. Research Project
Ground-breaking nature, ambition and feasibility

Starting, Consolidator and Advanced

Ground-breaking nature and potential impact of the research project
To what extent does the proposed research address important challenges?
To what extent are the objectives ambitious and beyond the state of the art (e.g. novel concepts and approaches or development across disciplines)?
How much is the proposed research high risk/high gain?

Scientific Approach
To what extent is the outlined scientific approach feasible (based on Extended Synopsis)?
To what extent is the proposed research methodology appropriate to achieve the goals of the project (based on full Scientific Proposal)?
To what extent does the proposal involve the development of novel methodology (based on full Scientific Proposal)?
To what extent are the proposed timescales and resources necessary and properly justified (based on full Scientific Proposal)?

---

2. Principal Investigator
Intellectual capacity, creativity and commitment

Starting and Consolidator

	Fully agree	Somewhat Agree	Somewhat Disagree	Strongly disagree
The PI has demonstrated the ability to propose and conduct ground-breaking research and his/her achievements have typically gone beyond the state-of-the-art.				
The PI provides abundant evidence of creative independent thinking				
The ERC Grant would contribute significantly to the establishment or where necessary, the further consolidation of the PI's independence and career.				
The PI is strongly committed to the project and demonstrates the willingness to devote a significant amount of time to the project (min 50% of the total working time on it and min 50% in an EU Member State or Associated Country) (based on full Scientific Proposal).				

NOTE: These criteria are subject to change during Horizon 2020.

Table 4.11 ERC Evaluation Criteria (Advanced Grant)

---

1. Research Project
Ground-breaking nature, ambition and feasibility

Advanced

Ground-breaking nature and potential impact of the research project
To what extent does the proposed research address important challenges?
To what extent are the objectives ambitious and beyond the state of the art (e.g. novel concepts and approaches or development across disciplines)?
How much is the proposed research high risk/high gain?

Scientific Approach
To what extent is the outlined scientific approach feasible (based on Extended Synopsis)?
To what extent is the proposed research methodology appropriate to achieve the goals of the project (based on full Scientific Proposal)?
To what extent does the proposal involve the development of novel methodology (based on full Scientific Proposal)?
To what extent are the proposed timescales and resources necessary and properly justified (based on full Scientific Proposal)?

---

2. Principal Investigator
Intellectual capacity, creativity and commitment

Starting and Consolidator

	Fully agree	Somewhat Agree	Somewhat Disagree	Strongly disagree
The track record of the PI is characterized by ground- breaking research and his/her achievements have typically gone beyond the state-of-the-art.				
The track record of the PI contains abundant evidence of creative independent thinking				
The PI has demonstrated sound leadership in the training and advancement of young scientists.				
The PI demonstrates the level of commitment to the project necessary for its execution and demonstrates the willingness to devote a significant amount of time to the project (min 30% of the total working time on it and min 50% in an EU Member State or Associated Country) (based on full Scientific Proposal).				

NOTE: These criteria are subject to change during Horizon 2020.

Table 4.12 Evaluation Criteria for FET Open and FET Proactive

FET Open and FET Proactive Evaluation Criteria		
Excellence	**Impact**	**Implementation**
Clarity of targeted breakthrough and its specific science and technology contribution towards a long-term vision.	Importance of the new technological outcome with regards to its transformational impact on technology and/or society.	Quality of the work plan and clarity of intermediate targets. Relevant expertise in the consortium.
Novelty, level of ambition and foundational character. Range and added value from interdisciplinarity. Appropriateness of the research methods.	Quality of measures for achieving impact on science, technology and/or society. Impact from empowerment of new and high potential actors towards future technological leadership.	Appropriate allocation and justification of resources (person-months, equipment, budget).
Threshold 4/5	**Threshold 3.5/5**	**Threshold 3/5**
Weight 60%	**Weight 20%**	**Weight 20%**

Table 4.13 Evaluation Criteria for FET Flagships

FET Flagships		
Excellence	**Impact**	**Implementation**
Degree of adherence to the programme of activities as envisioned in the framework partnership agreement Soundness of scientific concept, quality of objectives and progress beyond the state-of-the-art Quality and effectiveness of the work plan (including milestones, flexibility and metrics to monitor progress) Quality of measures for the coordination of activities across the Flagship Initiative, in particular to ensure overall continuity and coherence of the initiative.	Contribution to the expected impacts listed in the work programme Extent to which the proposal makes use of complementarities, exploits synergies, and enhances the overall outcome of related regional, national, European and international research programmes Effectiveness of measures for use of results, management of intellectual property and dissemination of knowledge Effectiveness of measures relating to human capital, education and training at European level Approach to address societal benefit and potential ethical and legal implications, including engagement with authorities and end-users	Quality of the governance, including management procedures and risk management Quality and relevant experience of the individual participants, and their contribution to the common goal Quality of the consortium as a whole (including complementarity, balance, involvement of key actors) Openness and flexibility of the consortium Appropriateness of the allocation and justification of the resources to be committed (e.g. in-kind

Facts and Figures about the Evaluation Process

Number of Pages
The Commission lists the maximum number of pages for each section of the proposal. Commission stresses (in bold) in the guidelines that: *"Expert evaluators will be instructed to disregard any excess pages."*

International evaluators
Due to the increased specialisation of the proposals, the Commission also selects international experts as evaluators. These people do not necessarily have to be names from the expert database.

Confidentiality
It is possible to submit proposals and to be an expert evaluator. The evaluators sign confidentiality agreements and list the proposals in which they are involved. Of course, the Commission prefers to select researchers who are not involved in proposals.

Payment to evaluators
Evaluators are paid a fixed fee for the evaluations. They are also paid travel expenses and per diem (daily rate) for meetings held in Brussels or Luxembourg. If an invoice is not sent within 45 days of the evaluation, the evaluator will not be paid. (Many evaluators do not send their invoices!). So why would people evaluate proposals and not invoice? Researchers do it for the expertise!

Evaluator's names will be published
The names of the evaluators are published. The names of the evaluators who evaluated individual proposals are NOT published.

Re-submission of Proposals
Proposals can be re-submitted. There is a question in Form A which asks whether the proposal has been submitted previously. If a proposal is rejected because of poor science then the researchers should not consider re-submitting the proposal. If the proposal is rejected because of weak management or unclear work plan then the researchers should consider re-submitting.

In 'Bottom Up' programmes (ERC, Marie Curie, FET), researchers are free to submit any type of proposal – rejected proposals can be resubmitted any time. In the 'Top Down' programmes (Pillar II and III) the topics change between calls and a resubmission is only possible when the topic appears in a future call.

"We give comments on the ESRs, not just scores, so that the consortia can take these comments into account and improve their proposals for a later call."
"ICT Call 3 involved three objectives 2.2, 4.3 and 4.4 which were defined exactly as in Call 1, consequently they were subject to substantial re-submission of unsuccessful proposals from the earlier call." Source: NCP Newsletter (ICT Programme)

When a proposal is resubmitted, it will be given to three new evaluators for evaluation. During the remote evaluation, these evaluators will not be given the results of the previous evaluation. At the consensus meeting, the results of the previous evaluation may be introduced.

In the case of one Irish research group they received a score of 10.5 on their first submission. They resubmitted and received a score of 12.5 – but were unsuccessful. On their third attempt the received a score of 14.5 and were funded.

How to become an Expert Evaluator

The Expert Database (Essential starting point)
The first step is to input details into the evaluator database. This can be found on the Participant Portal. Various reports claim that there are over 100,000 names in the expert database. This is only a starting point. The project officers in the Commission are constantly trying to select high quality experts.

Become the best (known) scientist in the field.
In other words, being a brilliant scientist is not enough! It is equally important to publish research work in magazines and journals that will be read by other European scientists and more importantly by the European Commission.

Speak at Conferences and Workshops
Participating in conferences as a speaker, chairperson or as an exhibitor is an essential way of demonstrating scientific expertise at a European level. A complete list of the conferences/workshops that have been funded by the European Commission can be found on http://ec.europa.eu/research/conferences/index_en.cfm

Become a Coordinator of a Framework project
The scientific officers in the European Commission know the project coordinators personally and are aware of their scientific expertise.

Obtain Recommendations from National Contact Points
The National Contact Points have direct contact with the scientific officers in the European Commission. A recommendation from a National Contact Point is one of the surest ways of becoming an evaluator.

Scarcity in some Categories of Evaluators
There is a shortage of evaluators in the following categories:

- **Female evaluators:** The evaluation panels must be balanced with regard to gender. The European Commission is under pressure to ensure that the gender balance exists. The following quotation comes from the Annual Monitoring report that the Commission sends to the European Parliament: *"Women accounted for 30% of the members of the monitoring panels for programmes, 28% of the members of external advisory groups, 22% of the members of programme committees and 27% of the evaluators for projects in the specific programmes."*

- **Industrial evaluators:** There is a shortage of evaluators from industry. Enterprises need to be aware of the advantages of being an evaluator.

Why bother being an expert evaluator?

Evaluating proposals is the best training course a researcher will ever receive on writing successful proposals. This involves approximately one week's work (some in the office and a consensus meeting in Brussels).

How Proposals should be Prepared

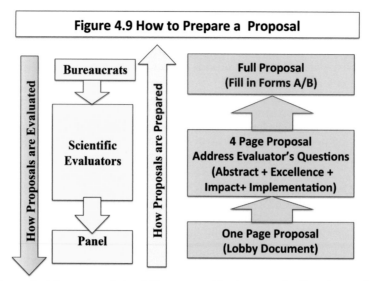

Figure 4.9 How to Prepare a Proposal

Figure 4.9 shows that the proposal should be prepared in the opposite direction to the evaluation process.

A one page proposal should first be prepared to assess whether or not the proposal would be accepted in the panel meeting.

If the feedback is positive, the consortium can then prepare a 'four page proposal'. This should have one page for:
- Abstract (one page)
- B1 Excellence Evaluator Question (one page)
- B2 Impact Evaluator Question (one page)
- B3 Implementation Evaluator Question (one page)

This should be checked with research support staff, experienced evaluators and National Contact Points. If the feedback is positive, the consortium should then proceed to prepare the full proposal.

The following Chapter will describe each of these steps.

Chapter 5: How to Write the 'Excellence' and 'Impact'

CONTENTS

'Excellence' in Horizon 2020
Concept and Approach
Ambition

'Impact' in Horizon 2020
History of 'Impact' in the Framework Programmes
Template for Writing 'Impact'
Examples of 'Impact' of Projects
Financial Plan for the Exploitation of Results

Chapter Webpage: www.hyperion.ie/impact.htm

B1 Excellence

1. Excellence
Your proposal must address a work programme topic for this call for proposals.
This section of your proposal will be assessed only to the extent that it is relevant to that topic.
1.1 Objectives
- *Describe the specific objectives for the project, which should be clear, measurable, realistic and achievable within the duration of the project. Objectives should be consistent with the expected exploitation and impact of the project (see section 2).*

1.2 Relation to the work programme
- *Indicate the work programme topic to which your proposal relates, and explain how your proposal addresses the specific challenge and scope of that topic, as set out in the work programme.*

1.3 Concept and approach
- *Describe and explain the overall concept underpinning the project. Describe the main ideas, models or assumptions involved. Identify any trans-disciplinary considerations;*
- *Describe the positioning of the project e.g. where it is situated in the spectrum from idea to application', or from 'lab to market'. Refer to Technology Readiness Levels where relevant. (See General Annex G of the work programme);*
- *Describe any national or international research and innovation activities which will be linked with the project, especially where the outputs from these will feed into the project;*
- *Describe and explain the overall approach and methodology, distinguishing, as appropriate, activities indicated in the relevant section of the work programme, e.g. for research, demonstration, piloting, first market replication, etc;*
- *Where relevant, describe how sex and/or gender analysis is taken into account in the project's content.*
  Sex and gender refer to biological characteristics and social/cultural factors respectively. For guidance on methods of sex / gender analysis and the issues to be taken into account, please refer to http://ec.europa.eu/research/science-society/gendered-innovations/index_en.cfm

1.4 Ambition
- *Describe the advance your proposal would provide beyond the state-of-the-art, and the extent the proposed work is ambitious. Your answer could refer to the ground-breaking nature of the objectives, concepts involved, issues and problems to be addressed, and approaches and methods to be used.*
- *Describe the innovation potential which the proposal represents. Where relevant, refer to products and services already available on the market. Please refer to the results of any patent search carried out.*

Evaluation Criteria (Research and Innovation Actions)
The following aspects will be taken into account, to the extent that the proposed work corresponds to the topic description in the work programme:
- *Clarity and pertinence of the objectives;*
- *Credibility of the proposed approach;*
- *Soundness of the concept, including trans-disciplinary considerations, where relevant;*
- *Extent that the proposed work is ambitious, has innovation potential, and is beyond the state of the art (e.g. ground-breaking objectives, novel concepts and approaches).*

NOTE: These questions will vary between actions and calls.

B 1.3 Concept and Approach

- *Describe and explain the overall concept underpinning the project. Describe the main ideas, models or assumptions involved. Identify any trans-disciplinary considerations;*
- *Describe and explain the overall approach and methodology, distinguishing, as appropriate, activities indicated in the relevant section of the work programme, e.g. for research, demonstration, piloting, first market replication, etc;*

Evaluator's Comments

The best way to explain how this section should be written is to list comments from Evaluation Summary Reports.

"The proposed developed methodology and work plan are insufficiently described."

"The S&T approach is not coherent with the identified objectives. The state of the art is not sufficiently described and contribution to advancement of knowledge and of technological progress is not clear."

"The methodology is weak and not sufficiently described, while technical limitations and risks have not been properly addressed."

"..the rationale presented does not cover all the scientific models that could influence this effect and therefore the ability for the proposed work to generate performance improvements of the targeted 30-50% is compromised."

"The technical solution...is not convincing."

"The proposal is also weak in describing a convincing methodology and work plan for research."

"..the detailed presentation does not convince how the objectives will be met and how the SMEs will achieve benefit in a realistic manner."

"The innovative character of this proposal is not clear as there are a large number of RTDs already working in this area."

"The proposal does not provide a full competitive analysis demonstrating the proposed level of innovation in relation to existing state-of-the art solutions."

"...quite a few framework programme projects, targeting the media and content domain, have proposed platforms and solutions addressing similar RTD issues,"

"One of the recognised problems is that the proposal is out of scope of the call,"

Source: Analysis Report on Framework 7 Evaluation

Gender Issues

Part B 1 (Excellence), Section 1.3 (Concept and approach) requests:

"Where relevant, describe how sex and/or gender analysis is taken into account in the project's content."
"Sex and gender refer to biological characteristics and social/cultural factors respectively. For guidance on methods of sex/gender analysis and the issues to be taken into account, please refer to http://ec.europa.eu/research/science-society/gendered-innovations/index_en.cfm ."

To understand this section of the proposal, it is necessary to understand the background to gender issues in Horizon 2020. Gender issues are an important part of the European Union Treaties, Policies, Actions and Research. The following is a summary of the background documents to the Gender question in Horizon 2020.

Articles of the Treaty:
- (Equality)
- (Discrimination)
- (Equity men/women)

European Union Policies:
- Com (96) 67 Mainstreaming of equality
- Com (97) 497 Gender issues in employment strategies
- Com (98) 131 Promotion of equality in the structural funds
- Com (98) 112 Promoting participation of women in EU R&D

Gender Activities in the Framework Programmes
- The Helsinki Group (civil servants from 29 countries)

Gender Issues in Horizon 2020:

Gender issues can be summarised as follows: Research FOR/BY/ABOUT Women in Science.

Research FOR Women: This is research that is specific to women e.g. cervical cancer.

Research BY Women: This relates to the number of women involved in the proposed work.

Research ABOUT Women: In a project, it may be possible to introduce a specific gender dimension to the project. For example, if the project focuses on diabetes, the gender aspect may be to investigate diabetes in men and diabetes in women. Similarly, a project on entrepreneurship may investigate entrepreneurship by men and entrepreneurship by women.

If there is NO gender aspect to the project state clearly that the issue was considered and that no gender aspect could be introduced to the project. Do not neglect to address the section on gender in the proposal.

The Big Picture

1.3 Concept and approach
- *Describe the positioning of the project e.g. where it is situated in the spectrum from idea to application', or from 'lab to market'. Refer to Technology Readiness Levels where relevant. (See General Annex G of the work programme).*

This question could be rephrased as: *'Describe the 'big picture' and indicate where the project is positioned'*. The 'big picture' is a very important part of the proposal as it helps the evaluator understand exactly the focus of the proposal. The 'big picture' will be used in Section B2 (Impact) to describe the potential impact of the proposal.

The 'idea to lab' or 'lab to market' can be described using Value Chains or Stakeholder Diagrams.

Value Chains

The terminology 'Value Chain' was mentioned by Michael Porter in his book *"Competitive Advantage: Creating and Sustaining superior Performance"* (1985). A Value Chain describes every step a business goes through - from raw materials to the eventual end-user. Examples of Value Chains will be shown in the following section. A Google search of 'Forestry Value Chain' or 'Photonics Value Chain' will present sample diagrams.

Figure 5.1 shows a Value Chain for the Photonics industry. It identifies the different business areas that are linked together.

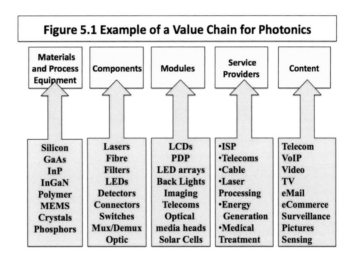

In 2009, the European Commission established a High Level Expert Group on Key Enabling Technologies (KETs). A Final Report was published in June 2011. In this 60 page document, the term 'Value Chain' can be found 38 times. The KET Report can be found on:
http://ec.europa.eu/enterprise/sectors/ict/files/kets/hlg_report_final_en.pdf

*"Asia is moving up traditionally European **value chains**. Huawei was founded in 1988 as a distributor of imported telecommunications switches. It is now n°2 worldwide in global mobile infrastructure equipment markets. In less than 20 years, Huawei has moved up the global telecommunications **value chain**, previously dominated by European global players such as Ericsson, Alcatel, Nokia and Siemens."*

*"In particular KETs have two specific characteristics that separate them from other "enabling technologies": they are embedded at the core of innovative products and they underpin strategic European **value chains**."*

*"KETs are of systemic relevance and feed many different **value chains**."*
*"It is observed that a combination of KETs is necessary at all levels of the **value chain** to the development and manufacturing of advanced innovative products."*

European Technology Platforms
http://cordis.europa.eu/technology-platforms/home_en.html

*"European Technology Platforms are an important weapon in the Commission's competitiveness arsenal and were set up to chart the strategic R&D path ahead for key European industries. ETPs cover the whole economic **value chain**, ensuring that knowledge generated through research is transformed into technologies and processes, and ultimately into marketable products and services."*

Stakeholder Diagrams

Stakeholder Diagram (or Stakeholder Analysis)
This is a diagram describing all the different actors (stakeholders) in a social, economic or political system. The diagram shows the relationship between the stakeholders and the objects (information, money, documents..) that flow between the them. Examples will be shown in the following sections. Other terms used are 'Stakeholder Analysis' and 'Stakeholder Mapping'.

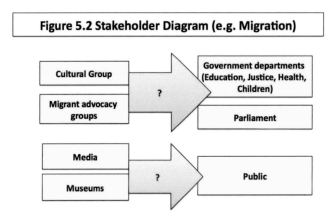

Figure 5.2 Stakeholder Diagram (e.g. Migration)

Active and Healthy Ageing
"The following stakeholders are represented:
– industry (medical devices, telecom, e-health, pharmaceuticals, nutrition);
– health and care providers (national and regional, local authorities, health care professionals);
– carers - formal and informal;
– users (including patients and older citizens);
– planners, implementers of health projects, regional authorities, academia, research, insurers and venture capital.

Source: The Pilot European Innovation Partnership on Active and Healthy Ageing (AHA)
http://ec.europa.eu/research/innovation-union/pdf/eip_staff_paper.pdf

"The multi-actor approach aims at more demand-driven innovation through the genuine and sufficient involvement of various actors all along the project: from the participation in the

planning of work and experiments, their execution up until the dissemination of results and the possible demonstration phase. The adequate choice of key actors with complementary types of knowledge (scientific and practical) should be reflected in the description of the project proposals and result in a broad implementation of project results. The multi-actor approach is more than a strong dissemination requirement or what a broad stakeholders' board can deliver: it should be illustrated with sufficient quantity and quality of knowledge exchange activities and a clear role for the different actors in the work. This should generate innovative solutions that are more likely to be applied thanks to the cross-fertilisation of ideas between actors, the co-creation and the generation of co-ownership for eventual results. A multi-actor project needs to take into account how the project proposal's objectives and planning are targeted to needs / problems and opportunities of end-users, and the complementarity with existing research. " (H2020 Work programmes)

When writing a proposal, it is important to begin by explaining the Value Chain (technology) or the Stakeholder Diagram (social sciences) to the evaluator. The next step is to identify exactly where the project will focus.

The Innovation Chain and the Value Chain

Figure 5.3 shows the relationship between the Value Chain and the Innovation Chain. These are two distinct activities. The Value Chain exists and is a business process. The aim of the Innovation Chain is to improve some aspect of the Value Chain.

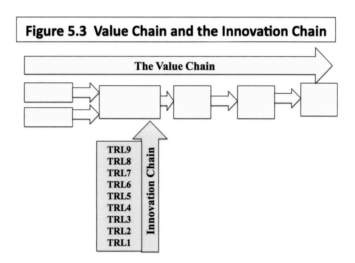

Figure 5.3 Value Chain and the Innovation Chain

TRL 9: Actual system proven in an operational environment
TRL 8: System completed and qualified
TRL 7: System prototype demonstrated in an operational environment
TRL 6: Technology demonstrated in a relevant environment
TRL 5: Technology validated in a relevant environment
TRL 4: Technology validated in the laboratory
TRL 3: Experimental Proof of Concept
TRL 2: Technology concept formulated
TRL 1: Basic Principles Observed
Source: Annex G (TRL) of the General Annexes of Horizon 2020

"Innovation enables European industries to position themselves at the upper end of the global value chain."
Source: Reviewing Community innovation policy in a changing world. Sept 2009

"Whilst European R&D is generally strong in new Key Enabling Technologies (KET), the High Level Group has observed that the transition from ideas arising from basic research to competitive KETs production is the weakest link in European KET enabled value chains."

"A new political approach and governance, that simultaneously incentivises innovation and cooperation, both through frameworks policies and funding, at crucial stages of European value chains."

Source: High Level Expert Group on Key Enabling Technologies Final Report June 2011
http://ec.europa.eu/enterprise/sectors/ict/files/kets/hlg_report_final_en.pdf

Figure 5.4 shows the position of the project in the Innovation Chain. It is clear from this diagram that the output of the project will be relevant to an organisation (or individual) working at TRL 4. This is an example of a 'Lead User'. The 'End User' is at the end of the Value Chain and may not benefit from the project for five to ten years.

When writing the proposal, it is important to explain these processes and people to the evaluators. Many evaluators are not familiar with the concepts of value chains, innovation chain, TRL, Lead User and End User.

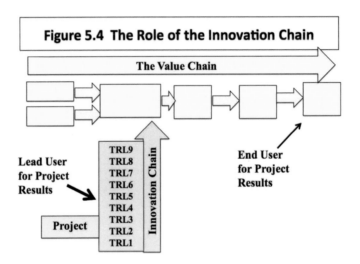

Lead User and End User
The 'Lead User' is the first user of the results from the project. The 'End User' is the long term user that will benefit from the development. Examples of these will be presented in the following sections. The concept of the 'Lead User' comes from a book by Eric von Hipple. Examples of this can be seen on www.leaduser.com. Lead Users are individuals who will be excited when the results are available. (If no individual is excited about the results then obviously the project is of no relevance).One way of finding these 'Lead Users' is to ask the researcher: ***Who is waiting urgently for these results?***

B 2 Impact

The title of this chapter is 'Writing Impact'. It would be better to describe it as 'How to Make an Impact'. The two key messages from this chapter are: (1) begin the proposal by writing the impact; (2) the researcher should not write the impact part of the proposal. The partner who will use the results from the project should write the impact part of the proposal. This chapter will also describe how a consortium can be structured around the concept of impact.

Background to 'Impact'

Impact is a political word. Some years ago Irish scientists were trying to convince the Minister of Science to spend one billion euro on research. At one meeting the Minister stated: *"With one billion euro, I can build 5000 houses for poor families. In four years, I will be able to see 5000 houses and 20,000 happy people with new homes. If I give you (scientists) one billion euro what will I see in four years?"* This is how many politicians think: We put money into something (research) and we expect results (impact).

On 30th November 2011, the European Commission sent a proposal to the European Parliament and the Council of Ministers requesting over 80 billion euro for Horizon 2020. The politicians asked for an 'Impact Assessment' report to justify why they should spend 80 billion euro on Horizon 2020. In this 52 page report (+ 112 pages of annexes), the Commission justified the potential impact of the investment in Horizon 2020.

The 'Impact Assessment' report can be found on
http://ec.europa.eu/research/horizon2020/pdf/proposals/horizon_2020_impact_assessment_report.pdf#view=fit&pagemode=none

The following is an example of a table from the Impact Assessment Report

"The overall results from the analysis of 726 projects under Evimp-2, representing €992 million of EU-funding, reveal the following: The projects have generated or are expected to generate the following results in the short term:
> ∞ *3 724 prototypes/demonstrators/pilots,*
> ∞ *747 new software tools,*
> ∞ *18 974 publications,*
> ∞ *2 152 doctorates,*
> ∞ *310 inputs into technical standards,*
> ∞ *423 inputs into EU legislation texts,*
> ∞ *1 077 patent applications,*
> ∞ *204 registered designs and other forms (IPR)*
> ∞ *the creation of 248 spin-off companies".*

Source: Impact Assessment Report for Horizon 2020 (30th November 2011)

"We have a lot of information about input data, but it is far more difficult to get reliable information on the output, in terms of what have been the scientific results of research, or its impact in terms of new jobs or competitiveness, or on increasing the wellbeing of European citizens - this is very, very difficult to assess."
Source: Court of Auditor's Special Report No 9/2007 on 'Evaluating the EU Research and Technological Development framework programmes. (30.1.2008)

"Experts in the field of impact assessment argue that the expected impacts of research are highly uncertain, often intangible, extremely variable in terms of scope, scale and timing and hence exceedingly difficult to quantify."
Source: ERIAB Report on Impact Assessment

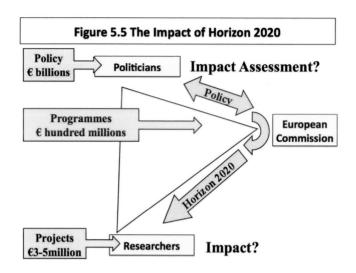

Figure 5.5 shows how the different players view impact. Politicians think in billions of euros. The European Commission programme planner think in hundreds of millions of euros and the researchers think in millions of euros. In fact, individual partners in projects think about their share of projects – which is normally in the range €300,000 to €500,000. These different concepts of impact can be seen in Figure 5.6.

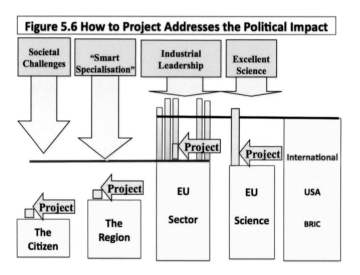

Societal Challenge Impact: the challenges in this project are long term (e.g. cancer, diabetes etc.) and the research project is one step in addressing the challenge.

Industrial Leadership Impact: the challenge is to establish Europe as the leader in different sectors or different technologies. The project focusses on increasing the technology readiness level by one or two steps.

Excellent Science Impact: the expected impact is that the projects will have 'scientific impact'. In particular, ERC projects should establish Europe as the scientific leader in the area of the project.

In Annex II of the Proposal for Horizon 2020 (30th November 2011) the following tables were included:

Table 5.1 Expected Impact of Excellent Science Programme

Specific Programme	Programme	Expected Impact
Pillar I **Excellent Science**	ERC	Share of publications from ERC funded projects which are among the top 1 % highly cited Number of institutional policy and national/regional policy measures inspired by ERC funding
	FET	Publications in peer-reviewed high impact journals Patent applications in Future and Emerging Technologies
	Marie Curie	Cross-sector and cross-country circulation of researchers, including PhD candidates
	Research Infrastructures	Research infrastructures which are made accessible to all researchers in Europe and beyond through Union support

Table 5.2 Expected Impact of Pillar II (Industrial Leadership)

Specific Programme	Programme	Expected Impact
Pillar II **Industrial Leadership**	Leadership in Enabling Industrial Technologies	Patent applications obtained in the different enabling and industrial technologies
	Access to Risk Finance	Total investments mobilised via debt financing and Venture Capital investments
	Innovation in SMEs	Share of participating SMEs introducing innovations new to the company or the market (covering the period of the project plus three years)

Table 5.3 Expected Impact of Pillar III (Societal Challenges)

Specific Programme	Programme	Expected Impact
Pillar III **Societal Challenges**	All Programmes	Publications in peer-reviewed high impact journals Patent applications Number of Union pieces of legislation referring to activities supported in the area of the different Societal Challenges

Impact in the Calls for Proposals

Each work programme in Pillar II and Pillar III (Top Down Programmes) is divided into areas and topics. Each topic is described in terms of 'specific challenge', 'scope' and 'expected impact'. Below are examples of the 'expected impact' published in a work programme.

Energy Programme

Area A3: Increasing energy performance of existing buildings through process and organisation innovations

Expected impact

Within the duration of the projects, activities should trigger the renovation of existing buildings towards Nearly Zero Energy Buildings, resulting in savings of at least 2.200 toe/year (25 GWh/year) per million EUR of EU support.

Further, activities should support the replication of best practices to raise quality and compliance in the construction, renovation and operation of buildings, resulting in savings of at least 5.000 toe/year (~57 GWh/year) per million EUR of EU support.

Activities should contribute to achieving the level of energy consumption in new buildings of 20-50 kWh/m2/year in 2020

Health Programme

Topic: Improving the control of infectious epidemics and foodborne outbreaks through rapid identification of pathogens

Expected impact

Better containment and mitigation of epidemics by competent authorities on the basis of a shared information system and global standards for rapid pathogen identification.

Consequent improved resource efficiency and reduction of economic impact of outbreaks (related to health care costs, market losses); facilitation of international trade, increasing competitiveness of European food and agricultural sector; reinforcement of food chain sustainability and enhancement of food security.

Contribution to the "Global Research Collaboration for Infectious Disease Preparedness" and its objective to establish a research response within 48 hours of an outbreak.

Inclusive and Innovative Societies

Topic: Early job insecurity and labour market exclusion

Expected impact

Research is expected to explore in a comprehensive way the short- and long-term consequences of job insecurity and unemployment of young people in order to analyse their impact on the economy, society and politics. These activities will contribute to an effective anticipation of the potential challenges facing the EU in the future allowing for an early policy response. Through a better understanding of the mechanisms driving the labour market, this research should lead to a more robust labour market policy in the EU as well as to a better informed economic, social and education policy. Activities under this topic will also shed light on broader societal questions related, for example, to demographic developments, population ageing, health and wellbeing, as well as the potential of economic development in the EU, both from the historical and the forward-looking perspective.

Secure Societies Programme

Topic: The role of new social media networks in national security

Expected impact: *Stakeholders should get a better understanding of the impact of social media for national security purposes. Proposers are encouraged to assess the positive and negative aspects, challenges and opportunities of engaging social media as well as how these tools could be used by national security planners.*

Innovation in SMEs Programme

Cluster animated projects for new industrial value chains
Expected impact:
Strengthen industrial leadership in Europe by reinforcing value chains that integrate innovative solutions in SMEs, along and across existing value chains.
Stimulate the creation of new globally competitive industrial value chains across Europe to accelerate the development of emerging industries in Europe, which will boost industrial competitiveness and underpin future economic growth, jobs, and progress towards a resource-efficient economy.
Further leverage and complement support for innovation in SMEs and other funding, which may be provided by national or regional authorities under the Cohesion funds. Contribute to smart specialisation strategies by capitalising upon concentrated and complementary competences for the development of new industrial value chains and emerging industries.
Provide a clear and measurable contribution to the innovation performance of the supported SMEs in the short-term – as revealed by indicators such as numbers of new or significantly improved products (goods and/or services), processes, new marketing methods, or new organisational methods –, and to its impact on resource efficiency and/or turnover. A wider impact is also expected in the medium-term.

Food Programme

Topic: Towards more resource-efficient food processing methods

Expected impact
The development of innovative and sustainable food processing methods will increase the competitiveness of the European food and drink industry, in particular SMEs, while minimising their ecological footprint. The research leads towards a resource-efficient economy via a notable reduction in water and energy use, less waste and an increased efficiency in the use of raw materials, which contributes to achieving the resource efficiency objectives for 2020 and beyond as planned in the "Roadmap to a resource-efficient Europe".

Transport Programme

Topic: Optimal use of transport data as a basis for smart mobility services

Expected impact
Research will contribute to unlocking the potential of vast amounts of transport data and solving problems related to interoperability, storage, processing and security. The resulting open co-modal, integrated transport information, communication and payment services will help to anticipate transport related problems, predict the amount of traffic, optimize investments and capacity use of the existing networks, develop optimal routes and schedules, alleviate congestion and reduce both emergency-response times and pollution levels.
Integrated ICT based services will offer new environmentally-friendly mobility options for European citizens and improve transport system's accessibility. At the same time, the possibility of remaining connected to the working environment and social networks will decrease the disutility of travel time, providing for additional consumer benefit.

Marie Skłodowska-Curie Actions (Expected Impact)

Marie Skłodowska-Curie Innovative Training Networks (ITN)
Expected impact:
- *ITN will create and contribute to high-quality innovative research and doctoral training, build capacity, and have a structuring effect throughout Europe and beyond.*
- *Through research training provided by the institutions from different countries, sectors and disciplines, this action will trigger cooperation between organisations from the academic and non-academic sectors.*
- *It will enhance skills development and knowledge-sharing, enhancing researchers' employability and providing them with new career perspectives.*
- *ITN will shape future generations of entrepreneurial researchers capable of contributing effectively to the knowledge-based economy and society.*
- *In the long term, it will also raise the attractiveness of research careers and encourage young people to embark on this career path.*

Marie Skłodowska-Curie Individual Fellowships (IF)
Expected impact:
- *Individual Fellowships are expected to add significantly to the development of the best and most promising researchers active in Europe, in order to enhance and maximise their contribution to the knowledge-based economy and society.*
- *The action will also strengthen the contact network of both the researcher and the host organisation.*
- *The fellowship will contribute to realising the full potential of researchers and to catalysing significant development in their careers in both the academic and non-academic sectors.*
- *Some researchers will be resuming a research career in Europe after a break, or reintegrating within Europe after living abroad.*

Marie Skłodowska-Curie Research and Innovation Staff Exchange (RISE)
Expected impact:
- *Research and innovation activities under RISE are expected to build or enhance new and existing networks of international and intersectoral cooperation. They will significantly strengthen the interaction between organisations in the academic and non-academic sectors, and between Europe and third countries.*
- *In terms of knowledge sharing and broad skills development, they will better align different cultures and expectations, with a view to a more effective contribution of research and innovation to Europe's knowledge economy and society.*

Marie Skłodowska-Curie Co-funding of regional, national and international programmes (COFUND)
Expected impact:
The COFUND scheme will on a voluntary basis exploit synergies between European Union actions and those at regional and national level, as well as with other actions at international level. The scheme will have a leverage effect on regional, national or international funding programmes for early-stage researchers and experienced researchers. This impact is expected to extend to:
- *enabling the relevant regional, national and international actors to contribute significantly to the development within their own setting of high quality human resources, by introducing and/or further developing the trans-national dimension of their offers;*
- *increasing the numerical and/or qualitative impact, in terms of supported researchers or working/employment conditions;*
- *combating fragmentation in terms of objectives, evaluation methods and working conditions of regional, national or international offers in this area.*

B 2.1 Expected Impacts

2.1 Expected impacts (Research and Innovation Actions)
Please be specific, and provide only information that applies to the proposal and its objectives.
Wherever possible, use quantified indicators and targets.
- *Describe how your project will contribute to:*
    - *the expected impacts set out in the work programme, under the relevant topic;*
    - *improving innovation capacity and the integration of new knowledge (strengthening the competitiveness and growth of companies by developing innovations meeting the needs of European and global markets; and, where relevant, by delivering such innovations to the markets;*
    - *any other environmental and socially important impacts (if not already covered above).*
    - *Describe any barriers/obstacles, and any framework conditions (such as regulation and standards), that may determine whether and to what extent the expected impacts will be achieved. (This should not include any risk factors concerning implementation, as covered in section 3.2.)*

Evaluation Criteria (Research and Innovation Actions)

The extent to which the outputs of the project should contribute at the European and/or International level to:

- o *The expected impacts listed in the work programme under the relevant topic;*
- o *Enhancing innovation capacity and integration of new knowledge;*
- o *Strengthening the competitiveness and growth of companies by developing innovations meeting the needs of European and global markets; and, where relevant, by delivering such innovations to the markets;*
- o *Any other environmental and socially important impacts (not already covered above);*

Effectiveness of the proposed measures to exploit and disseminate the project results (including management of the IPR), to communicate the project, and to manage research data where relevant.

Evaluation Criteria: Impact (Marie Curie)

Marie Curie Actions use different guidelines. The focus on Marie Curie is on the development of the careers of researchers.

ITN (Innovative Training Networks) –Impact Evaluation Criteria
Enhancing research- and innovation-related human resources, skills, and working conditions to realise the potential of individuals and to provide new career perspectives.
Contribution to structuring doctoral / early-stage research training at the European level and to strengthening European innovation capacity, including the potential for:
- a) *meaningful contribution of the non-academic sector to the doctoral/research training, as appropriate to the implementation mode and research field;*
- b) *developing sustainable joint doctoral degree structures (for EJD projects only).*

Individual Fellowships – Impact Evaluation Criteria
Enhancing research- and innovation-related human resources, skills and working conditions to realise the potential of individuals and to provide new career perspectives.
Effectiveness of the proposed measures for communication and results dissemination.

2.2 Measures to maximise impact

a) Dissemination and exploitation of results

- *Provide a draft 'plan for the dissemination and exploitation of the project's results' (unless the work programme topic explicitly states that such a plan is not required). For innovation actions describe a credible path to deliver the innovations to the market. The plan, which should be proportionate to the scale of the project, should contain measures to be implemented both during and after the project.*
  Dissemination and exploitation measures should address the full range of potential users and uses including research, commercial, investment, social, environmental, policy making, setting standards, skills and educational training. The approach to innovation should be as comprehensive as possible, and must be tailored to the specific technical, market and organisational issues to be addressed.
- *Explain how the proposed measures will help to achieve the expected impact of the project. Include a business plan where relevant.*
- *Where relevant, include information on how the participants will manage the research data generated and/or collected during the project, in particular addressing the following issues:*
  - *What types of data will the project generate/collect?*
  - *What standards will be used?*
  - *How will this data be exploited and/or shared/made accessible for verification and re-use? If data cannot be made available, explain why.*
  - *How will this data be curated and preserved?*
  You will need an appropriate consortium agreement to manage (amongst other things) the ownership and access to key knowledge (IPR, data etc.). Where relevant, these will allow you, collectively and individually, to pursue market opportunities arising from the project's results.
  The appropriate structure of the consortium to support exploitation is addressed in section 3.3.
- *Outline the strategy for knowledge management and protection. Include measures to provide open access (free on-line access, such as the 'green' or 'gold' model) to peer-reviewed scientific publications which might result from the project.*
  Open access publishing (also called 'gold' open access) means that an article is immediately provided in open access mode by the scientific publisher. The associated costs are usually shifted away from readers, and instead (for example) to the university or research institute to which the researcher is affiliated, or to the funding agency supporting the research.
  Self-archiving (also called 'green' open access) means that the published article or the final peer-reviewed manuscript is archived by the researcher - or a representative - in an online repository before, after or alongside its publication. Access to this article is often - but not necessarily - delayed ('embargo period'), as some scientific publishers may wish to recoup their investment by selling subscriptions and charging pay-per-download/view fees during an exclusivity period.

b) Communication activities

- *Describe the proposed communication measures for promoting the project and its findings during the period of the grant. Measures should be proportionate to the scale of the project, with clear objectives. They should be tailored to the needs of various audiences, including groups beyond the project's own community. Where relevant, include measures for public/societal engagement on issues related to the project.*

Evaluation Criteria:
The extent to which the outputs of the project should contribute at the European and/or International level to:
  - o *Effectiveness of the proposed measures to exploit and disseminate the project results (including management of the IPR), to communicate the project, and to manage research data where relevant.*

Terminology used to describe 'Impact'

Deliverables:
Deliverables are contractual outputs used to justify payments in the project. They are usually defined as documents so they can be submitted to the funding agency.

Results
'Results' refers to any tangible or intangible output of the action, such as data, knowledge and information whatever their form or nature, whether or not they can be protected, which are generated in the action as well as any rights attached to them, including intellectual property rights;
Example: Development of the GSM (wireless) draft standard

Outcomes:
Outcomes describe how the 'Lead Users' process the outputs.
Example: Adoption of the GSM Standard

Impact
Impact is the long term socio-economic benefit to a wide community of 'End Users'.
Example: GSM standard leads to new products, new business and increased quality of life of European citizens.

Exploitation and Use:
Exploitation means the utilisation of results in further research activities other than those covered by the action concerned, or in developing, creating and marketing a product or process, or in creating and providing a service, or in standardisation activities. An exploitation and use plan must describe how the results of the project will be promoted to communities of 'Lead Users'. Examples will be provided in the following sections.

Dissemination
Dissemination means the public disclosure of the results by any appropriate means (other than resulting from protecting or exploiting the results), including by scientific publications in any medium. Dissemination is used to promote the project and the expected outcomes to all stakeholders.

The following table can be used as a methodology to define the outcomes and long term impact. **Please note that this is a methodology. It is not a good idea to put a table like this in your proposal.** It is better to write the outcome and impact in text. An example will be presented at the end of this chapter.

Table 5.4 How to Convert Outputs to Outcomes to Impact

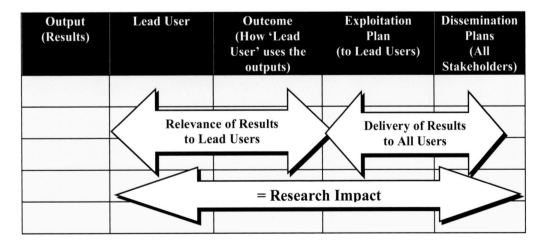

Output (Results)	Lead User	Outcome (How 'Lead User' uses the outputs)	Exploitation Plan (to Lead Users)	Dissemination Plans (All Stakeholders)
	Relevance of Results to Lead Users		Delivery of Results to All Users	
	= Research Impact			

Table 5.5 Example: Exploitation of Software Results

Deliverable	Lead User	Lead User Terminology	Exploitation	Dissemination
Software	Software Developer	Code, modules, Objects..	Internet (Open Source)	App Social Media
Software	Test User	System	Alpha version	Free
Software	Industrial Pilot	IT System	Pilot site (beta)	Magazine article

Table 5.6 Examples: Exploitation of Scientific Data

Deliverable	Lead User	Lead User Terminology	Exploitation	Dissemination
Instrument data	Sensor designer	Calibration curve	Service manual	Magazine Articles
Engine data	Engineer	Performance data	Manual	Portal
Results of tests	Medical researchers	Screening criteria	Training Courses	Online Training
Data	Public official	Indicators or Legislation limits	Conferences	Portal
Scientific data	Standards body	Factual data	Technical committee	Magazine Articles
Database	Researcher	Portal or Search Engine	Internet	Portal

Table 5.7 Examples: Exploitation of Scientific Documents

Deliverable	Lead User	Lead User Terminology	Exploitation	Dissemination
Report	Engineer	Design Specification	Handbook	Commercial Sales
Process improvement	Production Engineer	Handbook or Guideline	Training Course	Commercial Courses
Description of the process	Production Manager	Operation manuals	Publications / Exhibitions	Commercial Sales
Draft standard to diagnose Billharzia	Research Hospitals (Doctors)	Standard Method to Diagnose Schistosomiasis	Handbook / Lectures	University courses

Table 5.8 Examples of Technological Developments

Deliverable	Lead User	Lead User Terminology	Exploitation	Dissemination
Battery Monitor	Solar Installer	Test Kit for Batteries	Spin-off company	Magazine + Online Articles
Membrane	Biomaterials Company	Non-inflammatory mesh	First trial	Magazine + Online Articles
Membrane	Desalination Engineer	Separator to remove pollutants from water	Licence	Exhibitions + Magazine Article
Gassing sensor	Battery Designer	Full charge detector	Pilot site	Exhibitions + Magazine Article

Checklist for Results, Lead Users, Routes for Exploitation and Funding

The following is a checklist of possible options. This is based on over 500 interviews with researchers.

Table 5.9 Checklists for Deliverables, Lead Users and Routes for Exploitation and Funding.

Checklist for Results	Checklist for Lead Users	Checklist Exploitation/ Dissemination	Checklist For Sources of Funding for Exploitation
Technical Development IT System Software New Material	**BUSINESS** Manufacturing Business Service Business	**EXPLOITATION** Further Research	Horizon 2020 SME Instrument Access to Finance
	POLICY MAKERS EU Policy Maker National Policy Maker Regional Policy Maker	Licence	EIB
Animal Model New Strains Molecular Candidates Cell Culture	**PUBLIC SERVICES** Public Services Public Health	Product -Demonstration -Pilot Site -Trials	Eureka
		Service - Consultancy	Structural Funds
Document	**RESEARCH CENTRES** University Research Centre	- Mentoring service - Training Course	National Funding
Demonstration Pilot Site	Research Centres Contract Research Organisation	Education	Regional Funding
		Research Facilities	
Data Database Knowledge Methodology Algorithm Expert System Protocol	**EDUCATION BODY** Universities Technical Colleges Secondary Schools Primary Schools		Business Angel Venture Capital Private
IPR Patent Copyright	**SOCIAL SERVICES** Public Social Services Voluntary Organisations Non-Governmental Organisation Individuals	**DISSEMINATION** Scientific Publications	
		Workshop Conference	
MEDIA Training Material CD ROM Video Website	**STANDARDS BODY** International Standards EU Standards National Standards	Publish Book Website	
	THE CITIZEN	Portal Search Engine	
Workshop Conference		Lectures	
Network			

Methodology to describe 'Impact'

The following is a procedure on how to write impact in Pillar II and Pillar III proposals.

a) Define the 'Big Picture' – what specific part of the 'Challenge' are you addressing
b) Show the Stakeholder Diagram (social sciences) or Value Chain (technology)
c) Identify the 'Lead Users' of the results
d) Define how the 'Lead User' will take the results to the next level
e) Select partners to cover the relevant TRLs
f) Select partners from the relevant part of the Value Chain or Stakeholder Diagram
g) Define the steps needed to bring about the long term Impact.

The above methodology is based on the author's experience in writing the impact part of proposals and also in interviewing researchers during 'proposal clinics'. It is also a good format for researchers to use in presenting (Power Point) their ideas to support staff or colleagues.

The following points must be noted (from experience):

The Big Picture
Researchers are trained to become experts in niches (and sometimes niches within niches). Because of this training, they seldom think about the 'big picture'. Sometimes lengthy discussions with researchers were required to determine what they considered to be the relevance of their research in addressing social or economic challenges.

Stakeholder Diagram or Value Chain
These are often totally new concepts to researchers. It is a good idea for an advisor to ask the researcher to draw the diagram and explain the Value Chain or Stakeholder Diagram. From experience, several attempts are required before the diagram is completed.

Lead User and End User
This can be a difficult concept for some researchers. Researchers normally think about the scientific community as their target audience. Scientists normally judge their performance on the number of publications in scientific journals, presentations at conferences or the number of PhD students trained. The concept of delivering scientific results to individuals outside of the scientific community is often a new experience.

"We are not asking people to predict the outcome of their research, we are asking people to contextualise that research. And the way to contextualise impact is for the researcher to pretend they are justifying to an Irish taxpayer why Irish taxpayer's money should be used to fund this research." Source: Science Foundation Ireland director general Prof Mark Ferguson as they rolled out its new strategy, Agenda 2020.

"Participants that do not have commercial/innovation goals at the start of the project are very unlikely to achieve any commercialisation (even if there are results)."
Source: The impact of publicly funded research on innovation: An analysis of European Framework Programmes for Research and Development

The above guidelines will be demonstrated in the following pages. The following examples will be used:

Technology Example: Photonics project

Social Science Example: Migration project

Writing Impact for a Technology Project

This example will describe how the potential impact of a photonics project should be written. The first step is to present the photonics Value Chain. An example is presented in Figure 5.7. This diagram shows that the project is focussing on developing new LEDs based on Gallium Arsenide (GaAs) for LED arrays.

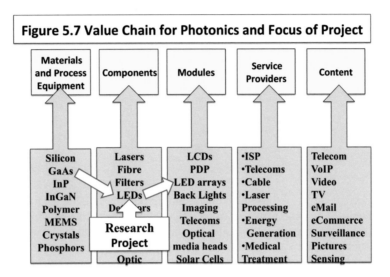

The next step is to draw the Value Chain based on the specific parts – in this example GaAs, LED and LED arrays.

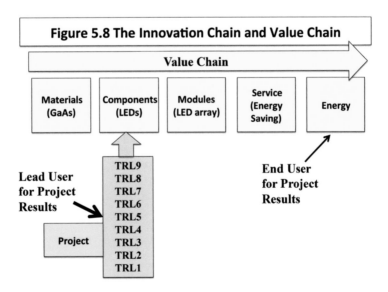

This diagram shows that the project is focusing on a development from TRL 2 to TRL 4. The Lead User is an organisation that operates at TRL 5 in GaAs based LEDs.

Selecting partners for the project.

Figure 5.9 show the possible construction of a consortium for this project.

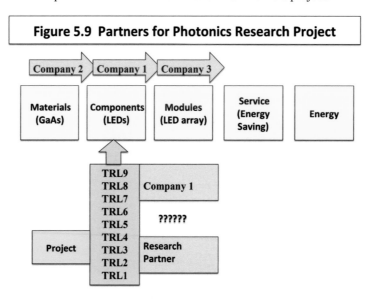

The research partners will develop the technologies from TRL2 to TRL4. Company 1 has been identified as a company that is interested in introducing the developed technology into the Value Chain. It is also a good idea to involve partners from the 'upstream' and 'downstream' of the Value Chain. These are not critical partners but they can bring valuable industrial experience to the project. These are identified as Company 2 and Company 3.

Figure 5.9 identifies a problem. Company 2 has a product development department that can work with technologies at TRL7 to TRL9. They do not have the capability to take TRL 4 results. If this project is presented, the Impact score in the evaluation will be low. It is necessary to find another partner who can work at TRL4 to TRL6 or find another Company 1 that can work with results at TRL 5.

Figure 5.10 shows a consortium where a Company 1 has been found that has a Research and Development department that works at TRL4 upwards.

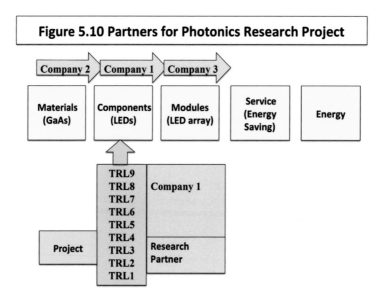

Large and Small Enterprises in European Projects

Finding SMEs with the capability to absorb TRL 4 results is difficult. These are research intensive SMEs. They are usually found as spin off companies from research centres or companies with venture capital investments.

In this project, Company 1 should be responsible for writing the impact in the proposals. The language they will use will be different to the language of the researchers.
Many companies are brought into projects where they are in the correct part of the Value Chain but they cannot use the results as they only operate at high Technology Readiness Levels. Experienced industrial evaluators will ask the following type of questions during the evaluation.

Where is your organisations situated on the relevant Value Chain?

What Technology Readiness Level are you able to use?

A number of studies on Innovation in SMEs have found that the number of European companies suitable for research projects is in the region of 5 to 7%. A famous UK study (NESTA report) entitled *'The Vital 6%'* found that 6% of UK businesses generated half of the new jobs between 2002 and 2008.

NESTA Report 'The Vital 6%'
http://www.nesta.org.uk/publications/reports/assets/features/the_vital_6_per_cent

Figure 5.11 shows how a company describe its suitability to a research project

Figure 5.11 How a Company should describe its role

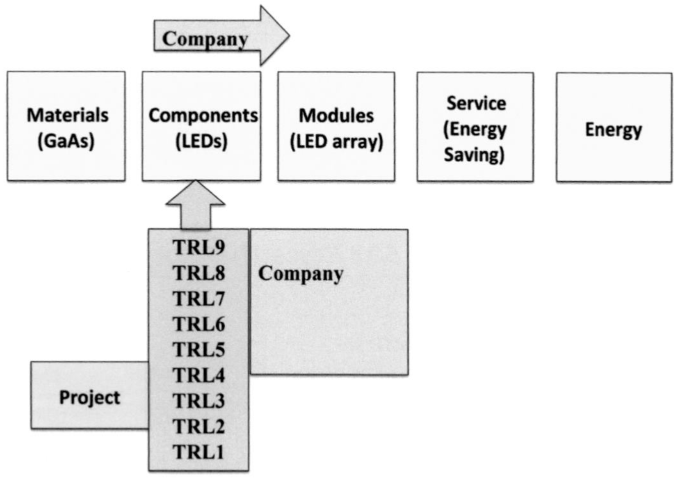

Writing Impact for a Social Science Project

Figure 5.12 shows the stakeholders in a migration project – cultural groups, advocacy groups, media, museums, Government departments and the media. The diagram also shows how the objects flow between the stakeholders - reports, information and data. This is a very simple example. In many social, economic and political science projects, there will be many more stakeholders and more complex interactions.

This should be the first diagram to appear in the proposal. Before convincing the evaluator, it is necessary to educate the evaluator on the big picture and on the stakeholders.

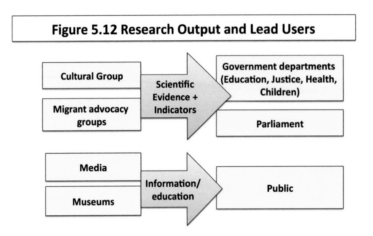

Figure 5.13 shows the role of the research project. It can be seen that the project will provide independent scientific evidence to the debate on migration. This diagram clearly identifies the 'Lead Users' as Cultural groups, migrant advisory groups, the media and museums. The diagram identifies the 'End Users' as Government departments, Parliament and the general public.

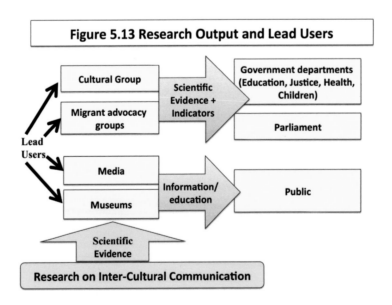

The methodology is applied to the project in the following steps.

Table 5.10 Expected Outputs (Results) from the Project

Outputs (Results)	Lead Users	Outcomes	Exploitation	Dissemination
Report on migration in the EU				
Data on migration in the EU				
Areas where further research is needed				

Expected Results

Report on migration in the EU: This report will summarise the main findings of the project. It will also provide a number of recommendations and options on how Member States and the European Union could address migration issues relating to Muslim communities.

Data on migration in the EU: Data on migration is complex as it involves 28 countries. This is further complicated when people move to another country and then return home. Data will be presented on these movements and predicted trends over the coming five years.

Areas where further research is needed: One of the aims of the proposed work was to identify where information on migration was weak and where further research was needed.

Table 5.11 Lead Users of the Results and the Outcomes

Expected Results	Lead Users	Outcomes	Exploitation	Dissemination
Report on migration in the EU	Policy Researchers (Cultural Groups) (Advocacy Groups) (Media)	Migration Trends in the European Union		
Data on migration in the EU	Policy Researchers (Cultural Groups) (Advocacy Groups) (Media)	Indicators of Migration in the European Union		
Areas where further research is needed	Funding Programme Directors	R&D Roadmap for Migration Research in the European Union		

In the steps shown in Table 5.11 the language of the researcher (Outputs) is converted into the language of the Lead Users (Outcome). Note that the language of the Lead User is defining the Outcomes in a format that can be delivered to the next step in the Stakeholder Diagram.

The final step is to exploit the results to communities of Lead Users – these are the people who will use the Outcomes immediately.

The Dissemination Plan is designed to promote the Outcomes to all the stakeholders.

Table 5.12 Lead Users of the Results and the Outcomes

Expected Results	Lead Users	Outcomes	Exploitation	Dissemination
Report on migration in the EU	Policy Researchers (Cultural Groups) (Advocacy Groups) (Media)	Migration Trends in the European Union	Official EU Publication Book on Migration in the EU	Through EU or National Publications
Data on migration in the EU	Policy Researchers (Cultural Groups) (Advocacy Groups) (Media)	Indicators of Migration in the European Union	Input to EU or National Policy Debates on Migration	Website Portal
Areas where further research is needed	Funding Programme Directors	R&D Roadmap for Migration Research in the European Union	Foresight Groups Lobby Groups Expert Groups	Directors of EU and National Funding Programmes

This table can now be converted into text. This can be used in the abstract and in the introduction to the B2 Impact section in the proposal.

Expected Results and Potential Impact

A report entitled 'Migration Trends in the European Union' would be of major importance to policy makers in the Ministries of Foreign Affairs (or External Relations) in all Member States of the European Union. This report could be used as the basis for policy debates and could outline possible strategies or make important recommendations on policy actions.

Scientific Evidence and Indicators of Migration in the European Union
Scientific evidence will be provided in a format that will support policy debates on migration in the European Union. Indicators will also be provided so that policy instruments can be monitored during implementation.

R&D Roadmap on Migration in the European Union
A roadmap will identify the research that should be undertaken over the following five years. This roadmap can be used by National and EU programme designers to identify topics for futures work programmes.

Scientific Publications
Scientific publications will be published in high impact journals to present the findings to the scientific committee. Five PhD theses will be prepared during this project.

Case Study: Writing 'Impact' of a Sensor Project

The aim of the project was to develop an infrared sensor to measure the concentration of hydrocarbons in drinking water. Annex 1 of the Water Framework Directive specifies 'Hydrocarbons' as one of the 'priority hazardous substances' that must be measured to meet the legislation. The sensors on the market cost around €3000 per sensor and only operate in laboratory conditions. The aim of this project was to develop a low cost infrared sensor that could work continuously on-site, with minimum maintenance.

The work involved coating a fibre-optic cable with a polymer, shining the infra-red light through the fibre-optic cable and measuring the refractive index. The level of hydrocarbons in water could be measured by calculating the change in refractive index.
TC147: Standardization in the field of water quality, including definition of terms, sampling of waters, measurement and reporting of water characteristics.

STEP 1: Draw the Value Chain

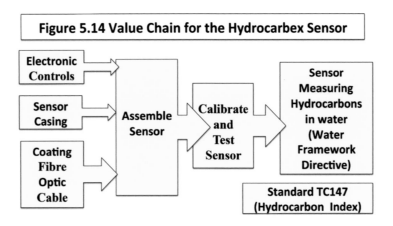

Figure 5.14 Value Chain for the Hydrocarbex Sensor

Step 2: Show what the research project is addressing

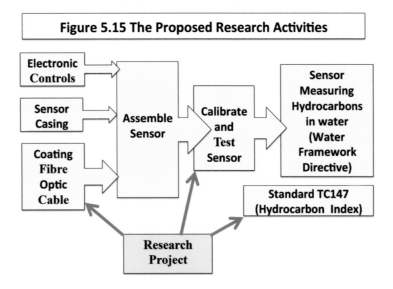

Figure 5.15 The Proposed Research Activities

Step 3: Identify the Lead Users of the Results

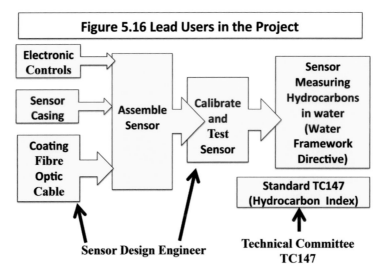

Figure 5.16 Lead Users in the Project

Table 5.13 Expected Outputs (Results) from the Project

Expected Results	Lead User	Outcomes	Exploitation	Dissemination
Prototype of sensor to measure hydrocarbons in water				
Scientific data on the performance of the sensor				
Document describing the sensor				

Expected Outputs (Results)
- *Technical prototype* of the sensor would be developed to prove that the concept proposed could be used to measure hydrocarbons in water.
- *Scientific data* would be collected from 150 hours of testing of the sensor.
- *Documents* would be written describing how to sensor was developed.

Actual Results

Technical Prototype: The project was very successful and it did prove that the concept could be used to measure hydrocarbons in water. However, the final 'sensor' was actually a table full of wires, laser beams and computers. It was supported by a team of technicians and supervised by the researchers from the project.

Scientific Data: The data was in a 'raw format' – collected directly from the sensor and stored in a database. Software was developed to analyse the data and produce statistical graphs for analysis.

Documents: Reports were written in a format specified by the Framework guidelines.

From a scientific point of view, the prototype, data and reports were perfectly suitable to prove the concepts and the project was considered a success.

Identify the 'Lead Users' of the results

Table 5.14 lists the 'Lead Users' for the different results. Note that the second result (Scientific data) has two different 'Lead Users.'

Table 5.14 Lead Users of the Results

Results	Lead User	Outcome	Exploitation	Dissemination
Prototype of sensor to measure hydrocarbons in water	Design Engineer from a company specialising in sensors for the water industry			
Scientific data on the performance of the sensor	Design Engineer from a company specialising in sensors for the water industry			
	ISO TC147 Technical Committee			
Document describing the sensor	Sensor design Engineer			

Lead User 1: Sensor design engineer in a company specialising in sensors for the water industry.

This was a company that specialised in the development and distribution of sensors for the water industry. They were in the process of updating their sensors to infrared based technologies – as this is what the market was demanding. In the company, one of the design engineers was responsible for the upgrading of the sensors for measuring hydrocarbons in water. This company was a partner in the project.

Lead User 2: ISO TC147 Technical Committee.

The standard for measuring hydrocarbons in water is ISO TC147. It is known as the 'Hydrocarbex Index'. The existing standard was not designed for infrared sensors. The data from the project would be used to update the Hydrocarbex Index. The next partner in the project was an individual who was a member of ISO TC147. In fact, this partner became the Scientific Coordinator of the project.

Outcome of the project: How the 'Lead User' describes the results?

The next step is to convert the description of the results into the language of the 'Lead User.' It is like converting a sentence from English to German or English to French. This conversion will describe the results in a format that is relevant to the needs of the 'Lead User.'

Table 5.15 Relevance of the Results to the 'Lead Users'

Outputs (Results)	Lead User	Outcomes	Exploitation	Dissemination
Prototype of sensor to measure hydrocarbons in water	Design Engineer from a company specialising in sensors for the water industry	Technical Prototype of a Hydrocarbex Sensor (TRL 4)		
Scientific data on the performance of the sensor	Product Development Engineer	Calibration Curve of the Hydrocarbex Sensor		
	ISO TC147 Technical Committee	Factual Data to upgrade the Hydrocarbex Index ISO TC147		
Document describing the sensor	Sensor design Engineer	Design Specification for the Hydrocarbex Sensor		

Technical Prototype of a Hydrocarbex Sensor

This is exactly how the sensor was described by the sensor design engineer in the company.

Calibration Curve of the Hydrocarbex Sensor

A calibration curve is needed to develop, manufacture, test and sell a sensor. It demands many hours of testing and is the key performance indicator for the sensor.

Factual data to upgrade the Hydrocarbex Index (ISO TC147)

'Factual data' is the terminology used in the development or upgrading of standards.

Design specification of the Hydrocarbex Sensor

Design Engineers work with functional specifications and design specifications. This is the language of their work.

(Note that the scientific data is described in two different ways-by the different 'Lead users').

Dissemination and Exploitation of Results

The final step is to identify how the results will be disseminated or exploited by the 'Lead Users.' If there is only one 'Lead User' in Europe then it is obvious that this project should not be funded by Horizon 2020. This is the column that defines the 'European Relevance' of the proposal.

Table 5.16 Dissemination/Exploitation of Results and Funding

Output (Results)	Lead User	Outcomes	Exploitation	Dissemination
Prototype of sensor to measure hydrocarbons in water	Design Engineer from a company specialising in sensors for the water industry	Technical Prototype of a Hydrocarbex Sensor (TRL 4)	Develop a Commercial Prototype (TRL 5-7)	SWIG (Sensors in Water Industry Group)
Scientific data on the performance of the sensor	Product Development Engineer	Calibration Curve of the Hydrocarbex Sensor	Publish Calibration Curve	Manual for Sensor Online forum
	ISO TC147 Technical Committee	Factual Data to upgrade the Hydrocarbex Index ISO TC147	Draft protocol for the upgrade of the Hydrocarbex Index ISO TC147	Promotion of Draft to National Members of Technical Committee
Document describing the sensor	Sensor design Engineer	Design Specification for the Hydrocarbex Sensor	Development of a commercial prototype	Manual Online Training

DO NOT INCLUDE A TABLE (like 5.16) IN THE PROPOSAL.
DESCRIBE THE TABLE USING TEXT AS FOLLOWS

Dissemination Route 1: SWIG (Sensors in Water Industry Group) www.swig.org.uk

The Water Framework Directive affects every water sensor company in Europe. The water sensor industry set up a network (SWIG) so that they could address the impact of the new water legislation and implement the upgrading of existing standards to meet new demands. SWIG held a workshop in Scotland on the topic '*How to Measure Hydrocarbons in Water.*' The report that issued from this workshop was the key document in writing the proposal.

Dissemination Route 2: ISO TC147 Technical Committee

The Scientific Coordinator was a member of ISO TC147 so the results of the project could be brought directly to the Technical Committee. Membership of Standards Committees is funded by national ministries of industry.

Exploitation Route 3: Development of a Commercial Prototype of the sensor

A 'Technical Prototype' is used to prove that the technical concept functions properly. A 'Commercial Prototype' is used to test the market and focuses on issues such as: Design, Costing, Protection of Intellectual Property, Pilot Testing and Demonstration.

How to Write the 'Impact' of the Project

The following text shows how the information contained in Table 5.16 was presented in the proposal. (Note that the information in Column 1 was not used).

Expected Result 1:
A technical prototype of an infra-red sensor that will measure hydrocarbons in water.

The sensor is expected to measure to an accuracy of 1000 ppb (parts per billion) and will cost less than €50 to manufacture. The Technology Readiness Level will be 4 (Technology validated in laboratory)

Lead Users of the sensor
The 'Lead Users' will be design engineers in companies that design and manufacture sensors for the water industry. One of the partners will define the industry requirements and will test the sensor in the laboratory and, in a pilot test site, on the river Severn, UK.

Exploitation/Dissemination Plan:
The results will be disseminated to the European Water Sensor Industry through SWIG (Sensors in Water Industry Group).

Funding of Exploitation/Dissemination:
The promotion of the results will be funded by SWIG.

Expected Result 2: Design Specification of the Hydrocarbex Sensor.

A detailed design specification of the sensor will be published. This will enable design engineers to build and test prototypes of the sensor. The document will also be used in patent applications.

Exploitation/Dissemination Plan:
This will be used in the ISO TC147 standard and will also be used to develop a commercial prototype of the sensor.

Funding of Exploitation/Dissemination:
The development of a commercial prototype of the sensor will be funded with private finance.

Expected Results 3: A Calibration Curve of the Sensor.

A calibration curve for the sensor based on 150 hours of tests will be produced. This is essential to the product development engineers who are working on further development of the commercial prototype and the reproduction of a range of test sensors for future pilot applications.

Exploitation Plan:
This will be exploited through the commercial prototype of the sensor.

Funding of Exploitation:
The development of a commercial prototype of the sensor will be funded with private finance.

Expected Result 4: Factual Data to upgrade the Hydrocarbex Index ISO TC147.

The factual data will be used to upgrade ISO TC147 so that the standard can be used for infrared sensors.

Dissemination Plan:
The Scientific Coordinator of the project is a member of the Technical Committee of ISO TC147. This will ensure an efficient transfer of the results from the project to the Technical Committee.

Funding of dissemination:
Membership of the Technical Committee is funded by the Irish Ministry for Enterprise, Trade and Employment.

Figure 5.17 shows the business plan for the sensor. This describes the different steps, time scales and expected sources of funding needed to bring this sensor to the market and to have a long term impact. From this project, a European company could become the leader in the market for infrared water sensors.

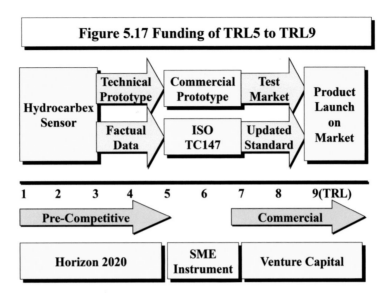

Step 1: Pre-competitive phase

This diagram clearly shows that Horizon 2020 will fund the first three years and will focus on 'pre-competitive' issues – technical prototype and generation of 'factual data'.

Step 2: Innovative phase

The next phase (after the project) will involve further development but will focus on more competitive issues – development and testing of commercial prototypes. This will be funded by public programmes that focus on 'innovation funding'.
Examples of innovation funding:
- SME Instrument (Horizon 2020)
- Private funding of company involved in the project

Step 3: Commercialisation

The final phase is a commercial phase where the product is launched on the market. As a purely commercial venture, this phase is funded by private sources. Examples of private sources of funding could be:
- Investment by company
- Venture capital
- Business angels

This is an example of how the potential impact could be written. The format is simple and it is clear to the evaluator that the researchers are thinking beyond the project.

Case Study: 'Impact' of an ERC Project

What impact will this project have on the scientific community?

In ERC projects, it is a good idea to present a diagram showing the scientific stakeholders and indicate where the project will contribute to a wider scientific community. The 'Lead Users' of basic research results are other scientists. These could be scientists from other disciplines or scientists who will use the results in more applied research applications. The other main users are lecturers who will use the new knowledge as the basis for post-graduate courses.

This example demonstrates how a similar approach can be used to explain the 'Impact' of a basic research project.

Table 5.17 Expected Results from a Basic Research Project

Output (Results)	Lead User	Outcome	Exploitation	Dissemination
Improved knowledge of nanostructures				
Scientific Data				
Reports on Results				

Expected Results

- *Improved knowledge of nanostructures:* Basic research is used to fill 'knowledge gaps' or to identify new approaches to old problems. The main result is 'knowledge'.
- *Scientific Data:* New knowledge needs scientific data to support the new theories or the new methods.
- *Reports on results.* Scientific reports are needed as part of the funding rules and also as a means of disseminating the results to the scientific community.

Table 5.18 Lead Users of Basic Research Results

Outputs (Results)	Lead User	Outcome	Exploitation	Exploitation
Improved knowledge of nanostructures	Basic/Applied Researchers	Scientific Publication on Nanostructures…		
Scientific Data	Basic/Applied Researchers	Validation or Reference Data		
Reports on Results	Academic Lecturers	Post-Graduate Course Material		

Table 5.19 Dissemination/Exploitation Plans and Funding

Outputs (Results)	Lead User	Outcomes	Exploitation	Dissemination
Improved knowledge of nanostructures	Basic/Applied Researchers	Scientific Publication on Nanostructures…	Direct contact with research groups who want the results	Scientific Publications Conferences
Scientific Data	Basic/Applied Researchers	Validation or Reference Data	Websites or Databases	Open Access
Reports on Results	Academic Lecturers	Post-Graduate Course Material	Master and PhD programmes	Online Training

Examples of Impact of Fundamental Research

Heinrich Rudolf Hertz comments on his discovery of electromagnetic waves:

"It's of no use whatsoever[...] this is just an experiment that proves Maestro Maxwell was right - we just have these mysterious electromagnetic waves that we cannot see with the naked eye. But they are there."

Asked about the ramifications (impact) of his discoveries, Hertz replied,
"Nothing, I guess."   Hertz also stated, "I do not think that the wireless waves I have discovered will have any practical application."

Source – Eugenii Katz, "Heinrich Rudolf Hertz". Biographies of Famous Electrochemists and Physicists Contributed to Understanding of Electricity, Biosensors & Bioelectronics.

In this example, the questions should have been: *Why is the scientific community so excited about this discovery?.* The answer is in the quotation: *"this is just an experiment that proves Maestro Maxwell was right."*

MP3 Music format: From Idea to Impact

Late 1970's
Prof. Dieter Seitzer (University of Erlangen-Nuremberg) first came up with the idea of high quality transmission of music over phone lines.Later he became Director of the Fraunhofer Institute for Integrated Circuits IIS. His first patent application for audio coding was rejected for being technically impossible.

1989: Patent for mp3 awarded
When the first mp3 standard was established there was very little interest from the entertainment industry. The first use of mp3 was by radio broadcasters to send audio files between studios using ISDN lines.

1994: The first prototype mp3 player came on the market in 1994

1997: Microsoft begins using mp3

1998: Era of mp3 players begins.

Today: Major impact

Source: Fraunhofer Institute – EARTO Impact Report (www.earto.eu)

Routes for Exploitation and Dissemination

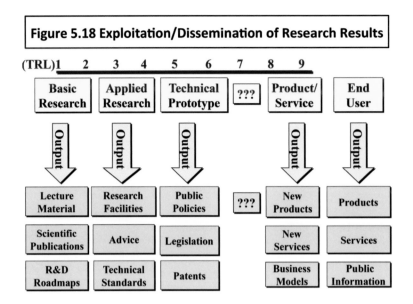

Figure 5.18 Exploitation/Dissemination of Research Results

Projects should include activities relating to the dissemination of knowledge and to the exploitation of the results. Figure 5.18 is a summary of routes of exploitation for different types of activities. These should include:

Intellectual property protection: protection of the knowledge resulting from the project (including patent searches, filing of patent (or other IPR) applications, etc.).

Dissemination activities beyond the consortium: publications, conferences, workshops and web-based activities aimed at disseminating the knowledge and technology produced.

Studies on socio-economic aspects: assessment of the expected socio-economic impact of the knowledge and of the technology generated. Analysis of the factors that would influence their exploitation (e.g. standardisation, ethical and regulatory aspects, etc.).

Activities promoting the exploitation of the results: development of the plan for the use and dissemination of the knowledge produced, feasibility studies for the creation of spin-offs, etc, "take-up" activities to promote the early or broad application of state-of-the-art technologies. Take-up activities include the assessment, trial and validation of promising, but not fully established technologies and solutions, easier access to and the transfer of best practices for the early use and exploitation of technologies. In particular, the projects will be expected to target SMEs.

A report by Tekes (www.tekes.fi), the Finnish funding agency for Innovation, demonstrates how Finnish research exploits the results of research.

"R&D projects and other investments carried out by Tekes gave rise to the following results: 999 academic dissertations, 2,451 publications, 732 patent applications, 465 new or improved products, 301 new or replaced service products and 187 new production processes. Results show that 3-5 years after the public input, there is a yield that is 10-30 times as great as the R&D investment."

PESTLE Impact Analysis

PESTLE analysis is the term used to describe the macro analysis of **P**olicy, **E**conomic, **S**ocial. **T**echnical, **L**egislation and **E**nvironmental. The same concept can be applied to Impact analysis. To write the 'Impact' of the proposal, researchers should investigate as to whether the project will have any of the following impacts

- Impact on **Policy** or Political Debates
- Impact on the European or Regional **Economy**
- **Social** Impact (jobs, education, quality of life etc.)
- **Technology** Impact (including contributions to technical standards)
- Impact on European Policy or European **Legislation**
- Impact on the **Environment**

PESTLE analysis is sometimes listed as:

TELES (Technical, Economy, Legislation, Environment and Social)
STEEPVE (Social, Technical, Environmental, Economy, Policy, Values and Education)
STEEPLED (Social, Technical, Environmental, Economy, Legislation, Ethics, Demography)

Websites for PESTLE Impact Analysis

Policy Websites
- Europa http://europa.eu
- OECD (Organisation for Economic Cooperation and Development) www.oecd.org

Economic Websites
- The Economist Magazine www.economist.org.
- Frost and Sullivan www.frost.com (This is the most comprehensive site)
- Dataquest www.dataquest.com (Mainly Information Technology reports)
- Forrester Research www.forrester.com
- IDC www.idc.com
- OVUM www.ovum.com

Social Websites
- European Social Policy http://ec.europa.eu/social/
- OECD website on social issues www.oecd.org/els/social/

Websites on Technology Trends and Technology Foresight
- Foresight studies: IPTS (Institute for Prospective Technological Studies) www.jrc.es

Websites for Technical Standards
- Cenorm www.cenorm.be
- Cenelec www.cenelec.be
- ISO www.iso.ch
- ETSI www.etsi.org
- ASTM www.astm.org

Websites for European Legislation
- EU Legislation http://europa.eu/eu-law/

Websites on Environmental Issues
- EU Environmental Policy http://ec.europa.eu/environment/index_en.htm

Financial Plan for Exploitation of the Results

"Provide a draft plan for the exploitation and dissemination of the results."
"For innovation actions describe a credible path to deliver the innovations to the market"
"Include a business plan where relevant."
(2.2 Dissemination and exploitation of results)

Proposal writers are expected to have a plan on how the results of the project will be delivered to the 'Lead Users.' The important point here is that researchers are not expected to exploit the results as part of the project. They are only expected to have a convincing exploitation plan. If the proposal is accepted, this exploitation plan will become a very important document.

Figure 5.19 is a graphical representation of the sources of funding available for research, development and innovation.

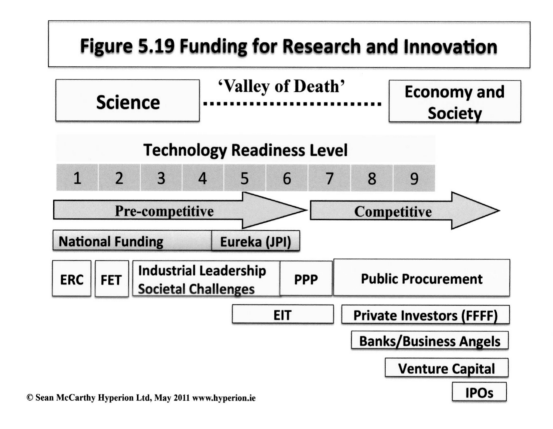

ERC (European Research Council)
FET (Future and Emerging Technologies)
PPP (Public Private Partnerships)
EIT(European Institute of Innovation and Technology)
FFFF (Founder, Friends, Fools and Family)
JPI (Joint Programming Initiatives)
IPO (Initial Public Offering)

Chapter 6: The One Page Proposal

CONTENTS

- Background to the One Page Proposal
- Uses of the One Page Proposal
- Structure of the One Page Proposal (Applied Research)
- Structure of the One Page Proposal (ERC)
- How to prepare a One Page Proposal

Chapter Webpage: www.hyperion.ie/onepageproposal.htm

The Role of the One Page Proposal

The One Page Proposal does not have to be submitted to the Horizon 2020 participant portal. It is a tool that can be used as the first stage in the preparation of any proposal. This chapter presents a format that is suitable to Pillar II and Pillar III of Horizon 2020. An outline of an ERC One Page Proposal is also presented.

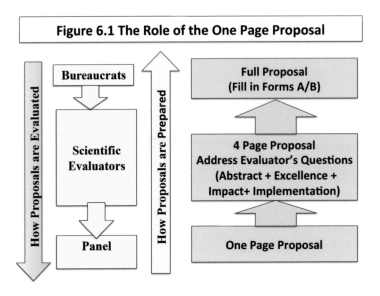

The following is a summary of the different uses of the One Page Proposal

Brainstorming an idea for a proposal
When beginning a proposal, most ideas are vague and unfocussed. The One Page Proposal format provides a list of issues to consider in a brainstorming session

Meeting with Research Support Staff
When a researchers discusses a new proposal with a research support staff, the first question will be '*What is the project about?*' The One Page Proposal contains all the information to explain the general concept to an advisor.

Meeting with a National Contact Point (NCP)
The National Contact Points are very familiar with the contents of the different programmes. They are also familiar with the results of previous calls for proposal. If a researcher has a meeting with an NCP, the researcher will be asked a number of questions to assess if the proposal is suited to Horizon 2020 programme. The information contained in the One Page Proposal will be exactly the information the NCP requires.

Meeting with a Project Officer (European Commission)
The Project Officer in charge of the work programme 'topic' is the person who selects the evaluators. Sometimes it is possible to meet with a Project Officer. This usually happens during existing projects or at workshops related to the calls for proposals. On one occasion, the author was coordinating a large project on an energy crop called Miscanthus. During a meeting with the project officer, a new proposal idea on Miscanthus was presented. The reaction of the project officer was *"We have already funded five projects on Miscanthus. I think we have done enough on Miscanthus for the moment."* After this, the consortium decided not to proceed with a new proposal. It was clear that even if the proposal received a score of 14.5, it would still be rejected at the panel meeting.

Project Officers will seldom comment negatively or positively on a proposal idea. However, if a coordinator has an opportunity to meet with a project officer, it is important for the coordinator to highlight the skills that would be needed to properly evaluate the proposal.

Initial contacts with potential partners (or competitors)
When draft work programmes are published, researchers study them to identify areas where their research could be funded. Potential partners can be contacted through existing networks, brokerage events or partner search databases. Researchers with ideas are attracted to other researchers with complementary ideas. The One Page Proposal is a useful tool to establish initial contacts with potential partners.
There is a possibility that some researchers, participating in the meeting, will be future competitors in proposals. This is why the One Page Proposal does not contain any of the scientific details of the project.

First item on the agenda of a consortium meeting
When researchers meet to discuss new proposals, they bring ideas to the table. Some present their ideas verbally, some by Power Point or some using unstructured notes. The One Page Proposal is a useful format for this first meeting. Following a call for proposals, the author attended a consortium meeting in Brussels to discuss a new proposal. After two hours of discussions, the meeting had turned into a scientific meeting – not a proposal writing workshop. The consortium agreed to use the One Page Proposal as the agenda for the discussion. After one hour, three versions of the One Page Proposal had been printed. At this point, the consortium agreed on the direction of the proposal. The project was eventually funded and every comment the evaluators made on the proposal referred back to the One Page Proposal.

Abstract of the Proposal
The One Page Proposal will eventually be converted into the abstract of the proposal. The abstract has three main functions:

- The Project Officer uses the abstract to select the evaluators for the proposal. Also, if the Project Officer receives 100 proposals for a topic, the only part of the proposal they will read will be the abstract.

- When an evaluator starts reading a proposal, the first text that is read is the abstract. The abstract must inform, convince and excite the evaluator in a very short period of time. If an evaluator has fifteen proposals to read, he/she begins by reading the abstracts of all the proposals. Often, the evaluator will start with the most interesting proposal – or the proposal with the best abstract.

- During the panel meeting, senior Commission personnel read the 'Consensus Report' from the evaluators. The only parts of the original proposal that will be in the 'Consensus Report' will be the Title, Acronym and the Abstract. During the panel meeting, '5 Key Questions' are asked. It is important that these are addressed in the abstract. Also, during the panel meeting, the 'Impact' is the key point of discussion so it is important that this is presented in the abstract.

Structure of the One Page Proposal

Structure of the 'One-Page Proposal'
1. Work Programme Topic and Funding Scheme
2. Title and Acronym
3. Objective of the proposal
4. Background to the proposal (5 Key Questions)
5. Expected Results and 'Lead Users' of the results (Impact)
6. Phases of the work (Simple list)
7. Organisations involved and their roles in the proposed work (List)
8. Expected costs and duration of the work.

This can be used as the agenda of the consortium meeting. The list can also be the slides of a Power Point presentation.

Preparation of the One Page Proposal

The list above shows the order in which the One Page Proposal is written. However, the order in which the One Page Proposal is prepared is as follows:

Preparation of the One Page Proposal
- Work Programme and Funding Scheme
- Expected Results and 'Lead Users' of the Results (Impact)
- Background to the proposal (5 key questions)
- Title and acronym
- Objective of the proposal
- Phases of the work
- Organisations involved and their roles
- Expected costs and duration of work.

An example of a One Page Proposal will be presented in the following page.

How to Prepare the One Page Proposal

In practice, the preparation of a One Page Proposal is done in the following way. This procedure is described in detail in the last page of this chapter.

Step 1: Present a Power Point presentation of the proposal idea (30 minutes)
Step 2: Present a Power Point presentation of the proposed idea (8 slides, 5 minutes)
Step 3: First draft of the One Page Proposal
Step 4: Refine the One Page Proposal during the writing of the proposal
Step 5: Convert the One Page Proposal into the Abstract of the proposal

Example of a One Page Proposal

Development of a Sensor to Measure Hydrocarbons in Water
(Hydrocarbex Project)

Work Programme (Topic) 3.x…   Funding Scheme: Research and Innovation Action

The aim of this proposal is to develop a technical prototype of an infrared sensor that will measure hydrocarbons in water. The sensor will use a fibre-optic cable, coated with a polymer and the level of hydrocarbon will be determined by measuring the changes in refractive index. The key research challenges will be: assessing the use of infrared to measure the level of hydrocarbons in water, identifying a range of polymers that could be used in the sensor and finally assessing the accuracy of the sensor.

Background to the project:
In 1999, the European Commission published legislation on water quality, known as the Water Framework Directive (COM 200/61). Annex 1 of this directive lists 11 parameters that must be continuously monitored to meet the directive. These are known as the 'priority hazardous substances'. One of these substances is Hydrocarbon. The sensors on the market today to monitor hydrocarbons in water are laboratory based, they require regular calibration and cost over €3,000 euro per sensor. If the water legislation is enforced it will cost the European water industry hundreds of millions of euro per annum just to measure this one parameter – hydrocarbons. The aim of this proposal is to develop a low cost, infrared based sensor that will measure hydrocarbons in water to meet the conditions of the directive. The sensor will be suitable for onsite monitoring, will require a minimum of calibration and will deliver data continuously.

Expected Results, Lead Users and Exploitation/Dissemination Plan,
A technical prototype of an infra-red sensor that will measure hydrocarbons in water:
The sensor is expected to measure to an accuracy of 1,000 ppb (parts per billion) and will cost less than €50 to manufacture. A detailed design specification of the sensor will be published. This will enable design engineers to build and test prototypes of the sensor. The document will also be used in patent applications. A calibration curve for the sensor based on 150 hours of tests will be produced. This is essential to the product development engineers for further development of the commercial prototype and the reproduction of a range of test sensors for future pilot applications. The lead users will be design engineers in companies that design and manufacture sensors for the water industry. One of the partners (Capital Controls Ltd., UK) will define the industry requirements and will test the sensor in their laboratory and in a pilot test site on the river Severn, UK. The results will be disseminated to the water sensor industry through SWIG (Sensors in Water Industry Group).
Factual Data to upgrade the Hydrocarbex Index (ISO TC147):
The factual data will be used to upgrade ISO TC147 so that the standard can be used for infrared sensors. The Scientific Coordinator of the project is a member of the Technical Committee of ISO TC147. This will ensure an efficient transfer of the results from the project to the Technical Committee.

Phases of Work: 1. Review of sensors on the market, 2.Specification of infrared sensor, 3.Identification of polymer to coat fibre-optic cable, 4.Testing of sensor, 5.150 hours calibration test, 6.Dissemination of Results (SWIG), 7.Exploitation plan for further development.

Partners: The proposal writers have been active in the development of infrared sensors and one of the industrial partners is a company that specialises in the development of sensors for the water industry. Coordinator Dublin City University, Partner 2 (Role infrared sensors), Partner 3 (Water Sensor Company), Partner 4 (Fibre-Optic Company), Hyperion (Impact Manager), etc.

Expected Budget: €6,000,000   Horizon 2020 contribution (Maximum €3,000,000)
Duration: 36 months

Impact Paragraph

The first item to be discussed in a new proposal is the Impact. This paragraph should answer the following questions.

- What results (new knowledge) are expected from the project?
- Who are the 'Lead Users' of these results?
- How do the 'Lead Users' describe these results? ('Relevance' to the 'Lead User')
- How will the results be delivered to the 'Lead Users'?
- How will the transfer of results to the 'Lead Users' be funded?

The concepts presented in Chapter 5 (Impact) can be used to write this paragraph.

Table 6.1 Dissemination/Exploitation of Results and Funding

Output (Results)	Lead User	Outcomes	Exploitation	Dissemination
Prototype of sensor to measure hydrocarbons in water	Design Engineer from a company specialising in sensors for the water industry	Technical Prototype of a Hydrocarbex Sensor (TRL 4)	Develop a Commercial Prototype (TRL 5-7)	SWIG (Sensors in Water Industry Group)
Scientific data on the performance of the sensor	Product Development Engineer	Calibration Curve of the Hydrocarbex Sensor	Publish Calibration Curve	Manual for Sensor Online forum
	ISO TC147 Technical Committee	Factual Data to upgrade the Hydrocarbex Index ISO TC147	Draft protocol for the upgrade of the Hydrocarbex Index ISO TC147	Promotion of Draft to National Members of Technical Committee
Document describing the sensor	Sensor design Engineer	Design Specification for the Hydrocarbex Sensor	Development of a commercial prototype	Manual Online Training

Expected Results, Lead Users and Exploitation/Dissemination Plan,
A technical prototype of an infra-red sensor that will measure hydrocarbons in water:
The sensor is expected to measure to an accuracy of 1,000 ppb (parts per billion) and will cost less than €50 to manufacture. A detailed design specification of the sensor will be published. This will enable design engineers to build and test prototypes of the sensor. The document will also be used in patent applications. A calibration curve for the sensor based on 150 hours of tests will be produced. This is essential to the product development engineers for further development of the commercial prototype and the reproduction of a range of test sensors for future pilot applications. The lead users will be design engineers in companies that design and manufacture sensors for the water industry. One of the partners (Capital Controls Ltd., UK) will define the industry requirements and will test the sensor in their laboratory and in a pilot test site on the river Severn, UK. The results will be disseminated to the water sensor industry through SWIG (Sensors in Water Industry Group).

Factual Data to upgrade the Hydrocarbex Index (ISO TC147):
The factual data will be used to upgrade ISO TC147 so that the standard can be used for infrared sensors. The Scientific Coordinator of the project is a member of the Technical Committee of ISO TC147. This will ensure an efficient transfer of the results from the project to the Technical Committee.

Background Paragraph

The 'Background' of the proposal should be written in the second paragraph. This should be five or six sentences long. The evaluator should gain a crystal clear idea of the background in around 20 seconds!

Educate the evaluator with facts and figures. Supply facts and figures including statistics (with references) and quotations. Arguments have to be so convincing (and true) that the evaluator is not able to disagree with them. (Bad proposals have no hope here. Only really good proposals survive this test).

The 5 Key Questions

The background should address all of the following questions and every answer must be supported with referenced facts or figures. These questions are not written in the proposal forms. They are, however, in the mind of every evaluator. During the panel meeting, the 5 Key Questions can be used to decide if a proposal is accepted or rejected.

Why bother? (What problem are you trying to solve?)
Is it a European priority? (Could it be solved at National level?)
Is the solution already available? (Product, service, by technology transfer)
Why now? (What would happen if the project was not funded?)
Why you? (Have you the best consortium to undertake this work?)

Why bother? (What problem are you trying to solve?)

This sentence should clearly identify the challenge which the proposal will address. The priorities (or policies) result from developments in Technology, Economics, Policy/Legislation, Environmental Concerns or Social Issues.

Is it a European priority? (Could it be solved at National level?)

The relevance of the proposal to policy documents, identified in Chapter 2, must be described. A reference to the size of the sector market in the EU would be useful. A comparison with the USA, China or Japan would be excellent.

The key websites in finding answers to questions 1 and 2 are:

- Europa General Search Engine http://europa.eu/geninfo/query/advSearch_en.jsp
- OECD (Organisation for Economic Cooperation and Development) www.oecd.org
- EU White Papers (Policy) http://ec.europa.eu/white-papers/
- EU Green Papers (Discussion documents for future policy) http://ec.europa.eu/green-papers/

Is the solution already available (product, service, by technology transfer)?

The researcher must clearly show familiarity with the state-of-the-art and the state of the market. References to the key industrial actors in the sector would be very impressive here.

Why now? (What would happen if the project was not funded?)

Why now? Was there some major technical or political development in the past number of years that makes this proposal necessary or urgent today? Or could the development wait another five years? The researcher must explain the urgency of the proposals.

The answers to questions 3 and 4 can be found on:

- Technology Platforms (Industry foresight) www.hyperion.ie/technology-platforms.htm
- Key Enabling Technologies www.hyperion.ie/ket.htm

Why you? (Have you the best consortium to undertake this work?)

Describe the consortium's activities and their relevance to the challenge being addressed in the proposal. Describe how all the expertise will be combined to address the proposed research.

Example 1: 5 Key Questions for the Hydrocarbex project

The European Commission published legislation on water quality, known as the Water Framework Directive (COM 200/61). Annex 1 of this directive lists 11 parameters that must be continuously monitored to meet the directive. These are known as the 'priority hazardous substances'. One of these substances is Hydrocarbon.

The sensors on the market today to monitor hydrocarbons in water are laboratory based, they require regular calibration and cost over €3,000 euro per sensor. If the water legislation was enforced it would cost the European water industry hundreds of millions of euro per annum just to measure this one parameter – hydrocarbons. The aim of this proposal is to develop a low cost, infrared based sensor that will measure hydrocarbons in water to meet the conditions of the directive. The sensor will be suitable for onsite monitoring, will require a minimum of calibration and will deliver data continuously.

The proposal writers have been active in the development of infrared sensors and one of the industrial partners is a company that specialises in the development of sensors for the water industry.

Example 2: 5 Key Questions for the SODIS Project
Solar Disinfection of Drinking Water (SODIS)

According to the World Health Organisation (WHO), over 1 billion people around the world have no access to any kind of treated drinking water. Every year 1.6 million people, most of them young children, die of diseases such as cholera which are attributable to a lack of access to safe drinking water and basic sanitation. Millions more are infected with water borne parasites. The United Nations Millennium Development Goals call for the proportion of people without access to safe drinking water and basic sanitation to be halved by 2015. Harnessing the power of the sun to disinfect water is nothing new; the technique was used in India 4000 years ago. In recent years, solar water disinfection has undergone something of a revival, as its ease of use and low costs make it ideal for use in poor, developing countries. The only equipment used in this project is a water bottle and a steady supply of sunlight. This work has been approved by WHO. In this project, research will be undertaken on the use of catalysts to speed up the process of disinfection and to provide WHO with scientific data to support their guidelines. The proposal writers have been working with WHO on this topic for over six years.

The writing of this short text involved a four hour discussion between all the partners. It was useful in identifying whether or not the proposed idea was convincing and, also, in helping the partners focus on the aims of the project.

The Title and the Acronym of the Project

The title should be based on the planned impact of the proposal. In this project the title should be:

Development of a Sensor to Measure Hydrocarbons in Water

The Acronym should be: **_Hydrocarbex Sensor_**

In selecting a title the following points should be taken into account:

- The title should be self-explanatory.
- The title could be used in a sentence and make sense to the 'Lead Users'
- The title is one of the last parts of the proposal that is written.

In the past, researchers created acronyms by selecting letters from the beginning of each word. This resulted in acronyms that had absolutely nothing to do with the proposal. This should be avoided. Table 6.2 shows examples of Titles and Acronyms for selected social science projects.

Table 6.2 Title and Acronyms for funded research projects

Title	Acronym
Social Platform on Research for Families and Family Policies	FAMILYPLATFORM
Gross Inequality Impacts	GINI
Work Organisation and Restructuring in the Knowledge Society	WORKS
A Micro-Level Analysis of Violent Conflict	MICROCON
Debates about Female Muslim Headscarves in Europe	VEIL
Platform of Local Authorities and Cities Engaged in Sciences	PLACES
Code of Conduct for Responsible Nanosciences and Nanotechnologies Research	NANOCODE
Science Teacher Education Advanced Methods	S-TEAM

Objective of the Proposal

This should be a short paragraph which clearly describes the aims of the proposed work.

"What is the research question?"

After this paragraph, the evaluator should have a perfect understanding of the aims of the work. This will take a lot of effort and rewriting. It is the most critical paragraph in the whole proposal. It should define the 'research question' that is addressed in the proposal.

The aim of this proposal is to develop a technical prototype of an infrared sensor that will measure hydrocarbons in water. The sensor will use a fibre-optic cable, coated with a polymer and the level of hydrocarbon will be determined by measuring the changes in refractive index. The key research challenges will be: assessing the use of infrared to measure the level of hydrocarbons in water, identifying a range of polymers that could be used in the sensor and finally assessing the accuracy of the sensor.

Structure of an ERC One Page Proposal

The One Page Proposal is not part of the official proposal to ERC. It is a tool to help the researchers begin the preparation of the proposal. When researchers are planning an ERC proposal, the following is the presentation that they should make to outline their project.

1. Call for Proposals
2. Type of Grant
3. Title and Acronym
4. Objective of the proposal
5. Background to the proposal
6. Overview of the proposed research and expected results
7. Principal Investigator
8. Expected costs and duration of the work.

Call for Proposals
This should indicate which call area:

> Life Sciences;
> Physical Sciences;
> Social Sciences and Humanities.

This paragraph should also indicate which 'ERC panel' in is most appropriate.

Type of Grant

> Starting Grant (2 to 7 years from PhD)
> Consolidator Grant (7 to 12 years from PhD)
> Advanced Grant (great than 12 years from PhD)

The '2 to 7 years' refers to the time from the date of the PhD to the date of the call for proposals deadline. (Note: these rules may change during the life of Horizon 2020).

Title and Acronym
These should reflect the research question or the expected research results.

Examples of funded ERC projects

Background
These are the questions that are in the minds of the reviewers when they start reading a proposal.

> *What new knowledge will this research produce?*
> *Has this the potential to establish Europe as the leader in the scientific field – in terms of publication and citations in high impact journals?*
> *Is the proposed research really beyond the state-of-the-art? (Strong argument needed here)*
> *Why now? Why was this work not done before now? (This is the killer question)*
> *Why you? Are you the best researcher to undertake this work?*

Overview of the proposed research and expected research results
This section should describe the key research approach, methodology, tools, data etc. It should also highlight the expected scientific results and how these would be used by other scientists.

Principal Investigator
Profile of the principal investigator – especially the researcher's background in the proposed research.

Estimated Cost and Duration
For example: ERC Contribution €1.5 million euro over a period of 5 years.

How to Prepare a One Page Proposal

The following is a procedure that has been tested in five different Universities (Cork, Galway, Helsinki, Linkoping and Erasmus, Rotterdam). It was designed as a tool for Research Support Staff.

Step 1: Presentation of the proposal (up to 30 minutes allowed).
A researcher should be invited to present the idea to an audience of researchers. In the above Universities, five different researchers were invited to present their proposal ideas. The format of the presentation was based on the One Page Proposal structure i.e.
1. Work Programme Topic and Funding Scheme
2. Title and Acronym
3. Objective of the proposal
4. Background to the proposal (5 Key Questions)
5. Expected Results and 'Lead Users' of the results (Impact)
6. Phases of the work (Simple list)
7. Organisations involved and their roles in the proposed work (List)
8. Expected costs and duration of the work.

During this workshop, the researcher should be questioned on all aspects of the idea. In many workshops, the researcher presented the idea in a lecture style i.e. telling not selling. At the end of the presentation, the key points of the proposal are highlighted. The researcher should now be aware of the weaknesses of their arguments.

When? This step can be done at any time. It can be done as a routine workshop when researchers are brainstorming ideas. The ideal time is when the draft work programmes are published and researchers are starting to think about ideas for proposals.

Step 2: Presentation of Proposal (8 slides, 5 minutes)
Following Step 1, the researcher should revise the presentation and focus only on 'educating and convincing' the evaluators. This presentation should use diagrams, fact and figures, quotations and tables to support the arguments. It is also a good idea not to invite the audience from Step 1. Following this presentation, the researcher should revise the presentation and present it to some colleagues for further comment.
When? This should be done immediately after Step 1.

Step 3: First Draft of the One Page Proposal
At this stage, the researcher should prepare the first draft of the one page proposal. This will be the starting point of the discussion with National Contact Points and Potential Partners.
When? This is done when the call for proposals is published and researchers are starting to prepare their proposals.

Step 4: Refine the One Page Proposal during the writing of the proposal
During the writing of the proposal, it is important to continuously update the One Page Proposal based on new discussions and new directions. This is a useful tool to keep the partners focussed on the core elements of the proposal

Step 5: Convert the One Page Proposal into the Abstract
This is done at the very end of the proposal writing process. When all the documentation is completed, it is necessary to review the One Page Proposal and then use the information to write an abstract that explains the key points of the proposal. Remember this abstract will be used:
- to select the evaluators for the proposal
- as the first page the evaluator read in the proposal
- during the panel meeting it is the only description of the proposal available

Obviously this procedure only works if the researcher uses all the time available to write the proposal.

Chapter 7: Writing the Proposal

CONTENTS

The Time Schedule for the Proposal
Phases of the Proposal Writing Process
Agenda for the Consortium Meeting
Templates for Distribution of the Writing

Chapter Webpage: www.hyperion.ie/h2020-writingtheproposal.htm

Writing the Proposal

The aim of the chapter is to streamline the proposal writing process and to offer a practical approach in writing Horizon 2020 proposals. The approach is based on the author's experiences in over 150 proposals to the Framework Programmes since 1980.

Writing a proposal is a project. Like any project, it needs a project manager ("proposal manager"), it needs a plan, it has deadlines and it has deliverables. As a project, it must have quality control procedures. The methodology presented in this chapter is only one way of writing a proposal. Proposal writers use different models – from the chaotic to the systematic.

The important message is that the life of a researcher involves regular periods of proposal writing. It is vital that a researcher adopts and develops a methodology for writing proposals.

This chapter shows that there are three distinct phases - the planning, the preparation and the writing phases.

Planning
Planning is something that is done on a continuous basis. Whenever a researcher gets an idea for a new proposal, it should be documented in some format. When a draft work programme is published, these ideas can be revisited and partners can be contacted to discuss possible collaboration.

Preparing
The preparation phase is the most important part. This is when the idea is discussed in detail. It is also the most interesting part as new ideas are discussed and new scenarios and approaches are examined.

Writing
The writing phase is the most tedious part. If the planning and preparation are done well, the writing can be streamlined. However, there is always an intense period before the deadline when one individual has to compile the proposal. Researchers might find this difficult to believe, but there are individuals who love this phase. They are usually called research managers or consultants.

All projects suffer from one weakness – projects involve people. People vary in performance, respect for deadlines and temperament. This is why all plans must be flexible and subject to revision. It also highlights the importance of selecting researchers who are scientifically excellent but who can also work in teams and respect deadlines. The performance of researchers at the proposal phase is often an indicator of how they will work if the proposal is successful.

Time available to write a proposal

Figure 7.1 shows the time available for planning, preparing and writing a proposal. The Draft Work Programmes are published up to six months before the call for proposals. These drafts indicate the areas and topics that will be covered in the call. At this stage, researchers should start planning their proposals. This usually involves contacting potential partners and discussing possible proposal ideas.

When the call for proposals is published, this is the time to start preparing and writing the proposal. This chapter describes how to use the time between the call and the deadline.

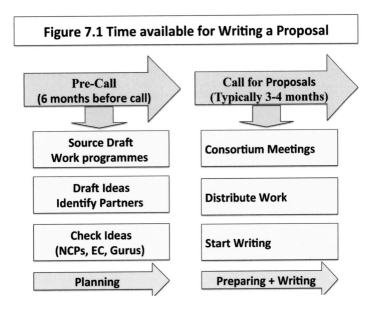

Draft Work Programmes Published

For 'bottom up' programmes (ERC, Marie Curie, FET, Innovation in SMEs), the researchers are free to submit any idea. During the planning phase, the focus is on identifying new ideas for proposals – or resubmitting previous proposals that were not successful.

For 'top down' programmes (Pillar II and Pillar III), planning should begin when the draft work programmes are published. Identifying relevant topics involves studying the work programmes. There are no short cuts to this process. In Horizon 2020, the work programmes cover periods of two years. This means, that for some topics, the researchers have up to two years advance notice.

During this period (pre-call), researchers meet to discuss possible proposals. These meetings are normally organised during conferences or as part of project meetings. This is also the period to attend workshops organised by the National Contact Points.

Who Prepares the Proposal?

The writing of a consortium proposal is structured according to Figure 7.2. The description in this section is the ideal scenario. In many cases, one partner writes the complete proposal - with other partners contributing little. This chapter shows how to efficiently distribute the writing of the proposal.

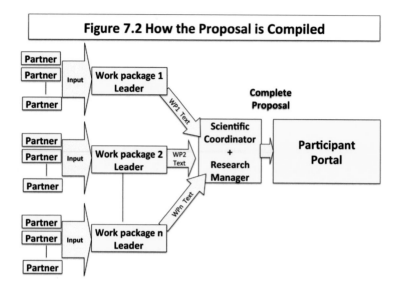

Figure 7.2 How the Proposal is Compiled

Scientific Coordinator

This is usually (but not always) the researcher who is promoting the idea for the proposal. In the proposal, this person is responsible for Part B1 (Excellence) and for selecting the scientific partners.

Research Manager

This person is responsible for compiling the proposal and the non-scientific parts of the proposal – especially the implementation section (B3). In some research centres, individuals are hired as 'Research Managers' and their work is to support the researchers. Sometimes they are referred to as 'Caddies' (from golf) or 'Sherpas' (from Mount Everest). Some consultancy firms provide professional services – either as paid consultancy or as a partner in the project.

Work Package Leaders

The project is divided into work packages (usually between six and nine work packages). A work package leader is responsible for the writing of the text describing the work package. The work package leaders are normally considered the 'core' partners in the project.

Partners

These are partners who are neither coordinators, research managers or work package leaders. For example, a project with 12 partners and nine work packages will have some partners who are not work package leaders. This is an ideal role for beginners in Horizon 2020 proposals.

A professor in a University in Dublin stated that she wrote two pages and received €380,000 euro for her role in a successful project. She was a work package leader with a very professional coordinator.

Table 7.1 Effort Needed to Write a Competitive Proposal

Project Phase	Average time spent by Coordinator	Average time spent by Work Package Leaders
Writing the Proposal	365 hours	80 hours
	48 days (7.5 hours per day)	

Table 7.1 was presented in the 2011 Annual Monitoring Report (Deloitte 2011). It estimates the time needed to prepare a European research proposal.

This table indicates that the coordinator and research managers spend 365 person hours preparing a proposal. Assuming 7.5 working hours per day, this is 48 days !

The work package leaders spend 80 person hours. Assuming that there are eight work packages this is approximately 10 hours per work package.

These are estimates. A consultant in Berlin (Dr. Susanne Rahner, Yggdrassel) keeps a time sheet when writing proposals. She presented the results of her recording at an EARMA (www.earma.eu) conference. The first proposal she coordinated needed 650 person hours (86 days !). She had to learn the procedures, forms and made many mistakes. Now, as an experienced coordinator, she estimates that it takes 350 person hours to prepare a proposal – close to the Commission's estimate.

However, Dr. Rahner also presented another interesting statistic. 45% of the effort in writing a proposal involved writing emails and especially delayed delivery (or non-delivery) of documentations by partners.

In the following sections, a plan will be presented to avoid these delays – by having more face to face meetings during the writing of the proposal.

Profile of a Professional Coordinator

The following are some of the criteria that must be considered when joining (or starting) a proposal:
- Does the coordinator have experience with previous Framework projects?
- Does the coordinator's organisation have excellent financial and legal experience to deal with all aspects of Horizon 2020 proposals/projects?
- Does the coordinator have personal contacts with the European Commission so that they can check the proposed idea?
- Has the coordinator received funding from their National Governments (or own organisation) to fund the writing of the proposal?
- Did the scientific coordinator evaluate Framework proposals in the past?
- Did the scientific coordinator participate in any European R&D networks, COST actions, Technology Platforms, Advisory groups?

Observation

If the idea is weak, nobody wants to be the coordinator or proposal writer. If the proposal idea is brilliant, and has a great chance of being funded, there will be a competition for the role of coordinator.

From the Call for Proposals to the Deadline

This section describes how organised coordinators write proposals. It describes, how, consortia who regularly win projects, prepare their proposals. It describes how some consultants support researchers in writing proposals.

The methodology is based on the concept presented in Chapter 4 (Evaluation) and repeated here in Figure 7.3. The preparation and writing of the proposals is divided into three steps; the one page proposal, the four page proposal and then the full proposal.

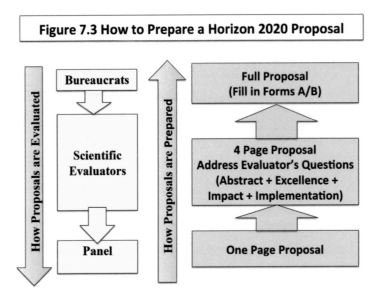

Figure 7.4 assumes that the period between the Call and the Deadline is twelve weeks. This period varies from twelve to sixteen weeks. Many researchers confuse 'preparing the proposal' with 'writing the text'. The writing part is easy if all the content is prepared beforehand.

In the following sections, the different steps will be presented.

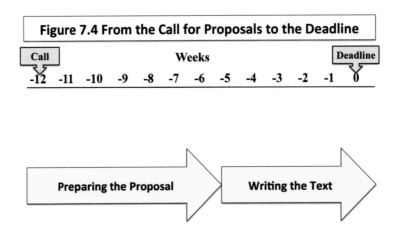

Call for Proposals Published

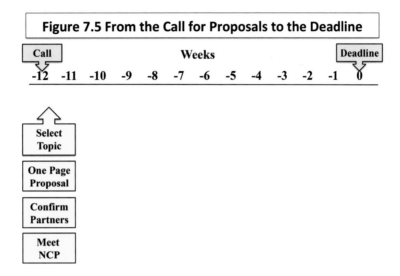

When the call for proposals is published, the researchers must re-read the topic as there can be changes between the draft and the official work programme. A single word can make a big difference e.g. photovoltaics versus photovoltaic systems.

Draft a One Page Proposal
The researcher who is promoting the idea should draft a one page proposal. This should be based on the discussions that were held before the call for proposals. It is a good idea to copyright the idea at this point by placing a copyright sign © at the footer of the page. There are several ways of declaring copyright. One is to have the document posted by registered post to the researcher's address. Do not open the letter. It is only useful in case proof of date is required in the future.

Contact Potential Partners
The researcher promoting the proposal should now contact all the potential partners and ask them to confirm two issues:
-    their willingness to participate in discussions on the proposal?
-    whether they are working on a competing proposal?
The email/letter should also request dates that suit the potential partners to meet and discuss the proposal.

Meet National Contact Points
Potential partners should meet their National Contact Points or attend any workshops on the programme that are held nationally. The aim of this is to collect as much information as possible about the call. Questions that should be asked at the events/meetings would be:
-    Will the standard evaluation criteria be used?
-    Will there be emphasis on any specific criteria? (e.g. impact)
-    Is there any emphasis on any region in Europe (e.g. South Eastern Europe)?
-    Is the topic selected for the proposal very competitive? This is based on experiences from previous calls for proposals.

Meeting with Project Officer of the European Commission
When the call for proposals is published, it is very difficult to meet with the relevant Project Officers. It is possible to meet Project Officers at official workshops held to promote the programme. These are usually held at national level. It is a good idea to ask all the partners whether they have personal contacts with Project Officers. For example, existing Coordinators of projects have direct contacts with the European Commission. Other examples would be experts on European research committees.

Consortium Meeting

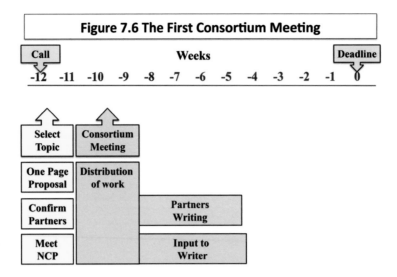

Figure 7.6 The First Consortium Meeting

It is very important to bring all the potential partners together to discuss the proposal. This meeting can identify those who are serious about the proposal and the discussion can be used to focus the proposed idea. Some consortia try to avoid this meeting by using Skype or other conferencing tools. These are useful as follow-on meetings but not for the initial meeting.

Duration of the first meeting?
The author has attended many of these meetings and they typically last one or two days. As most of the people attending the first meeting will be senior researchers, it is a good idea to limit it to a one day meeting – in a location that is accessible to everyone. The Nordic countries have a very nice model – the lunch to lunch meeting. Meet on day 1 at lunchtime. Discuss the proposal during the afternoon and evening dinner. Meet again on the following morning and finish at lunch time.

Where should the consortium meeting be held?
The most common meeting location is in Brussels. Most European Countries have national offices based in Brussels. (These can be found on www.iglortd.org). These National offices provide meeting rooms and may also be able to provide extra information on the call. In exceptional situations, they can invite a representative of the European Commission to the meeting. Other locations could be a place that is easily accessible (e.g. London) or the research base of the researcher promoting the idea.
Each partner is responsible for travel and accommodation costs during the writing of the proposal. Some countries (e.g. Ireland) provide a travel grant for researchers participating in proposals.

Who should be invited to the first meeting?
The researcher promoting the proposal usually decides who to invite. Researchers usually invite people from their own network of contacts. This will be discussed in detail in Chapter 8 (Where to find the best partners).

Preparation for the first meeting
It is important that the researcher promoting the idea prepares for the first meeting. The following section provides an agenda for the meeting. It is a good idea to prepare draft 'One Page Proposals' and Draft answers to the 'evaluators questions' to stimulate the debate.

Agenda for the Consortium Meeting

Item 1: Selection of the Work Programme Topic

In the case of 'top down' programmes, the partners must agree on which topic is most suitable for the proposed idea. In some meetings, the topic is first discussed – and then the researchers try to find an idea that fits the topic. It is better to have a brilliant idea and then find a topic than the other way around.

In some cases, an idea may fit into one or more topics. It is necessary to decide which topic is most suitable. Chapter 4 (Evaluation) showed a table indicating that there is a variation in the level of competition between different topics.

Item 2: Agree on the One Page Proposal

This is based on the agenda described in Chapter 6 (One Page Proposal). Normally, this discussion lasts over one hour. The One Page Proposal should be printed out and everyone must agree on it before proceeding. As the discussion progresses, the One Page Proposal should be continuously revised. This will eventually become the abstract of the proposal.

Item 3: The Evaluator's Questions

In each call for proposals, the documentation includes a description of the evaluation process and the evaluation criteria. This was described in Chapter 4 (Evaluation). A standard set of evaluation criteria is published. Extra criteria may be added to each call or emphasis may be placed on individual criteria (e.g. impact or implementation).
The criteria should be circulated before the meeting to all the participants. It is also a good idea for the coordinator to provide a Power Point presentation on possible arguments for each criteria.

In Chapter 4 (Evaluation), it was shown that the best approach to discussing the evaluation criteria would be:
> B2 Impact
> B1 Science
> B3 Implementation

This discussion could take several hours. It is the core activity of the first meeting. This information will be used to produce the four page proposal (abstract, excellence, impact and implementation).

Item 4: The Plan for Writing the Proposal

The first consortium meeting should be held 10 weeks before the deadline. On the following page, a template is presented identifying the different tasks to be completed and the deadlines.

Item 5: The Writing Team

One individual is selected to write the text. This is usually the researcher promoting the proposal – or one of the researcher's team. It is a good idea that one person has overall responsibility for the proposal. Many will contribute but one will be responsible for the final submission.

The Plan, developed in Item 4, lists the organisations that are responsible for each part of the proposals. This section should indicate who exactly will write the different sections.

Item 6: Review of the Proposal before Submission

It is a good idea that individuals are asked to review the proposal before it is submitted. These should be people who are not involved in the writing of the proposal ('fresh eyes'). Table 7.4 includes a list of possible people who could be invited to review the proposal.

Table 7.2 Division of Work (Horizon 2020 Proposals)

Job to be done	Responsible Person	Deadline
Overall responsibility for submission of the proposal		
PART A		
Acknowledgement of receipt form		
Form A1: Summary		
Form A2: Partner details	Each partner	
Project Effort form		
Form A3: Summary of costs		
PART B		
1. Scientific and/or technical quality relevant to call		
1.1 Concepts and objectives		
1.2 Progress beyond the state- of- the- art		
1.3 S/T methodology and associated work-plan		
2. Impact		
2.1 Expected Impacts		
2.2 Dissemination of project results		
Exploitation of project results		
Management of intellectual property		
3. Implementation		
3.1 Management Structure and procedures		
3.1a Work-package List		
3.1b Deliverables List		
3.1c Description of each work-package	WP Leaders	
3.2a List of Milestones		
3.2b Critical Tasks		
3.5a Summary effort table		
Gantt Chart	Manager	
Pert Chart		
3.2 Individual Participants	Each partner	
3.3 Consortium as a whole		
Subcontractors?		
International Partners?		
Future additional partners?		
3.4 Resources to be committed		
Cost		
Other sources of income for the work		
4. Ethical Issues		
5. Consideration of gender aspects		
6. Security Issues		

Note: This is a template to help in writing the proposal. It is NOT part of the proposal.

Table 7.3 Division of Scientific Work

Work Package	Work package Name	Writer	*Contributors to the Work package*
WP1			
WP2			
WP3			
WP4			
WP5			
WP6			
WP7			
WP8			
WP9			

Table 7.4 Experts to review the proposal

Document	Name of Expert	Organisation	*Who will contact them?*
Proposal Summary		National Contact Point	*Coordinator*
Proposal Summary		National Delegates	
Full Proposal		Consultant	
B1 Excellence		Scientific Expert	
B2 Impact		Lead User	
B3 Implementation		Research Manager	
Financial Part A		Financial Expert	
Pre-screening		Proposal reviewers	
Proof reading		Science Writer	

These tables can be downloaded as a Word file on www.hyperion.ie/divisionofwork.doc

Note: This is a template to help in writing the proposal. It is NOT part of the proposal.

The Four Page Proposal

In Chapter 4 (Evaluation) the evaluation criteria used by the Evaluators was presented. It described how the evaluators agreed the scores in the 'Consensus Reports'. At this stage of the proposal writing process (seven weeks before the deadline), the partners should agree on the 'four page proposal'.

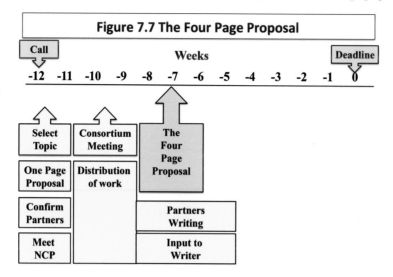

Figure 7.7 The Four Page Proposal

Structure of the Four Page Proposal

Abstract (One Page)
This should be written in the format outlined in Chapter 6 (One Page Proposal). It should also follow the guidelines i.e. number of words.
- It will be used to select the evaluators for the proposal
- It will be the first text the (tired) evaluator will read
- During the panel meeting, it will be the only document describing the project

B1: Excellence (One Page)
This page will be the first page of B1 in the proposal. It will be the first page the evaluator will read and it should convey the most important scientific points. This has to be perfect. It should be revised and revised until the message is convincing. This is when proposals based on weak ideas or with weak science will die.

B2: Impact (One Page)
Many evaluators are confused with the concept of 'impact'. This one page must be written in journalistic style and must both educate and convince the evaluator of the potential impact of the proposals. This should be based on the information provided in Chapter 5 (Impact).

B3: Quality of the Implementation (One Page)
This one page must provide a simple and convincing description of the plan to implement the project. As this will be the first page of B3 in the proposal, it must present the key messages of the plan. These are described in Chapter 9 (Implementation).

This is a critical stage in the preparation of the proposal. If the partners are totally convinced with the arguments in the four page proposal, they should proceed to the next stage. If the partners are not convinced, two options must be considered: revise the four pages or terminate the proposal.
If the partners decide to proceed, the four page proposal should be continuously updated as the writing proceeds. They will eventually be the first pages that the evaluator will read in each section of the final proposal.

NOTE: the four page proposal is NOT part of the formal submission of the proposal. It is a tool to streamline the writing of the proposal.

All Inputs from the Partners

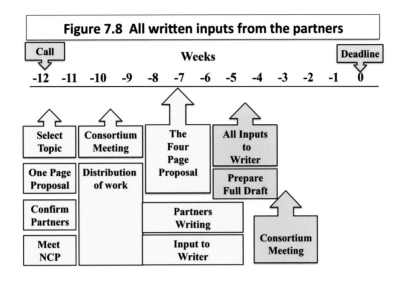

Figure 7.8 All written inputs from the partners

Five weeks before the deadline, the proposal writer should have all inputs from the partners. At this point, the first draft of the proposal can be circulated to the partners.

Final Consortium Meeting

Four weeks before the deadline, a meeting of the consortium should be held. The most important partners at this meeting are the work package leaders. This is a critical meeting. The agenda of this meeting is very simple. The coordinator or proposal writer reads the proposal page by page and welcomes comments. Any comments must be sent by email during the meeting. Some consortia hold this meeting online. The author always organised a meeting where partners sat around a table.

A suggested format would be the following:

Abstract
Title: Any comments
Paragraph 1: Introduction. The proposal writer reads the paragraph and welcomes comments
Paragraph 2: Background. Same as above
Etc.

B1 Scientific Excellence
B1: Paragraph 1: The proposal writer reads the paragraph and welcomes comments.
B1: Paragraph 2: etc.
Etc.

This might sound tedious but it is the most efficient way of reviewing the proposal. It is also providing the partners with an opportunity to study the text and identify additions to the proposal. It also gets rid of the hundreds of emails that are normally associated with proposal writing.

At the end of this workshop, the proposal writer will have many comments on the draft proposals. The writer should also have all the emails sent by the partners during the meeting. This information allows the writer to spend the following weeks compiling the final proposals.

Writing and Reviewing the Text

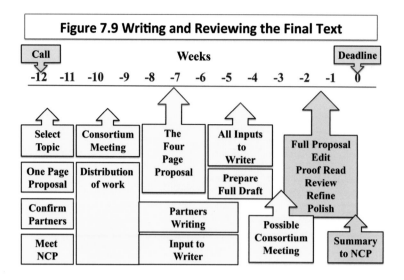

Figure 7.9 Writing and Reviewing the Final Text

Final Preparation of the Proposal

During the final weeks before the deadline, the proposal writer will complete the proposal. This period focusses on refining the document, the layout and presentation. It is an intensive writing period for the proposal writers. A person who has not been involved in the proposal should be asked to review the proposal.

During this period, some research centres organise a full evaluation of the proposal – involvingthree experienced evaluators, a consensus meeting and the preparation of an Evaluation Summary Report. This is then used to further improve the proposal

When the complete proposal is submitted, it is a good idea that all the partners send a summary of the proposal to the relevant National Contact Points. The summary should use the One Page Proposal format.

The plan for reviewers that was prepared 10 weeks before the deadline can now be implemented.

Table 7.4 Experts to be consulted on the proposal

Document	Name of Expert	Organisation	*Who will contact them?*
Proposal Summary		National Contact Point	*Coordinator*
Proposal Summary		National Delegates	
Full Proposal		Consultant	
B1 Excellence		Scientific Expert	
B2 Impact		Lead User	
B3 Implementation		Research Manager	
Financial Part A		Financial Expert	
Pre-screening		Proposal reviewers	
Proof reading		Science Writer	

Chapter 8: Where to find the Best Partners

CONTENTS

Who can participate?
Categories of Partners
The role of Small and Medium Sized Enterprises
Where to find the 'Best Partners'
A Strategy for Beginners

Chapter Webpage: www.hyperion.ie/h2020-partners.htm

Introduction

Some research organisations appear to be like magnets for EU Framework funding – and others may submit several proposals and not receive a single grant. It is not favouritism on the part of the European Commission. The research organisations that are successful in EU Framework Programmes have excellent scientists and their scientists are active in science policy, science promotion and commercialisation of scientific results. This chapter presents a profile of research organisations that are successful in the EU Framework Programmes. The profile could be helpful as a basis for promoting a researcher at European level – and in finding the best partners for the consortium.

Two issues are considered in this chapter:
- Where to find suitable partners based on their expertise and ability to work in a consortium (Professionalism)
- Which type of partner (University, Company..) and geographical locations are allowed to participate (Rules)

The Profile of Professional Partners

Selecting partners is the single most important task when planning a proposal for Horizon 2020. The researchers, who are continuously successful in the Framework Programmes, are excellent scientists – but they do more than science. They work as 'experts' with the Commission, they are members of European Research Associations, they participate actively in conferences and they contribute to technical standards. These are researchers who realise that writing proposals is only part of the process.

Criteria for selecting individuals for projects:

- Trust and respect between partners. This is why many successful consortia consist of a core group of researchers who have developed a level of trust over many years of cooperation. For beginners, this means that a period of networking and demonstrating expertise and professionalism is necessary before being invited into high level consortia;
- Scientific Excellence based on proven track record and reputation;
- Capacity to undertake the work proposed in the project;
- Timely delivery of documents during the proposal writing. Remember participation in a proposal is an opportunity to impress future partners. Delayed and low standard documentation can ruin a researcher's reputation;
- Understanding the bureaucratic processes of the European Commission;
- Willingness to work in a team (consortium). Many researchers prefer to work alone;
- Personal traits. Good personality and ability to add enthusiasm to the team.

Many researchers do not participate in European projects, mainly because they have sufficient funding at national level. It is necessary to identify researchers who are willing to work on European projects. The following is a list of sources. The links to these sources can be found on www.hyperion.ie/h2020-partners.htm

Where to find Partners

Existing Framework partners (and especially Coordinators)
It is important to identify the researchers that are already receiving EU R&D contracts in a scientific area. In particular, the coordinators of the contracts must be identified.
Funded projects can be found on the Participant Portal

EU R&D Associations
Many research sectors have established EU Research Associations to communicate their priorities to the European Commission. The European Commission works closely with these associations.
Website: www.hyperion.ie/euassociations.htm.

COST Actions
COST is an initiative funded by Horizon 2020. COST does not fund research. COST funds the bringing together of national researchers. According to the COST website, over 30,000 researchers meet annually at conferences and workshops.
Website: http://www.cost.eu/

Technology Platforms
The Technology Platforms (described in Chapter 2) are used by industry to identify the research challenges that will face European enterprises over the coming years. They are ideal sources of partners for Horizon 2020 projects.
Website: www.hyperion.ie/technology-platforms.htm

EU Funded Conferences and Workshops
The European Commission funds conferences and workshops that are relevant to the research priorities. These conferences are used to promote the results from the Framework Programmes and they have an input to the design of future work programmes.
Website: http://ec.europa.eu/research/conferences/index_en.cfm

European Research Infrastructures
The European Commission funds 'European Research Infrastructures' as part of the Framework programmes. These are very rare, expensive and important research laboratories in Europe. These laboratories receive funding so that researchers can access the facilities free of charge. Researchers from these laboratories make excellent partners for Horizon 2020 projects as the Commission has already identified their organisations as exceptional centres.
Website: http://cordis.europa.eu/infrastructures/projects.htm

Technical Standards Committees
Many European researchers participate on Standards 'Technical Committees.' The Standards bodies identify areas where new standards are required or where scientific data ('factual data') is needed to support the standards. Researchers involved in these committees make excellent project partners as they provide an important route for exploiting the results through standards.
Website: www.cenorm.be

Evaluators from the Framework Programmes
The European Commission publishes the names of the researchers who act as 'Expert Evaluators' for the Framework Programmes. These researchers are also good partners as they understand the evaluation process.
Website: http://cordis.europa.eu/fp7/experts.htm

Partner Search Service

A partner search service where researchers can input their details and hope that some consortium will invite them into proposals. This service could be used to find partners with a specific skill.

Networks of National Contact Points (e.g. Ideal-ist)

The National Contact Points have established networks. An example is the ICT network – Ideal-ist. This is a search engine designed to find partners for the ICT programme. It circulates proposal ideas that are looking for specific skills. Researchers can put their details in the system and receive regular updates.
Website: www.ideal-ist.net

Writers of EU Reports and Studies

The European Union produces thousands of 'policy documents'. They often use scientific experts to prepare these documents. These researchers are normally listed in the Annex of the reports.
Website: http://europa.eu/geninfo/query/advSearch_en.jsp

By analysing all of the above websites, researchers can easily compile a list of the key European researchers in each scientific field. Note that the same ten or fifteen names will appear regularly in the different activities outlined above. These are usually the best partners.

How many partners in a project?

In Horizon 2020, a 'partner' is any legal entity - any organisation that is legally registered. This includes research centres, universities, enterprises, non-governmental organisations etc. The European Commission only signs contracts with legal entities.

The Rules of Participation state that "*at least three legal entities must participate, each of which must be established in a Member State or associated country, and no two of which may be established in the same Member State or associated country.*"

Exceptions specified in the work programme.

- Some Coordination and Support Actions (CSA) can have one partner. This will be specified in the call for proposals.

- Marie Skłodowska-Curie Fellowships. The individual fellowship involves only the Host. Some Marie Skłodowska-Curie Networks could involve a single partner.

- ERC projects have only one partner (except Synergy projects)

- International Cooperation projects need two partners from the Member States/associated countries and two partners from the ICPC Countries. In the case of large ICPC countries (e.g. China), partners from two regions are accepted.

- If a number of organisations form a legally binding 'Group' that meets the minimum criteria then the 'Group' may act as a sole participant in the project.

These definitions can be found in the *Rules of Participation*

Which Countries can participate in Horizon 2020?

The list of countries that may participate in Horizon 2020 is defined in Annex A of the General Annexes. It also presents the terminology used in the definition of countries. During Horizon 2020, some of these rules may change.

The 28 Member States of the European Union (MS)

Austria, Belgium, Croatia, Denmark, Finland, France, Germany, Greece, Italy, Ireland, Luxembourg, Portugal, Spain, Sweden, The Netherlands, United Kingdom, Poland, Hungary, Slovakia, Czech Republic, Slovenia, Malta, Latvia, Lithuania, Estonia, Bulgaria, Romania, Cyprus.

The Associated Countries (AC)

These are countries that make a financial contribution to Horizon 2020. Research organisations from these countries participate in Horizon 2020 under the same conditions as research organisations from the Member States.

- **Associated Countries that have an International Agreement with the EU**
  Norway, Liechtenstein, Iceland, Israel and Faroe Islands
- **Switzerland** has a bilateral agreement with the European Union
- **The Associate Candidate Countries** Turkey, Serbia, FYROM (Former Yugoslav Republic of Macedonia), Montenegro, Albania, Bosnia-Herzegovina, Moldova. (This list may expand during Horizon 2020)

Third Countries

A Third Country is a country that is not a Member State of the European Union. Therefore, by using this European Commission definition, the United States of America is classified as a 'Third Country.' The Third Countries that can receive funding from Horizon 2020 are:

International Cooperation Partner Countries (ICPC)

- **Developing Economies:** Africa, Pacific, Asia, Latin America
- **Emerging Economies:** Mexico and South Africa
- **Mediterranean Partner Countries (MPC):** Algeria, Egypt, Jordan, Lebanon, Libya, Morocco, Palestine administered areas, Syrian Arab Republic, Tunisia
- **Eastern European and Central Asian Countries (EECA):** Armenia, Azerbaijan, Belarus, Georgia, Kazakhstan, Kyrgyz Republic, Moldova, Russia, Tajikistan, Turkmenistan, Ukraine and Uzbekistan

(This list may change during Horizon 2020)

ERC Proposals: The Host of the Frontier Research grant (ERC) must be based in an EU/Associated Country but there is no regulation governing the nationality of the team members.

EU Scientific Co-operation Agreements http://ec.europa.eu/research/iscp/index_en.cfm

The EU has scientific cooperation agreements with USA, Canada, Argentina, South Africa, Australia, China, India, Russia, Chile, Mexico, Ukraine and Brazil. These agreements define the scientific areas where the European Union would like to cooperate.
"The level of cooperation is such that around 20% of the projects funded by FP7 include at least one international partner in its consortium. Around 5.4% of all FP7 participants come from 'third countries', with the top five sources being Russia, the USA, China, India and South Africa.
Source: Commissioner Maire Geoghegan Quinn 2013

USA, Canada and Australia

The European Union has signed Scientific Cooperation Agreements with USA, Canada and Australia. Research organisations from these countries CAN participate in Horizon 2020 under the following conditions:

- They do not receive funding from Horizon 2020 – they receive funding from their own national programmes.
- They participate on a 'project by project' basis.

Exceptions:

Research organisations from USA, Canada and Australia can receive funding from Horizon 2020 if:

- They can show that their expertise is not available in Europe or that their expertise is essential to the project
- If it is specified in the work programme or in the bilateral agreement between the EU and the country.

Note: Microsoft (Germany), IBM (Zurich) and Intel (Ireland) are European companies and participate as German, Swiss and Irish partners.

The Joint Research Centres http://ec.europa.eu/dgs/jrc/

The European Commission has seven research institutes of its own, known as the Joint Research Centres (JRC). The JRC Website states that '*The JRC supports policy makers in the conception, development, implementation and monitoring of policies.*'

These research centres are located in five different sites throughout the EU (Belgium, Germany, Italy, The Netherlands and Spain). Even though they are part of the European Commission, they can participate as partners in Horizon 2020 projects. If the grant is awarded, the Commission makes payments to the Joint Research Centre directly (not through the coordinator as with other partners).

The Joint Research Centres are:

- Institute for Reference Materials and Measurement (IRMM)
- Institute for Transuranium Elements (ITU)
- Institute for Energy (IE)
- Institute for the Protection and Security of the Citizen (IPSC)
- Institute for Environment and Sustainability (IES)
- Institute for Health and Consumer Protection (IHCP)
- Institute for Prospective Technological Studies (IPTS)

International Organisations (e.g. World Health Organisation, UNESCO, FAO)

International organisations can participate in Horizon 2020, if it can be shown that their participation is essential to the objectives of the proposal. The rules of participation are either based on an agreement between the Commission and the organisation or the rules of the country in which the organisation is located.

European International Organisations www.eiroforum.org

These are organisations that are established as European Research Centres. They include:

- CERN (http://welcome.cern.ch/welcome/gateway.html)
- EMBL (www.embl.org)
- ESA (www.esa.org)
- EUREKA (www.eureka.be)
- ILL (www.ill.fr)
- ESO (www.eso.org)
- ENO (www.eno.org).

Small and Medium Sized Enterprises

Definition of an SME

An SME is defined as a company with less than 250 employees, less than 40 million euro annual turnover and no more than 25% equity by a non-SME. The definition can be seen on:
http://ec.europa.eu/enterprise/enterprise_policy/sme_definition/decision_sme_en.pdf

SMEs in the European Union

SMEs represent over 99% of all EU enterprises and 66% of total EU employment.
SMEs receive special attention in Horizon 2020. There are four categories of Enterprises in Horizon 2020 and these are shown in Table 6.2.

Table 6.2 Categories of SMEs and their Roles in Horizon 2020 Projects

Category	Role in Horizon 2020	Research Activities	Programme
High Research Intensive Sectors (Biotechnology, Aerospace Information Technology)	Technology Provider Lead Users of results	In-house research	Pillar II Pillar III TRL 5 to TRL 9
High Technology Sector (Materials, Machinery, Services to Industry)	Lead Users of Results	In-house research Outsource non-core research	Pillar II Pillar III (TRL 7,8,9)
Low Technology Intensive Sectors (Agro-Industry, Textile, non-technical services)	End Users of Results/ Training/ Dissemination	Outsource all research	No Opportunities
No Technology Sectors	New Knowledge	None	No Opportunities

Research intensive sectors represent only 3% of European Enterprises. The Low Technology Sectors and the No Technology Sector represent over 90% of enterprises in Europe.

Rules of Participation
The Rules defining the participation of different organisations are printed below (verbatim).

Article 8 Independence
1. Two legal entities shall be regarded as independent of each other where neither is under the direct or indirect control of the other or under the same direct or indirect control as the other.
2. For the purposes of paragraph 1, control may, in particular, take either of the following forms:
(a) the direct or indirect holding of more than 50 % of the nominal value of the issued share capital in the legal entity concerned, or of a majority of the voting rights of the shareholders or associates of that entity;
(b) the direct or indirect holding, in fact or in law, of decision-making powers in the legal entity concerned.
3. For the purposes of paragraph 1, the following relationships between legal entities shall not in themselves be deemed to constitute controlling relationships:
(a) the same public investment corporation, institutional investor or venture-capital company has a direct or indirect holding of more than 50 % of the nominal value of the issued share capital or a majority of voting rights of the shareholders or associates;
(b) the legal entities concerned are owned or supervised by the same public body.

Article 9 Conditions for participation
The following minimum conditions shall apply:
(a) at least three legal entities shall participate in an action;
(b) three legal entities shall each be established in a different Member State or associated country; and
(c) the three legal entities referred to in point (b) shall be independent of each other within the meaning of Article 8.
2. For the purposes of paragraph 1, where one of the participants is the JRC, or an international European interest organisation or an entity created under Union law, it shall be deemed to be established in a Member State or associated country other than any Member State or associated country in which another participant in the same action is established.
3. By way of derogation from paragraph 1, the minimum condition shall be the participation of one legal entity established in a Member State or associated country, in the case of:
(a) European Research Council (ERC) frontier research actions;
(b) the SME instrument, where the action has a clear European added value;
(c) programme co-fund actions; and
(d) justified cases provided for in the work programme or work plan.
4. By way of derogation from paragraph 1, in the case of coordination and support actions and training and mobility actions, the minimum condition shall be the participation of one legal entity.
5. Where appropriate and duly justified, work programmes or work plans may provide for additional conditions according to specific policy requirements or to the nature and objectives of the action, including inter alia conditions regarding the number of participants, the type of participant and the place of establishment.

Article 10 Eligibility for funding
1. The following participants are eligible for funding from the Union:
(a) any legal entity established in a Member State or associated country, or created under Union law;
(b) any international European interest organisation;
(c) any legal entity established in a third country identified in the work programme.

2. In the case of a participating international organisation or in the case of a participating legal entity established in a third country, neither of which are eligible for funding according to paragraph 1, funding from the Union may be granted provided that at least one of the following conditions is fulfilled:
(a) the participation is deemed essential for carrying out the action by the Commission or the relevant funding body;
(b) such funding is provided for under a bilateral scientific and technological agreement or any other arrangement between the Union and the international organisation or, for entities established in third countries, the country in which the legal entity is established.

Chapter 9: How to Write the Quality and Efficiency of the Implementation

CONTENTS

Overview of Implementation Plan

Work plan

Management structure and procedures

Operational capacity of individual participants

Consortium as a whole

Resources to be committed

Chapter Webpage: www.hyperion.ie/h2020-implementation.htm

B3.1 Work plan

The following is an example of text from a call. The exact text may vary between actions and between calls for proposals. The exact text will be defined in each call.

3.1 Work plan — Work packages, deliverables and milestones
Please provide the following:
- *brief presentation of the overall structure of the work plan;*
- *timing of the different work packages and their components (Gantt chart or similar);*
- *detailed work description, i.e.:*
- *graphical presentation of the components showing how they inter-relate (Pert chart or similar).*
  - *a description of each work package (table 3.1a);*
  - *a list of work packages (table 3.1b);*
  - *a list of major deliverables (table 3.1c);*

Give full details. Base your account on the logical structure of the project and the stages in which it is to be carried out. Include details of the resources to be allocated to each work package. The number of work packages should be proportionate to the scale and complexity of the project.

You should give enough detail in each work package to justify the proposed resources to be allocated and also quantified information so that progress can be monitored, including by the Commission.

You are advised to include a distinct work package on 'management' (see section 3.2) and to give due visibility in the work plan to 'dissemination and exploitation' and 'communication activities', either with distinct tasks or distinct work packages.

You will be required to include an updated (or confirmed) 'plan for the dissemination and exploitation of results' in both the periodic and final reports. (This does not apply to topics where a draft plan was not required.) This should include a record of activities related to dissemination and exploitation that have been undertaken and those still planned. A report of completed and planned communication activities will also be required.

If your project is taking part in the Pilot on Open Research Data4, you must include a 'data management plan' as a distinct deliverable within the first 6 months of the project. A template for such a plan is given in the guidelines on data management in the H2020 Online Manual. This deliverable will evolve during the lifetime of the project in order to present the status of the project's reflections on data management.

Evaluation Criteria for the Quality of Implementation

Experts will indicate whether the participants meet the selection criterion related to the operational capacity, to carry out the proposed work, based on competence and experience of the individual participant(s);

Coherence and effectiveness of the work plan, including appropriateness of the allocation of tasks and resources;

Complementarity of the participants within the consortium (when relevant);

Appropriateness of the management structures and procedures, including risk and innovation management.

(These evaluation criteria may change during Horizon 2020)

The success of any project depends on the science, the work plan and the implementation of the work. This chapter describes how to write the 'Implementation' (Part B 3). Templates for all of these diagrams can be found on www.hyperion.ie/templates.htm. This Chapter focusses on the Pillar II and Pillar III proposals.

Comments by Evaluators on Implementation

The following are comments from Evaluation Summary Reports (ESR)

...the allocation of the resources is not clear

The use of resources is overestimated and some of the claimed consumables of the partners are not sufficiently justified

The overall project management is inadequate and no management work package is planned in the work plan

There is no methodology for monitoring and reporting progress,

Conflict resolution and decision making mechanism are not convincing.

The contribution of the coordinating SME to the leadership of most work packages and to most key activities may be a risk for the project; this may limit the other partners' involvement in the project. Two partners do not appear in the work plan.

The experience in the leadership of European projects of the co-ordinator is not sufficiently presented.

The allocation of resources for demonstration activities is overestimated.

No mechanisms for conflict resolution seem to be in place

The proposal does not show a strong interest and commitment of the participating SMEs and it looks as if the RTD performers are in the driver's seat rather than the SME participants.

A far bigger project is needed to guarantee the success and achievement of all deliverables.

...the data presented in the proposal is not sufficient or in some cases erroneous (financial) information (refers to another project) is provided.

The individual participant description is very short and some participants are missing

Scientific Skills and Partners

The first diagram that should be drawn when planning the work is a description of the skills needed in the project and a list of partners undertaking the different tasks. Some proposals use a 'Skills Matrix' (Skills versus Partners). Figure 9.1 is an example of the skills needed in an 'eLearning' proposal. This diagram clearly shows the different skills and technologies that are needed in the project and how they are integrated. It also shows the roles of the partners.

Figure 9.1 Skills and Partners in the Project

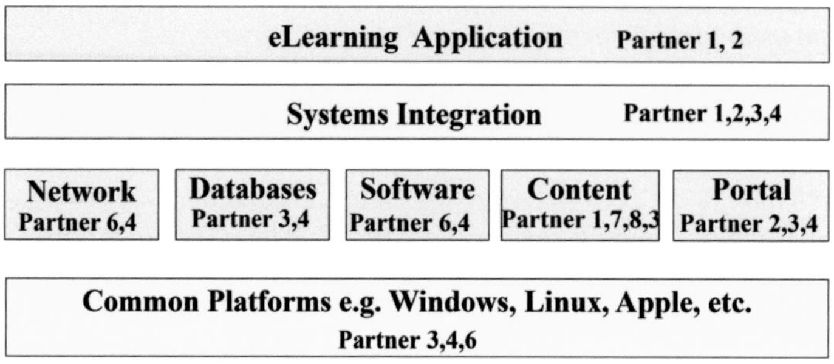

eLearning Application	Partner 1, 2

Systems Integration	Partner 1,2,3,4

Network Partner 6,4	Databases Partner 3,4	Software Partner 6,4	Content Partner 1,7,8,3	Portal Partner 2,3,4

Common Platforms e.g. Windows, Linux, Apple, etc.
Partner 3,4,6

Work Breakdown Structure

The Work Breakdown Structure (WBS) describes the division of the project into work packages. The work packages can be sub-divided into 'tasks' and the 'tasks' should be built around the deliverables. Figure 9.2 shows a template that can be used to illustrate this breakdown. The topics are organised into logical work packages.

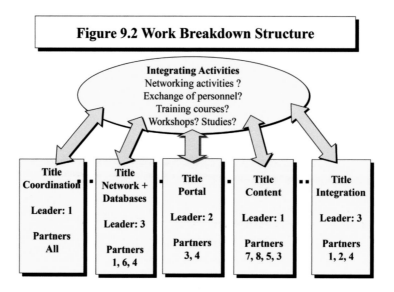

Figure 9.2 Work Breakdown Structure

The PERT Chart

The links between the work packages can be seen on the PERT (Programme Evaluation and Review Techniques) Chart. This is the most important diagram when describing the management of a project. Figure 9.3 shows the relationship between the work packages.

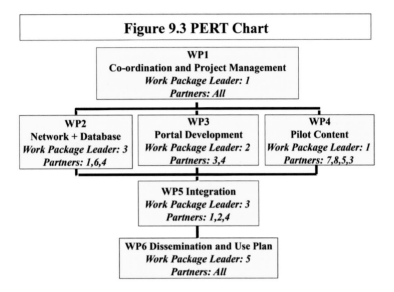

Figure 9.3 PERT Chart

Rules for PERT Charts

- The division of the work must be logical. It must also be clear that the focus of the management is on the Work packages and Deliverables.
- The guideline specifies that there should be a Work package on 'Coordination and Management' (not necessarily Work package 1).
- The guideline specifies a Work Package for Exploitation or Dissemination.
- The Leader of each work package and the partners involved (in order of priority) should be identified.

Evaluation of the Pert Chart

- If all partners are in all work packages then, it is obvious, that the distribution of work was not discussed.
- If there is only one partner per work package, it will appear as six small projects under the umbrella of one project (not a good idea).
- If one partner is involved in everything, this partner may have underestimated the work involved – usually a beginner. Consider Partner 3 in Figure 9.3. This partner is leading two work packages and is involved in every work package. This is not wise.
- Ideal: Each partner should lead one work package and be involved in two others. This is not a strict rule, but it is a good 'rule of thumb'. It helps to focus partners on a small number of integrated tasks rather than a range of small unrelated tasks. (Partner No. 5).
- Floating partners! Consider Partner Number 4 in Figure 9.3. Partner 4 does not lead any work package and is the least important partner in most work packages. In fact, Partner Number 4 is floating. These people can join a project for three years and contribute very little. The evaluators are always searching for these partners. Partner No. 4 could be a very experienced scientist. If this is the case, then his/her low input into the project must be explained.

The Gantt Chart

The Gantt Chart defines the time scales for the different work packages. An example (from a different project) is presented in Figure 9.4. This can be drawn using Excel. (www.hyperion.ie/templates.htm).

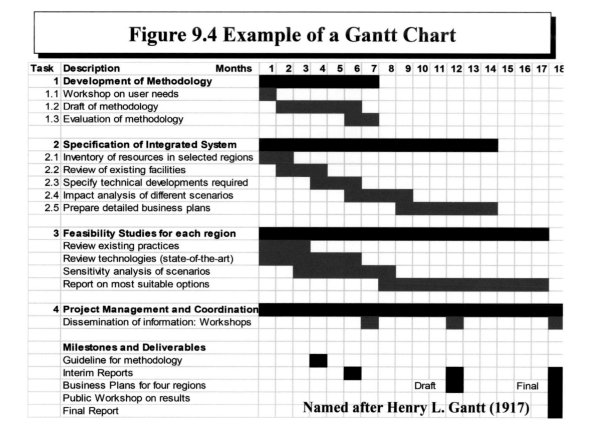

Figure 9.4 Example of a Gantt Chart

Tables in Part B3 of the Proposal

Using the diagrams from the previous pages, it is now possible to complete the tables presented in Part B3 of the proposal. The diagrams shown above (or the descriptions presented) should match the tables shown in the following pages.

Table 3.1a Work Package Description

Each work package from the PERT Chart must be described in the following format.

Table 3.1a Work Package Description

Work Package No		Start date or starting event:											
Work Package Title													
Participant Number													
Person-months per participant													

Objectives

Description of Work (where appropriate, broken down into tasks), lead partner and role of participants

Deliverables (Brief description and month of delivery)

It is very important to put effort into the final layout of the document. It should look professional. This extra effort should make it easy for the evaluator to understand the management plans of the proposal.

If the proposal is accepted, these tables will be very important in the negotiation of the grant agreement. The final grant agreement will include tables 3.1a.

Deliverables: A good tip is to have one Major Deliverable and one Minor Deliverable. This is not an official rule or guideline but a practical one.

The European Commission has refined this table over 23 years of running the Framework Programmes. It is a very logical table and could be used in any research (or commercial) project.

Table 3.1b Work Package List

Table 3.1b is a summary of the work packages.

Table 3.1b Work Package List

No. (1)	Work Package Title	Lead Participant Short Name	Person months	Start Month	End Month

Information that must be transferred from the Pert Chart to the Work Package List

1. Work package number (WP1 to WPn)

2. Work package title (Titles from Work Breakdown Structure and Pert Chart)

3. Type of Activity:
    RTD: Research and Technological Development
    DEM: Demonstration
    REP: First market replication
    MGT: Management
    PDE: Activities to prepare for the dissemination and/or exploitation
    OTHER: Other activities specified in Call

4. Lead Participant (From PERT Chart) – leading the work package

5. Total number of person months allocated to each work package (Details of the 'Person months' can be found in Table 3.1c)

6. Start Month and End Month (These are found in the Gantt Chart)

Table 3.1c Deliverables List

In Horizon 2020, 'Deliverables' are the 'payment criteria'. In Table 3.1c, the Commission is asking that the 'payment criteria' for the project be defined. In Horizon 2020 projects, there are two types of deliverables. The 'Grant Deliverables', such as the annual reports, are specified in the grant agreement. Secondly, the 'Scientific (or Project) Deliverables' are produced in the project. Table 3.1c is a list of the 'Scientific (or Project) Deliverables'. A rule of thumb should be, one major deliverable and one minor deliverable per work package. Each deliverable should be linked to a 'task'.

Table 3.1c List of Deliverables

No. (1)	Deliverables Name	WP No.	Lead Partner	Type	Dissemination Level	Delivery Date

Deliverable No: 1.1 = Deliverable 1 from Work package 1
WP No: Work package Number (from Table 3.1a)
Type: R=Document, report (excluding periodic and final reports)
    DEM: Demonstrator, pilot, prototype, plan designs
    DEC: Websites, patent filing, press and media actions, videos etc.
    Other: Software, technical diagram, etc.
Dissemination Level: PU=Public, CO=Confidential CI= Classified
Delivery Date: Month 1 = start of project

Defining Deliverables

It is important to have clearly defined deliverables. The European Commission likes to have reports as deliverables. For example, if a workshop is organised, the workshop report should be the deliverable. If a prototype sensor was developed, the deliverable would be a report on the performance of the sensor.

Avoid specifying a scientific target as a deliverable. As the research progresses, it may be discovered that the scientific targets cannot be met.

For example in the following project the researchers specified that the consortium would develop *"a sensor that would measure hydrocarbons in water to an accuracy of 20 parts per billion."* Half way through the project, the partners realised that the target of *20 parts per billion* was unrealistic. They had to revise the agreement to change the deliverable. It would have been better if the deliverable had been described as *"150 hours scientific data to assess the accuracy of the sensor in parts per billion."* (In this instance, the 150 hours test is realistic and achievable).

Think SMART **(Specific, Measurable, Achievable, Realistic Targets).**

3.2 Management Structure and Procedures

- *Describe the organisational structure and the decision-making (including a list of milestones (table 3.2a))*
- *Explain why the organisational structure and decision-making mechanisms are appropriate to the complexity and scale of the project.*
- *Describe, where relevant, how effective innovation management will be addressed in the management structure and work plan.*
  Innovation management is a process which requires an understanding of both market and technical problems, with a goal of successfully implementing appropriate creative ideas. A new or improved product, service or process is its typical output. It also allows a consortium to respond to an external or internal opportunity.
- *Describe any critical risks, relating to project implementation, that the stated project's objectives may not be achieved. Detail any risk mitigation measures. Please provide a table with critical risks identified and mitigating actions (table 3.2b)*

Figure 9.5 shows a possible structure for a **large** project consortium. The *Scientific Committee* includes the names of the scientists representing the different partner organisations. The *Management Group* lists the consortium manager and the managers of the work packages. The *Advisory Board* is made up of senior personnel from the partner organisations, external experts and may include the scientific officer of the project (European Commission). In the Consortium Agreements on www.iprhelpdesk.eu, all of the roles are defined and rules of operation are proposed. This is the best source for descriptions of the consortium structure.

Additional partners may be added later in the project. In particular, if SMEs are expected to join at a later stage, they should be listed here. These could include companies that are interested in commercially exploiting the results.

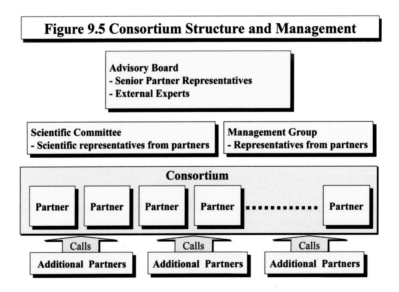

Figure 9.5 Consortium Structure and Management

Cost of Management:

The Commission does not give any guideline on the % of the funding that should be allocated to management. A good 'rule-of-thumb' would be 5% to 7% - depending on the complexity of the project. The management costs should never exceed 7%.

For smaller projects the diagram in Figure 9.6 is sufficient. Most projects do not have a '*Governing Assembly*' or '*Scientific Committees*' or '*Management Groups*'. Figure 9.6 clearly shows the Scientific Coordinator and the Project Manager. The Scientific Coordinator is responsible for the scientific direction of the project and the Research Manager is responsible for all non-scientific issues. Table 9.1 summarises the responsibilities of the Project Manager.

Figure 9.6 Structure of the Consortium (Small project)

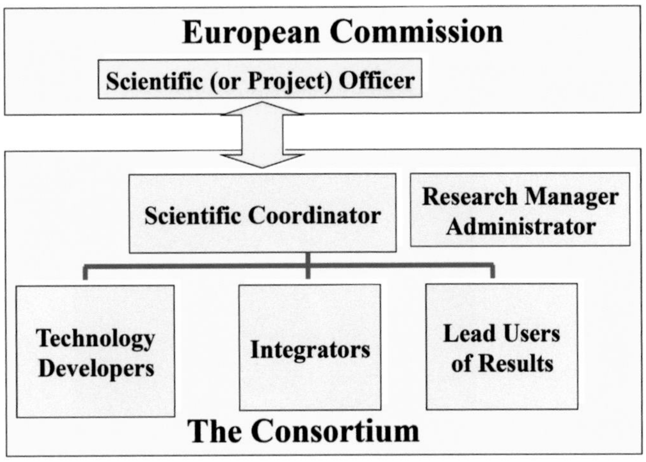

European Commission

Scientific (or Project) Officer

Scientific Coordinator

Research Manager Administrator

Technology Developers

Integrators

Lead Users of Results

The Consortium

Table 9.1 Responsibilities of the Project Manager:

Category of work	Specific responsibilities
Grant Issues	Grant Deliverables (and their deadlines) Milestones (especially Annual reviews, Mid-term reviews and Final review)
Financial Issues	Certificate on the financial statement Audits requested by the European Commission Management Justification of Costs (annually) Summary Certified Statement Payments and Distribution of Money to Partners
Legal Issues	Project Core Grant Agreement Model Grant Agreement (General Conditions) Consortium Agreement Change in Consortium (Calls for Proposals for new partners)
Management Issues	Work Flow and Scheduling of work Communication between partners and the European Commission Change Control Procedures Management of Conflicts Reporting Dissemination of Information
Political Issues	Exploitation of Results, Measurement of Impact, Innovation Activities, Gender and Equality Issues, Ethical Issues, Safety Issues, Links with Education (at all levels), Involvement of Small and Medium Enterprises Promotion of Results to Society

Table 3.2a List of Milestones

'Milestones' *refer to control points in the project that help to chart progress. Milestones may correspond to the completion of a key deliverable, allowing the next phase of the work to begin. They may also be needed at intermediary points so that, if problems have arisen, corrective measures can be taken. A milestone may be a critical decision point in the project where, for example, the consortium must decide which of several technologies to adopt for further development.*

A 'Milestone' is used to measure progress. The word comes from a stone that was used to tell travellers how many miles they had travelled or how many miles they had yet to travel.

In Horizon 2020, milestones are defined as *'control points where decisions are needed with regard to the next stage of the project'*. The milestone could be a meeting, a demonstration of software, a report or an occasion where several technologies are integrated and demonstrated.

Table 3.2a List of Milestones				
Milestone Number	Milestone Name	Related Work Package (s)	Estimated Date	Means of Verification

'Means of verification'
Show how you will confirm that the milestone has been attained. Refer to indicators if appropriate. For example: a laboratory prototype that is 'up and running'; software released and validated by a user group; field survey completed and data quality validated.

Table 3.2b Critical Risks

To understand this issue, it is necessary to understand the difference between an 'engineering project' and a 'scientific project'. In an engineering project, a clear deliverable is expected from the project. For example: *'a sensor with an accuracy of 20 parts per billion'* or *'a solar cell with an efficiency of 18%'*. If this target is not achieved then the engineering company will not be paid. This contract is judged solely on the results.

In a scientific research project, there are some 'unknowns'. It is not proposed that the research will find a solution or 'fill a knowledge gap'. The aim of the proposal is to 'apply the best scientific expertise and facilities' to solve the problem or to acquire new knowledge.

When researchers are writing a proposal, it is important to identify the risk in the project. In one project, where a sensor was being developed, the risk in the project was defined as *'the level of bonding between the polymer and the fibre-optic cable'*. If the project found a polymer that made a perfect bond, then the accuracy of the sensor could reach 20 parts per billion. A weaker bond would only result in an accuracy of 1,000 parts per billion. The aim of the project was to assess the highest accuracy of the sensor.

Table 3.2b Critical Tasks

Description of Risk	Work Package(s) involved	Proposed risk-mitigation measures

Potential Risks could be:

- **Scientific:** Knowledge may not be available or could not be developed
- **Technical:** Objectives may be beyond state-of-the art technologies
- **Economic:** Solutions may be too expensive to achieve results
- **Legislation:** Approach cannot be used due to existing legislation
- **Ethical:** Solution may infringe ethics rules
- **Social:** Approach not socially acceptable

Part B 3.3 Consortium as a whole

3.3 Consortium as a whole

The individual members of the consortium are described in a separate section 4. There is no need to repeat that information here.

- *Describe the consortium. How will it match the project's objectives? How do the members complement one another (and cover the value chain, where appropriate)? In what way does each of them contribute to the project? How will they be able to work effectively together?*

- *If applicable, describe the industrial/commercial involvement in the project to ensure exploitation of the results and explain why this is consistent with and will help to achieve the specific measures which are proposed for exploitation of the results of the project (see section 2.3).*

- ***Other countries****: If one or more of the participants requesting EU funding is based in a country that is not automatically eligible for such funding (entities from Member States of the EU, from Associated Countries and from one of the countries in the exhaustive list included in General Annex A of the work programme are automatically eligible for EU funding), explain why the participation of the entity in question is essential to the carrying out of the project.*

The evaluator is asked to comment on the: '*Complementarity of the participants within the consortium*'.

These questions are addressed using Figure 9.7 (also shown at the beginning of the Chapter).

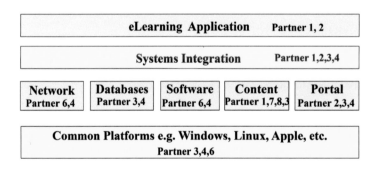

Figure 9.7 Skills and Partners in the Project

Table 9.2 Skills Matrix (not official form – only recommendation)

Skill	Partner	Role of Partners
Common Platform	Partner 3	Windows Platform
	Partner 4	Linux Platform
	Partner 6	Apple Platform
Network	Partner 6	Development of network interfaces
	Partner 4	Network Standards
Databases	Partner 3	Oracle
	Partner 4	Other databases
Software	Partner 6	Describe role
	Partner 4	Describe role
Content	Partner 1	Describe role
	Partner 7	Describe role
	Partner 8	Describe role
	Partner 3	Describe role
Portal	Partner 2	Describe role
	Partner 3	Describe role
	Partner 4	Describe role
Systems Integration	Partner 1	Describe role
	Partner 2	Describe role

"If applicable, describe the industrial/commercial involvement in the project to ensure exploitation of the results and explain why this is consistent with and will help to achieve the specific measures which are proposed for exploitation of the results of the project (see section 2.3)."

The diagram presented in the Impact part of the proposal (B2) can be used here to show the roles of each partner in the exploitation and use of the results.

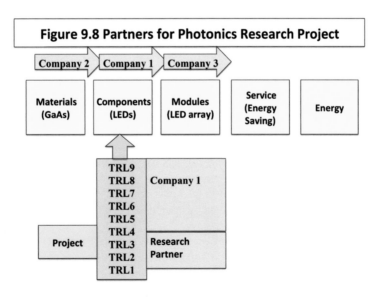

Figure 9.8 Partners for Photonics Research Project

Part B 3.4 Resources to be Committed

Please make sure the information in this section matches the costs as stated in the budget table in section 3 of the administrative proposal forms, and the number of person/months, shown in the detailed work package descriptions.

Please provide the following:
- *a table showing number of person/months required (table 3.4a);*
- *a table showing 'other direct costs' (table 3.4b) for participants where those costs exceed 15% of the personnel costs (according to the budget table in section 3 of the administrative proposal forms).*

Table 3.4a Summary of Staff Efforts

"Please indicate the number of person/months over the whole duration of the planned work, for each work package and for each participant. Identify the work package leader for each WP by showing the relevant person-month figure in bold."

Table 3.4a Summary of Staff Effort

No	Partner	WP1 pm	WP2 pm	WP3 pm	WP4 pm	WP5 pm	WP6 pm	Total pm
1	Partner 1	20	9.5	0	39	0	3	72
2	Partner 2	26	8	3	12	13	3	65
3	Partner 3	12	0	2	3	45	3	65
4	Partner 4	19	3	3	6	6	1	38
5	Partner 5	32	1.5	0	2	1.5	1	38
6	Partner 6	20	0	67	46	20	43	196
7	Partner 7	22	38	4	12	4	3	83
8	Partner 8	26	0	0	6	6	4	42
	Total	177	60	79	126	95.5	61	599

Distribution of work

Table 3.4a is a summary of the information contained in the different work package descriptions. It is a very important table as it summarises how the work is distributed between the partners. In the example shown in the following table, a clear problem can be identified with Partner 6. This partner has a total of 196 person months – far greater than any other partner. This must be explained in the proposal.

Both of these tables can be combined by adding extra columns to Table 3.4a The extra columns are:
- **Total** Expected Cost of Partners (this is taken from Form A2)
- **Budget/Work Ratio**: Divide Total Cost by Effort (person months)
- **Country**: The salaries of people vary between countries.

Table 3.4b 'Other direct costs'

'Other direct costs' refers to travel, equipment, other goods and services and large infrastructures.

"Please complete the table below for each participant if the sum of the cost for 'travel', 'equipment', and 'goods and services' exceeds 15% of the personnel costs for that participant (according to the budget table in section 3 of the proposal administration forms."

Table 3.4b 'Other direct costs'

Participant Number/ Short Name	Cost (€)	Justification
Travel		
Equipment		
Other goods and services		
Total		

Please complete the table below for all participants that would like to declare costs of large research infrastructure under Article 6.2 of the General Model Agreement6, irrespective of the percentage of personnel costs. Please indicate (in the justification) if the beneficiary's methodology for declaring the costs for large research infrastructure has already been positively assessed by the Commission.

Large research infrastructure means research infrastructure of a total value of at least EUR 20 million, for a beneficiary. More information and further guidance on the direct costing for the large research infrastructure is available in the H2020 Online Manual on the Participant Portal.

Participant Number/ Short Name	Cost (€)	Justification
Large Research Infrastructure		

The Budget / Work Ratio

This is not a calculation specified in Part B of the proposal but it is a very important calculation for participants in projects. For the evaluator, it provides a lot of valuable information in assessing the proposed work. Researchers should write the proposal assuming that the proposal will be approved and that the budget allocated to them perfectly matches the work they have to undertake. In other words, the 'Budget' matches the 'Work'.

Figure 9.9 shows how the budget/work ratio can be calculated. This excel spreadsheet can be found on www.hyperion.ie/templates.htm.

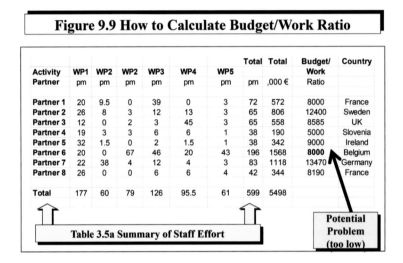

Figure 9.9 How to Calculate Budget/Work Ratio

Activity Partner	WP1 pm	WP2 pm	WP2 pm	WP3 pm	WP4 pm	WP5 pm	Total pm	Total ,000 €	Budget/ Work Ratio	Country
Partner 1	20	9.5	0	39	0	3	72	572	8000	France
Partner 2	26	8	3	12	13	3	65	806	12400	Sweden
Partner 3	12	0	2	3	45	3	65	558	8585	UK
Partner 4	19	3	3	6	6	1	38	190	5000	Slovenia
Partner 5	32	1.5	0	2	1.5	1	38	342	9000	Ireland
Partner 6	20	0	67	46	20	43	196	1568	**8000**	Belgium
Partner 7	22	38	4	12	4	3	83	1118	13470	Germany
Partner 8	26	0	0	6	6	4	42	344	8190	France
Total	177	60	79	126	95.5	61	599	5498		

Table 3.5a Summary of Staff Effort

Potential Problem (too low)

Variation in Budget/Work ratio between countries

The costs in the proposal are based on the ACTUAL costs in the partner's country. A researcher in Germany will cost more than a researcher in Ireland – who will cost more than a researcher in Poland.

Partner 6 in Figure 9.9 has a problem. Even though this partner has the most work (196 person months) and the highest costs (€1568k), the budget to work ratio is only €8000 per person month. For a company in Belgium, it is normally greater than €10,000 per person month.

The budget/work ratio is only used a 'quick check'. It can be used to determine whether the balance of work and money between the participants is correct. A further table is needed to understand the detailed costs and to explain how each partner's individual budget is calculated.

Software and Templates for Project Management

At the proposal stage, it is not necessary to use specialised Project Management software. Microsoft Project is excellent for producing the PERT charts and Gantt charts and, if it is available, it should be used.

For researchers who are not familiar with Project Management software, the diagrams can be produced with PowerPoint, Excel and Word. The templates shown in this chapter can be found on www.hyperion.ie/templates.htm.

The Consortium Agreements have an excellent description of how projects should be managed, the responsibilities of the different partners, the structure of the consortium and the decision making process. It also shows how conflicts and changes in the project should be dealt with by those involved. The Consortium Agreements can be found on the IPR-Help Desk www.iprhelpdesk.eu.

Software Tools for Writing the Management Plan:

The diagrams presented in this chapter were drawn using Power Point and the GANTT Chart was drawn using Excel. There are a number of companies on the market offering software tools– specifically adapted to Framework proposals and projects. The following is a list of some of these software tools. The author is not familiar with these tools. This is only a list – not a recommendation.

- GABO:milliarium mbH & Co. KG http://www.gabo-mi.com
- EFAMT Professional www.efamt.si
- PRODIGE www.prodige.com
- Vitamib www.vitamib.com
- Project Coordinator www.projectcoordinator.net Example on www.sustainablebridges.net
- Eurescom (IST projects) http://www.eurescom.de/services/
- Armines http://www.armines-euromanagement.fr
- BAL.PM www.bal-pm.com.

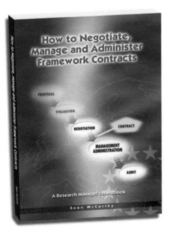

Details of Handbooks on www.hyperion.ie/books.htm

Section B4 Members of the Consortium

Section 4: Members of the consortium
This section is not covered by the page limit.
The information provided here will be used to judge the operational capacity.

4.1. Participants (applicants)

Please provide, for each participant, the following (if available):
- *a description of the legal entity and its main tasks, with an explanation of how its profile matches the tasks in the proposal;*
- *a curriculum vitae or description of the profile of the persons, including their gender, who will be primarily responsible for carrying out the proposed research and/or innovation activities;*
- *a list of up to 5 relevant publications, and/or products, services (including widely-used datasets or software), or other achievements relevant to the call content;*
- *a list of up to 5 relevant previous projects or activities, connected to the subject of this proposal;*
- *a description of any significant infrastructure and/or any major items of technical equipment, relevant to the proposed work;*
- *[any other supporting documents specified in the work programme for this call.]*

4.2. Third parties involved in the project (including use of third party resources)

Please complete, for each participant, the following table (or simply state "No third parties involved", if applicable):

Does the participant plan to subcontract certain tasks (please note that core tasks of the project should not be sub-contracted)	Y/N
If yes, please describe and justify the tasks to be subcontracted	
Does the participant envisage that part of its work is performed by linked third parties*?	Y/N
If yes, please describe the third party, the link of the participant to the third party, and describe and justify the foreseen tasks to be performed by the third party	
Does the participant envisage the use of contributions in kind provided by third parties (Articles 11 and 12 of the General Model Grant Agreement)?	Y/N
If yes, please describe the third party and their contributions	

*A third party that is an affiliated entity or has a legal link to a participant implying a collaboration not limited to the action. (Article 14 of the Model Grant Agreement).

The evaluation criteria: '*Experts will indicate whether the participants meet the selection criterion related to the operational capacity, to carry out the proposed work, based on the competence and experience of the individual participant(s).*'

The following Template could be used for each participant.
(Suggestion only – not Commission document).

Name of Organisation:
Expertise Relevant to the proposed work:
Specific Role in the Project:

Work package	Title of Work package	Role in the Work package

Profile of Key Personnel:

Name	Relevant Expertise

Ethical Issues in Horizon 2020 Proposals

Section 5: Ethics and Security
This section is not covered by the page limit.

5.1 Ethics
If you have entered any ethics issues in the ethical issue table in the administrative proposal forms, you must:
• submit an ethics self-assessment, which:
- *describes how the proposal meets the national legal and ethical requirements of the country or countries where the tasks raising ethical issues are to be carried out;*
- *explains in detail how you intend to address the issues in the ethical issues table, in particular as regards:*
- *research objectives (e.g. study of vulnerable populations, dual use, etc.)*
- *research methodology (e.g. clinical trials, involvement of children and related consent procedures, protection of any data collected, etc.)*
- *the potential impact of the research (e.g. dual use issues, environmental damage, stigmatisation of particular social groups, political or financial retaliation, benefit-sharing, malevolent use , etc.).*

• provide the documents that you need under national law(if you already have them), e.g.:
- *an ethics committee opinion;*
- *the document notifying activities raising ethical issues or authorising such activities*

If these documents are not in English, you must also submit an English summary of them (containing, if available, the conclusions of the committee or authority concerned).
If you plan to request these documents specifically for the project you are proposing, your request must contain an explicit reference to the project title.

Ethical Review of Proposals
The primary aim of the ethics question is to prevent Horizon 2020 funding being used for research that contravenes fundamental rights.

Ethical Review Panel

This is a special panel of experts selected by the European Commission from the 'expert' database (described in Chapter 4 –Evaluation). The review process is overseen by the 'Ethics Review Team' of the European Commission. The 'Ethics Review Team' is part of the Governance and Ethics unit of DG Research.

5.2 Security
Please indicate if your project will involve:
- *activities or results raising security issues: (YES/NO)*
- *'EU-classified information' as background or results: (YES/NO)*

Article 37.1 of Model Grant Agreement. *Before disclosing results of activities raising security issues to a third party (including affiliated entities), a beneficiary must inform the coordinator — which must request written approval from the Commission/Agency;* Article 37. *Activities related to 'classified deliverables' must comply with the 'security requirements' until they are declassified; Action tasks related to classified deliverables may not be subcontracted without prior explicit written approval from the Commission/Agency.; The beneficiaries must inform the coordinator — which must immediately inform the Commission/Agency — of any changes in the security context and — if necessary —request for Annex 1 to be amended (see Article 55).*

Chapter 10: Legal and Financial Issues

CONTENTS

The Rules of Participation
The Model Grant Agreement
The Consortium Agreement
European Economic Interest Group
Subcontractors in Framework 7
The Financial Rules
How the Financial Rules are applied
Intellectual Property Rights

Introduction

The Legal and Financial Rules of Horizon 2020 are described in the *Rules of Participation*, the *Model Grant Agreements* and the *Financial Guidelines*. This Chapter provides an overview of these complex issues. Detailed financial and legal information is not contained in this Chapter as it would require several hundred pages.

The Rules of Participation

Figure 10.1 shows the key documents that define the legal and financial rules. The *Rules of Participation* are first agreed between the Politicians and the European Commission. Following this the *Model Grant Agreement* is prepared. This defines who can participate, how much funding partners can receive and the ownership of intellectual property.

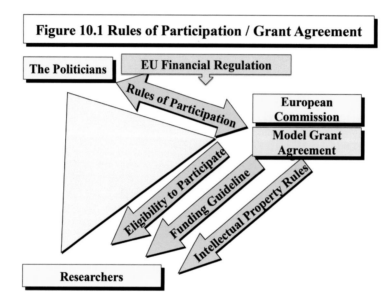

Figure 10.1 Rules of Participation / Grant Agreement

INTRODUCTORY PROVISIONS
> *Article 1 Subject matter and scope*
> *Article 2 Definitions*
> *Article 3 Confidentiality*
> *Article 4 Information to be made available*

GENERAL PROVISIONS
> *Article 5 Forms of funding*
> *Article 6 Legal entities that may participate in actions*
> *Article 7 Independence*

GRANTS: AWARD PROCEDURE
> *Article 8 Conditions for participation*
> *Article 9 Eligibility for funding*
> *Article 10 Calls for proposals*
> *Article 11 Joint calls with third countries or with international organisations*
> *Article 12 Proposals*
> *Article 13 Ethics review*
> *Article 14 Selection and award criteria*
> *Article 15 Evaluation review procedure*

MODEL GRANT AGREEMENT
This can be found on the Participant Portal

Grant Agreements and Consortium Agreements

If the proposal is successfully evaluated, the European Commission (EC) 'negotiates' a Grant Agreement with the consortium. If the negotiations are successful, the European Commission signs a Grant Agreement with the Coordinator. A Consortium Agreement is agreed between the partners. Figure 10.2 shows the link between the Commission Grant Agreement and the Consortium Agreement.

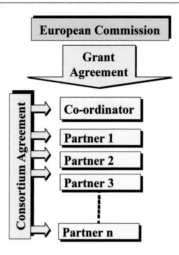

Figure 10.2 Grant Agreement and Consortium Agreement

The Grant Agreement and the Consortium Agreement contain the legal and financial rules that will be needed if the proposal is successful. These documents describe how the project should be managed, how the ownership of Intellectual Property will be decided and what the liability of each partner will be if the project is terminated. As a coordinator, it is very important to have a thorough working knowledge of these documents. This non-scientific part of the proposal/project is completed by the 'Research Manager' or the legal and financial support staff in the organisation.

Terminology used in the Grant Agreement and Consortium Agreement

'Beneficiary'	Partner signing the grant agreement (i.e. the legal entity)
'Parties'	Beneficiaries and Commission (i.e. everyone signing the agreement)
'Participant'	Broader term covering subcontractors, tenders, beneficiaries etc.

The term 'Partner' is used to describe an organisation that is a member of the consortium.

The IPR Help-Desk

The European Commission has funded a special 'help-desk' to assist organisations with questions on Intellectual Property Rights

> IPR-Helpdesk http://www.iprhelpdesk.eu/

The Commission stresses that while it funds the IPR-Helpdesk, the Commission is not responsible for the advice given by the helpdesk.

Model Consortium Agreements

The Consortium Agreement is an agreement between the partners on how the project will be managed, how the work will be distributed, how disputes will be handled, how the ownership of the intellectual property will be decided. The Consortium Agreement should be thought of as the 'Rules of the Consortium'.

The Consortium Agreement is not a European Commission document.

It is a legal document prepared by the consortium. In Horizon 2020, the Consortium Agreement must be produced before the European Commission signs the Grant Agreement – unless the work programme specifies that it is not necessary. The Consortium Agreement is used by the European Commission to transfer 'decision making' to the consortium and to give the consortium more freedom in deciding how the project should be managed.

The European Commission does not provide a model – but they do provide a check-list of issues that should be included in the Consortium Agreement. A number of 'Model Consortium Agreements' have been developed by European groups. These can be found on the IPR-Helpdesk http://www.iprhelpdesk.eu/ . A Simplified Consortium Agreement can be found on DESCA www.desca-fp7.eu.

Key Issues in the Consortium Agreement:

- Internal organisation of the consortium
- Distribution of the Community financial contribution
- Additional rules for dissemination and intellectual property rights
- The settlement of disputes (including the abuse of power)
- Liability, indemnification, confidentiality arrangements

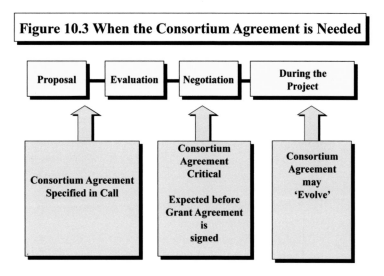

Figure 10.3 When the Consortium Agreement is Needed

The need for a Consortium Agreement is specified in the Call for Proposals. During the negotiation phase, the Commission will insist on having a signed Consortium Agreement before the Grant Agreement is signed with the consortium. During the project, the Consortium Agreement may 'evolve' based on changes in the partners, knowledge generated etc.

Consortium Agreement Checklist

The following is the checklist provided by the Commission. This checklist is used to create the Model Consortium Agreements described in the previous section.

General Information
Preamble
Subject of the Agreement

Technical Provisions
- Technical Contribution of each partner
- Technical Resources made available
- Production Schedule
- Maximum efforts
- Modification procedures

Rules for Dissemination and Use
- Confidentiality
- Ownership of results
- Legal protection of results (patent rights)
- Commercial exploitation of results
- Obligation to use

Dissemination of knowledge
- Publications

Background patents, know-how/info.
- Sub-licences

Organisational provisions
- Committees
- Co-operation supervision
- Revision of the Agreement

Financial Provisions
- Financing plan
- Modification procedures
- Mutual payments
- Selection of costs to be listed under the management activity heading

Legal Provision
- Legal co-operation status
- Terms of the agreement
- Penalties for non-compliance
- Applicable law/dispute settlement
- Secondment of personnel

European Economic Interest Group

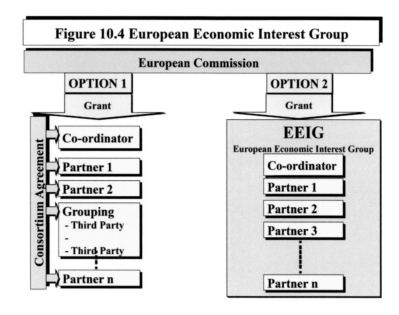

Figure 10.4 European Economic Interest Group

In a **European Economic Interest Group (EEIG)** the consortium is established as a formal legal entity. The commission signs the grant agreement with the EEIG rather than the coordinator.

EEIGs have existed since 1985 (Council Regulation No 2137/85). An EEIG allows companies from different countries to establish a legal body equivalent to a European Company.

Detailed information on EEIGs can be found on
http://europa.eu.int/comm/internal_market/en/company/company/news/783.htm

Article 10 (Rules of Participation)
"Where the minimum conditions for an indirect action are satisfied by a number of legal entities, which together form one legal entity, the latter may be the sole participant in an indirect action, provided that it is established in a Member State or associated country."

Other forms of 'Groupings' are also possible, provided they are legally recognised. In Figure 10.4 one of the 'Partners' is a 'Group'. The members of the Group are defined as 'Third Parties'.

European Grouping of Territorial Cooperation (EGTC) (Regulation 1082/2006/EC)

The EGTC is a legal instrument that enables regional and local authorities from different member states to set up cooperation groupings with a legal personality.

Subcontractors in Horizon 2020

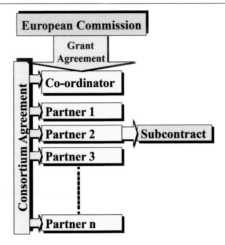

Figure 10.5 Horizon 2020 Rules for Subcontractors

The rules for subcontractors are very specific in Horizon 2020.

*   Subcontractors can be paid 100% of their costs
*   Subcontractors are NOT partners in a Horizon 2020 projects
*   A Competitive tendering process must be used (best price/quality)
*   Core elements of the work cannot be subcontracted (for example the management cannot be subcontracted)
*   Partners may not subcontract to other partners (except in exceptional circumstances)
*   Conditions of the EC grant agreement are applicable to the subcontractor (confidentiality, communication of data, payments, and audits). This must be clearly specified in the subcontract

Subcontracts should be kept for non-core elements of the projects such as conference organisation and some training courses.

"A subcontractor is a third party which has entered into an agreement on business conditions with one or more of the beneficiaries, in order to carry out some part of the work of the project without the direct supervision of the beneficiary and without a relationship of subordination."

"Subcontracts may only cover the execution of a limited part of the project. The award of subcontracts must be duly justified in Annex I (Technical Annex)"

"Contracts entered into prior to the beginning of the project that are according to the beneficiary's usual management principles may also be accepted."

Source: Court of Auditors Report 2012

How EC Financial Contribution is Calculated

The best way, to understand how the European Commission (EC) contribution to a project is calculated, is to use a real example. Figure 10.6 shows an example of a project that is planning to spend €230,200.

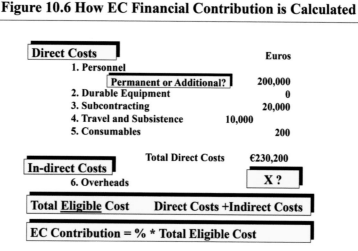

Figure 10.6 How EC Financial Contribution is Calculated

Direct Costs		Euros
1. Personnel		
Permanent or Additional?		200,000
2. Durable Equipment		0
3. Subcontracting		20,000
4. Travel and Subsistence	10,000	
5. Consumables		200
	Total Direct Costs	€230,200
In-direct Costs		
6. Overheads		X ?
Total Eligible Cost	Direct Costs +Indirect Costs	
EC Contribution = % * Total Eligible Cost		

Terminology Used in Horizon 2020 Finances

Direct Costs. These costs are directly related to the project:
- Personnel in Horizon 2020, both permanent and additional, can be charged to the project. Staff paid from Framework projects must keep 'Time sheets' to verify the costs charged against the project. Staff who are 100% working on a project do not need to keep timesheets;
- Equipment – equipment is allowed to depreciate over the life of the project;
- Subcontracting (described in previous section);
- Travel and subsistence;
- Consumables.

How Direct Costs are calculated: The direct costs are based on the 'actual' costs in each country. For example, if a researcher working in a German organisation and another researcher in a Latvian organisation are both carrying out exactly the same work, then the costs charged by the German partner will be based on German salaries and the costs charged by the Latvian partner will be based on Latvian salaries. The following is one of the most common questions in Framework projects:

> **Question:** *How much can we charge for personnel, travel, consumables etc.?*
> **Answer**: *The costs that are allowed in your country.*
> **Exceptions**: In the Marie Skłodowska-Curie programme, the amount paid to the Fellows is defined in the work programme.

Indirect Costs (or Overheads): These are costs that are not directly related to the project such as rent, heating, communications. (This is described in more detail in the following page).

Total Eligible Costs = Direct Costs + Indirect Costs
Horizon 2020 Contribution to the project = % of Total Eligible Costs

The EC financial contribution depends on the type of organisation and the activity. The above rules are defined in: Rules of Participation.

Overheads ('Indirect Costs')

In Horizon 2020, a flat rate of 25% is used to calculate overheads.

There is no strict definition of overheads. It generally refers to incurred costs that are not directly related to a project. The most common overhead elements are:
- Non-productive personnel costs (personnel that do not generate income)
- Rent
- Heating, lighting
- Communications (websites, IT system)

Funding Rates

In Horizon 2020, two funding rates are used:

Research Activities: 100% of eligible costs

Innovation Activities: 70% of eligible costs

For public non-profit research organisations, Innovation activities are funded at 100%

Non-eligible costs:

The following list, of non-eligible costs – provided by the European Commission:
- Profit ('*The Community financial contribution to reimburse eligible costs shall not give rise to a profit*')
- Interest owed
- Provision for future losses or charges
- Costs declared, incurred or reimbursed from another Community project
- Return of capital
- Debt and debt service charges
- Excessive or reckless expenditure

Example: 25% Overhead and 100% Funding

Figure 10.7 shows an example of how the European contribution is calculated for a research project (100% funding) and where overhead is calculated at 25% of eligible costs.

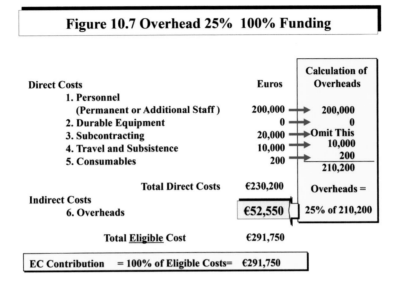

Figure 10.7 Overhead 25% 100% Funding

Example: 25% Overhead and 70% Funding

Figure 10.8 shows an example of how the European contribution is calculated for an innovation project (70% funding) and where overhead is calculated at 25% of eligible costs.

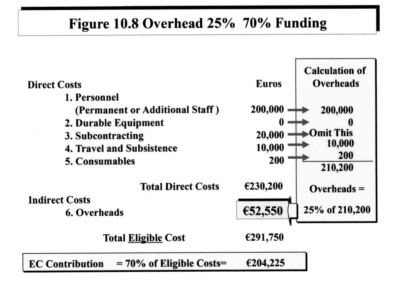

Figure 10.8 Overhead 25% 70% Funding

NOTE: This handbook is not a financial handbook. In the financial guidelines, more detailed information is available on the financial rules. These examples are only included to explain the method of calculation only.

Rules on Intellectual Property Rights (IPR)

The Rules on Intellectual Property Rights in Horizon 2020 projects are defined in:
- Rules of Participation
- Model Grant Agreement
- Consortium Agreements which define more specific rules on IPR

The European Commission also funds an IPR-Helpdesk that provides information on all aspects of IPR issues. This can be found on www.iprhelpdesk.eu

This section of the handbook only provides an overview of the key concepts on Intellectual Property Rights in Horizon 2020.

Definitions (from Rules of Participation and Model Grant Agreements)

Results: (Results generated in the project)
"Results means the results, including information, whether or not they can be protected, which are generated by the indirect action concerned. Such results include rights related to copyright, design rights, patent rights, plant variety rights or similar forms of protection."

Background (Intellectual property generated before the project starts)
"Background means information which is held by participants prior to their accession to the grant agreement, as well as copyrights or other intellectual property rights pertaining to such information, the application for which has been filed before the accession to the grant agreement, and which is needed for carrying out the indirect action or for using the results of the indirect action."

Dissemination
"Dissemination means the disclosure of results by any appropriate means other than that resulting from the formalities for protecting it, and including the publication of results in any medium."

Use
"Use means the direct or indirect utilisation of results in further research activities other than those covered by the project, or for developing, creating and marketing a product or process, or for creating and providing a service."

Table 10.4 IPR in the *Rules of Participation*

RULES GOVERNING EXPOLOITATION AND DISSEMINATION OF RESULTS
Article 38 Ownership of results
Article 39 Protection of results
Article 40 Exploitation and dissemination of results
Article 41 Transfer and licensing of results
Article 42 Background
Article 43 Access rights principles
Article 44 Access rights for implementation
Article 45 Access rights for exploitation
Article 46 Access rights for the Union and the Member States

Chapter 11: What is your Strategy for Horizon 2020?

CONTENTS

Introduction

How many research organisations have a formal written strategy for Horizon 2020? How many individual researchers have a personal strategy for Horizon 2020? Horizon 2020 is about science and people. It is not just about EU institutions, websites and proposal documents. The researchers who are successful in Horizon 2020 are involved in a wide variety of EU activities. They network at a European level and, more importantly, they maintain networks. Successful researchers use four mechanisms to promote their expertise: Publications, conference presentations, proposals and projects. This chapter presents a checklist for the writing of a simple but practical strategy for Horizon 2020.

An Organisation's Strategy for Horizon 2020

The following are examples of statements that could be used in a research organisation's strategy for Horizon 2020. The examples are based on discussions with research organisations. *(The comments in italics are actual quotations from research managers).*

- *'To access European Union Funding for research activities.'* One of the problems with this simple objective is that the researchers may concentrate on obtaining any grants rather than focusing on the research priorities of the organisation.

- To establish the research group as the European (or International) scientific leader in a scientific area *('to be the best in our field')*. It is important that the scientific areas are well defined (a niche within a niche).

- To access new technologies relevant to the organisation's areas of excellence *('to avoid missing the train')*.

- To work with the best research partners in the European Union. *('to be the preferred partner of the best scientists in our field')*.

- To provide better education and training to graduates and post-graduates. *('We want our graduates to excel in any interview, anywhere in the world')*.

- To promote the organisation's scientific and technical excellence to the scientific/technical community *('more conferences, more publications, more website hits...')*.

- To ensure that the research results are used by enterprises and society *('getting value from our research efforts')*

- To provide relevant support to researchers *('to streamline the process of proposal writing, grant negotiation and project management/administration')*.

The strategy should also refer to the activities that the organisation will **NOT** undertake in Horizon 2020. For example:

- Specific tasks in the project. One University clearly informed its researchers that they were not to *'act as coordinators in Horizon 2020 projects'*
- Subcontracting. (*'We will utilise only internal resources in the project'.)*
- Applied Research Centres *('We will not participate in ERC')*

A Strategy for Individual Researchers

An individual researcher (or a small research group) should have a strategy that answers all of the following questions:

- Which scientific niche (or even 'niche within a niche') best suits the researcher involved? It is important to clearly define the scientific area where the researcher's expertise is the best and where it complements researchers from other research centres.

- Which Horizon 2020 Priorities (sub-programmes) are relevant to the researcher? Identify all of the 'topics' – not just the main programmes.

- Which type of grants will be used? A simple strategy could be the following: *We will focus on Research and Innovation Projects. We will use Coordination and Support Actions to fund workshops and small conferences. We will use CSA to fund our research networks. We will use Marie Skłodowska-Curie Fellowships to hire researchers in our organisation and we will use the Research Infrastructure programme to access facilities not available in our research centre.*

- Which 'Calls for Proposal'? Each programme will have (typically) one call for proposals each year. An example of a strategy could be*: In 2014 we will focus on CSA to establish links with potential partners, in 2015 we will set up a CSA to establish a formal network. This should lead to a Research and Innovation Project in 2016.*

- Which Roles in the Projects? Scientific Coordinator? Work package leader? Consortium Manager? Exploitation Manager?

- Which partners? This is a most critical issue and will require a thorough analysis. Which companies and, in particular, which SMEs (Small and Medium Enterprises) could be included in the project? Should international partners be included?

- What support staff is available? Examples include: Who will write the Gender dimension of the proposal? Who will take care of the ethical issues, the consortium agreement etc.?

- Which sources of information? Horizon 2020 proposals require arguments in science, economic relevance, social relevance, relevance to European Union policies etc. Which are the best sources of information for these sections of the proposal? For this information see www.hyperion.ie/h2020-proposalwebsites.htm.

A Strategy for Beginners (Networking)

Website for Beginners use www.hyperion.ie/beginners.htm

Beginners find it difficult to become a 'preferred partner'. The following is a simple (but slow) strategy. It assumes that the researcher has scientific expertise in some niche. If not, the researcher will not get past Step 2. An example of a beginner in Renewable Energy will be used to illustrate the strategy.

Step 1: Clarify the Scientific Niche of the Researcher

The researchers need to clarify the scientific niches where they excel (or more importantly the niche within a niche). An example could be the *Development of Computer Models to Design and Simulate Photovoltaic (solar) Systems*. It is possible to have a number of niches.

Step 2: Identify who's who in the Scientific Niche?

Analyse the websites presented in Chapter 8 (Partners) to identify the key individuals in the scientific area and the individuals involved in the specific niche. In particular identify:
* The Unit in the European Commission (and if possible, the scientific officers).
* The researchers who are already winning in this area (especially the coordinators)
* The 'gurus' who advise the European Commission on research policy in the niche.

Step 3: Join the relevant European Associations and Networks.

Join the relevant European Association or Network where the individuals, identified in Step 2 can be found. This is the single most important step in the process. The best Associations have very strict admission criteria. A list of European research associations is presented in www.hyperion.ie/euassociations.htm. In the Renewable Energy example, an association entitled: The EUREC Agency (European Renewable Energy Research Centres) www.eurec.be represents the top 40 renewable energy research centres in Europe.

Step 4: Establish a role in the European Scientific Community

Participate in the relevant Association and Network activities. These include scientific meetings, conferences and discussion groups. The aim here is to identify 'Who's Who?' and, more importantly, to identify the scientific areas where excellent scientists exist. 'Gaps' in the scientific field or topics where the scientific quality is not excellent can also be identified. From this, the researcher will find one or two niches. Researchers should aim to be the 'preferred partner' in these topics.

Step 5: Promote scientific expertise to future partners

The researcher must demonstrate and promote expertise in the chosen scientific niches. This should be done initially through visits to research centres and sharing of scientific results. Young researchers must submit papers to seminars, conferences and association magazines. Any presentation by a researcher must be prepared to the highest standards. After a conference a researcher must report on:
* Scientific advances reported in the conference
* Reaction to the researcher's presentation, poster or exhibition
* Ideas for future proposals
* Key people identified (and met) who could become partners in future proposals

Step 6: Become a 'guru' on Horizon 2020

Study the Horizon 2020 procedures, work programmes and background policy documents. Become a 'guru' on Horizon 2020 in the scientific niche. Many experienced researchers may be novices on Horizon 2020 procedures.

Step 7: Participate first as a partner – then move to the role of coordinator

Submit proposals for small activities such as Workshops, Fellowships and Small Research Projects. Participate as a 'Partner' at the beginning but aim to become a 'Scientific Coordinator' in the future.

Step 8: Submit high quality proposals

During the proposal preparation, the researcher must demonstrate scientific knowledge and professionalism to the partners. This is essential at all times.

Step 9: Demonstrate scientific expertise to future partners

A research project is the best way of planning for future proposals. Each existing project must be seen as a mechanism to demonstrate scientific expertise and professionalism. It must also show an ability to solve problems and to propose innovative solutions. It is also an important opportunity to demonstrate willingness to work as part of an international consortium. Researchers, when they are searching for partners for new proposals, will always endeavour to work with the people they know and respect.

Step 10: Go to Step 4,5,6,7,8 and 9.
This is a continuous process for an active researcher.

A Strategy for Beginners (Funding)

The following is a practical funding strategy for beginners.

1. Access **research infrastructures** through the Research Infrastructure programme http://cordis.europa.eu/infrastructures/projects.htm.

2. **Join an existing Network**. Search for for 'Coordination Actions in the project website.

3. Find a **Marie Skłodowska-Curie Host Fellowship** where there is funding available for Fellows. EURAXESS http://ec.europa.eu/euraxess/index.cfm/jobs/index

The relevant Web Pages can be found on www.hyperion.ie/beginners.htm. This website will be updated with new links as Horizon 2020 progresses.

A Strategy for Small and Medium Sized Enterprises

Small and Medium Sized Enterprises (SMEs) must understand the benefits and costs of their involvement in Horizon 2020 projects. For an SME, the key points to remember are:

- Horizon 2020 is not a market in which to bid for grants, complete the job and make a profit. Horizon 2020 funding is in the form of 'grants' that are designed to help the European Commission implement policies. SMEs can help the European Commission in creating jobs and in improving the competitiveness of European industry. For this, the European Commission is willing to cover some of the costs of the effort.
- An SME cannot make a profit from Horizon 2020 projects.
- The costs incurred in the preparation of a proposal cannot be claimed in the grant.

Why would an SME participate in a Horizon 2020 project? An evaluation of SME involvement in previous Framework Programmes listed the following reasons for participation:

- To access technologies relevant to the company's business
- To promote the expertise of the company to future clients
- To establish contacts with experts and suppliers of technologies throughout the European Union
- To help the company transform from being a regional company to being a European company

The best strategy for an SME is to obtain funding for research and development that is already part of the company's development plan.

The key programmes that are relevant to SMEs are:
- SME Instrument in Pillar II and Pillar III
- SME as a partner in research projects in Pillar II and Pillar III
- Eurostars for Research Intensive SMEs
- Marie Curie (RISE) for exchange between research centres and SMEs.

These programmes are described in Chapter 3 (The Research Priorities).

Conclusion

Strategies are useless pieces of paper unless implemented. A strategy is not a once in a lifetime exercise – it must be regularly updated to reflect changes in internal research priorities, changes in funding rules or changes in funding priorities. The important issue is that a general strategy exists and that it is communicated throughout the research organisation.

Research organisations and individual researchers should be able to answer the following questions:

- How will the success of participation in Horizon 2020 be measured?
- How will the failure of involvement in Horizon 2020 be measured?
- What is the greatest concern of the organisation regarding Horizon 2020?
- What are limitations of the researchers and the limitations of the organisation when setting out to participate in Horizon 2020?

Annex I: Webpages used in the Handbook

These can be found on **www.hyperion.ie/h2020-proposalwebsites.htm**

Module 1: Overview of Horizon 2020

Official Documents on Horizon 2020

- Horizon 2020 Website http://ec.europa.eu/research/horizon2020/index_en.cfm?pg=home
- Participant Portal http://ec.europa.eu/research/participants/portal/page/home
- European Commission Presentation of Horizon 2020 (Prezi)
- Horizon 2020 Online Magazine http://horizon-magazine.eu/
- Draft Work programmes (Link)

How to Stay up-to-date

- National R&D Offices in Brussels www.iglortd.org
- EU R&D Associations www.hyperion.ie/euassociations.htm
- Linkedin Group 'Horizon 2020' led by EARTO **(Link)**
- CORDIS Website http://cordis.europa.eu/fp7/home.html
- Euractiv (General EU News service) www.euractiv.com
- Cordis News CORDIS News http://cordis.europa.eu/news/en/home.html
- Europa Website http://europa.eu (or Search Google europa.eu 'topic')
- Register on IPR Helpdesk http://www.iprhelpdesk.eu/user/register
- Research Europe www.researchresearch.com

Module 2: How to Lobby for Horizon 2020

Mapping + Lobbying for Horizon 2020 www.hyperion.ie/h2020-mapping.htm

Horizon 2020 Beginner's Website www.hyperion.ie/beginners.htm

The Technology Platforms www.hyperion.ie/technologyplatforms.htm

EIP (European Innovation Partnerships) www.hyperion.ie/eip.htm

KET (Key Enabling Technologies) www.hyperion.ie/ket.htm

Module 3: Research Priorities in Horizon 2020

- EIT (European Institute for Innovation and Technology) www.hyperion.ie/eit.htm
- FET (Future and Emerging Technologies) www.hyperion.ie/fet.htm
- European Research Council (ERC) http://erc.europa.eu/
- Public Private Partnerships www.hyperion.ie/ppp.htm
- Joint Programming www.hyperion.ie/jointprogramming.htm
- Joint Technology Initiatives www.hyperion.ie/jti.htm
- Lead Market Initiatives www.hyperion.ie/lmi.htm
- Public Procurement www.hyperion.ie/publicprocurement.htm
- SBIR (Small Business Innovation and Research) (USA) www.hyperion.ie/sbir.htm

Module 4: How Horizon 2020 Proposals are Evaluated

How Horizon 2020 Proposals are Evaluated www.hyperion.ie/h2020-evaluation.htm

Module 5: How to Write the Impact of a Horizon 2020 Proposal

How to write the 'Impact' of the Proposal www.hyperion.ie/impact.htm

Module 6: The One Page Proposal

The One Page Proposal www.hyperion.ie/onepageproposal.htm

The 5 Key Questions www.hyperion.ie/fivekeyquestions.htm

Module 7: How to Streamline the Writing of a Horizon 2020 Proposal

How to Streamline the Writing of a Proposal www.hyperion.ie/writingtheproposal.htm

Module 8: Where to find the Best Partners

Where to find the best partners **www.hyperion.ie/h2020-partners.htm**

Module 9: How to Write the Implementation Plan

How to write 'Implementation' Plan www.hyperion.ie/h2020-implementation.htm

Gender Issues www.hyperion.ie/gender.htm

Ethical Issues www.hyperion.ie/ethics.htm

Templates for Proposals and Projects **www.hyperion.ie/templates.htm**

Module 10: The Legal and Financial Rules

- Draft Rules of Participation http://eur-lex.europa.eu/LexUriServ/LexUriServ.do?uri=COM:2011:0810:FIN:en:PDF
- Simplification in Horizon 2020 (fact sheet)

www.hyperion.ie/h2020-proposalwebsites.htm

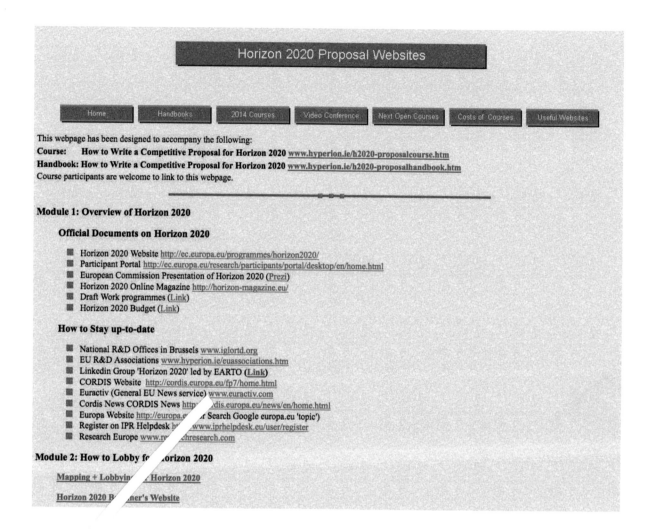

Training Courses on Horizon 2020

How to Write a Competitive Proposal for Horizon 2020 (half-day course)

This one-day course is designed for researchers. Details of the course can be found on www.hyperion.ie/h2020-proposalcourse.htm
Courses can be delivered as In-house courses (in the research centres) or as Open Courses (where individuals attend). Details on how to organize In-house courses and details on how to attend Open Courses can be found on www.hyperion.ie.

Training Course for Horizon 2020 Advisors (3-days)

The aim of this training course is to develop the skills of Horizon 2020 Advisors to provide effective support services to researchers in Universities and Research Centres.

Following the training course, the Horizon 2020 Advisors will be able to:
- provide a detailed explanation of all aspects of Horizon 2020
- assist researchers in preparing proposals for Horizon 2020
- assist researchers in sourcing information for proposals
- assist researchers in identifying 'best' partners
- help researchers to streamline proposal writing (using templates)

Who should attend?
This training course is relevant to individuals who are appointed as Horizon 2020 advisors in Research Centres and in Universities.

Details of Horizon 2020 Advisors course on www.hyperion.ie/h2020-advisorscourse.htm
Details of next training courses on www.hyperion.ie

Training Courses offered by Hyperion Ltd.

How to Write a Competitive Proposal for Horizon 2020

How to Negotiate, Manage and Administer Framework Projects

How to Write a Plan for Using and Dissemination of Research Results

How to Present Research Activities to Business Executive, Public Officials and Politicians

Details of all of these training courses can be found on www.hyperion.ie

www.hyperion.ie